THE PROBLEMS OF MODERNITY

WARWICK STUDIES IN PHILOSOPHY AND LITERATURE

General editor: David Wood

In both philosophical and literary studies much of the best original work today explores both the tensions and the intricate connections between what have often been treated as separate fields. In philosophy there is a widespread conviction that the notion of an unmediated search for truth represents an oversimplification of the philosopher's task, and that the language of philosophical argument requires its own interpretation. Even in the most rigorous instances of the analytic tradition, a tradition inspired by the possibilities of formalization and by the success of the natural sciences, we find demands for 'clarity', for 'tight' argument, and distinctions between 'strong' and 'weak' proofs which call out for a rhetorical reading – even for an aesthetic of argument. In literature many of the categories presupposed by traditions which give priority to 'enactment' over 'description' and oppose 'theory' in the name of 'lived experience' are themselves under challenge as requiring theoretical analysis, while it is becoming increasingly clear that to exclude literary works from philosophical probing is to trivialize many of them. Further, modern literary theory necessarily looks to philosophy to articulate its deepest problems and the effects of this are transmitted in turn to critical reading, as the widespread influence of deconstruction and of a more reflective hermeneutics has begun to show. When one recalls that Plato, who wished to keep philosophy and poetry apart, actually unified the two in his own writing, it is clear that the current upsurge of interest in this field is only re-engaging with the questions alive in the broader tradition.

The University of Warwick pioneered the undergraduate study of the intertwinings of philosophy and literature, and its recently established Centre for Research in Philosophy and Literature has won wide respect. This new Series brings the work of the Centre to a larger public in volumes which combine a sense of new direction with traditional standards of intellectual rigour. The Series will be further developed by the inclusion of monographs by distinguished academics.

THE PROBLEMS OF MODERNITY

ADORNO AND BENJAMIN

Edited by

ANDREW BENJAMIN

ROUTLEDGE
London and New York

First published 1989
by Routledge
11 New Fetter Lane, London EC4P 4EE
29 West 35th Street, New York, NY 10001

© 1989 University of Warwick

Set in 10/12pt Baskerville by
Hope Services, Abingdon, Oxon, Great Britain
and printed by T. J. Press (Padstow) Ltd, Padstow, Cornwall

British Library Cataloguing in Publication Data

The Problems of modernity : Adorno and
Benjamin.—(Warwick studies in philosophy
and literature).
1. Culture – Philosophical perspectives
I. Title   II. Series
306'.01

Library of Congress Cataloging in Publication Data

The Problems of Modernity.
(Warwick studies in philosophy and literature)
Bibliography: p.
Includes index
1. Adorno, Theodor, W., 1903–1969.
2. Benjamin, Walter, 1892–1940.
I. Benjamin, Andrew E. II. Series.
B3199.A34P74   1988   193   88–11435
ISBN 0–415–01066–7

1-11-91

CONTENTS

CONTENTS

NOTES ON THE
CONTRIBUTORS

ANDREW BENJAMIN is Lecturer in the Department of Philosophy, University of Warwick. He has published widely in various areas of philosophy.

JAY BERNSTEIN is Lecturer in Philosophy at the University of Essex. He has published *The Philosophy of the Novel: Lukacs, Marxism and the Dialectics of Form*, University of Minnesota Press, Minneapolis 1984.

ANDREW BOWIE is Lecturer in Humanities at Cambridge College of Arts and Technology. He has a book forthcoming on German aesthetic theory.

PETER DEWS is Lecturer in Humanities at Cambridge College of Arts and Technology. Amongst his publications are *Logics of Disintegration: Post-Structuralist thought and the claims of critical theory*, Verso, London 1987 and *Habermas, Autonomy and Solidarity. Interviews with J. Habermas*, Verso, London 1986. He is also an editor of *New Left Review* and *Radical Philosophy*.

JOANNA HODGE is Lecturer in Philosophy at the University of York. She has published a number of papers on Kristeva, Adorno and feminist philosophy. She has a forthcoming book on Heidegger and ethics.

PETER OSBORNE teaches philosophy at Middlesex Polytechnic and the Polytechnic of the South Bank. He has published papers on Adorno, Bloch, Hegel and Marx. He is also an editor of *Radical Philosophy*. He is preparing a book on Marxism and the 'end of philosophy'.

JOHN RIGNALL is Senior Lecturer in the Department of English, University of Warwick. He has published widely in the field of literary studies.

JANET WOLFF is Reader in the Department of Sociology, University of Leeds. Her many publications include *Hermeneutic Philosophy and the Sociology of Art*, Routledge & Kegan Paul, London 1975; *Aesthetics and the Sociology of Art*, Allen & Unwin, London 1983; *The Art of Women*, Macmillan, London 1986.

IRVING WOHLFARTH is Professor of Comparative Literature at the University of Oregon. He has published papers on Benjamin, Flaubert and Laclos. Recently he edited a special edition of *New German Critique*, Number 39, Fall 1986, devoted to studies of Benjamin's Arcades Project. He has a forthcoming book on Benjamin.

INTRODUCTION

A. E. BENJAMIN

The philosophical problem of modernity has begun to occupy a central and privileged place within contemporary philosophical and intellectual concerns. It is a problem made more urgent by the possibility advanced by Jean-François Lyotard that modernity as a project is over and what should now be of central concern is the postmodern. The papers in this volume are situated at precisely this point of tension. The concentration on Adorno and Benjamin attests to the fact that their work is of great importance to a philosophical engagement with the problem of modernity.

The papers by Andrew Bowie, Peter Osborne and Jay Bernstein are positioned around the question of the aesthetic. In each paper Adorno features as the central philosophical figure. For Bowie Adorno's writings on music provide the way into a general discussion of the place of music within any assessment of modernity. Peter Osborne has provided one of the most systematic presentations of Adorno's aesthetics to be published since the translation of the *Aesthetic Theory*[1] into English. Osborne situates his presentation of Adorno in relation to the work of Peter Burger and Fredric Jameson. One of Osborne's major concerns is to explicate what is at stake in Adorno's term 'autonomous art'. It is precisely this term that is central to Jay Bernstein's evaluation of the critique of Adorno that stems from the writings of Jurgen Habermas and Albrecht Wellmer. Bernstein's point against them and in favour of Adorno is that they misunderstand what is at stake in the work of art being autonomous. Each of these three papers exemplifies the contemporary importance of Adorno's work. Peter Dews[2] deploys Adorno in order to develop a critique of what he identifies as a poststructuralist conception of subjectivity. Dews' aim is, in part, to guard the conception of identity inherent in modernism from its fragmentation within the postmodern. His paper presents a valuable corrective to any quick claim that the unity of identity has been overcome.

Within Janet Wolff's[3] examination of the exclusion of women from certain conceptions of modernity, there lies an inherent questioning of the gendered nature of modernity. Taking Walter Benjamin's conception of the *flâneur* she shows how it is an essentially male construct whose inclusion as a dominant image within modernity works to exclude the *flâneuse*. Joanna Hodge argues that the structure of the debate between modernism and postmodernism needs to be rethought so as to include the category of gender. In an original reading of Adorno and Deleuze she presents an effective challenge to any complacent understanding of the problem of modernity. Fundamental to this reassessment is the work of Julia Kristeva.

John Rignall, Andrew Benjamin and Irving Wohlfarth examine specific themes or 'motifs' within the work of Walter Benjamin. Rignall rightly identifies the part played by the theme of realism within Benjamin's work as well as in modernity. He traces, with meticulous care, Benjamin's concern with realism throughout a number of his texts. Andrew Benjamin, focusing on the themes of tradition and experience, seeks to locate in Benjamin's presentation of them, the limit of modernity itself. He concludes by arguing that plotting their limit opens up the possibility of thinking the postmodern. Irving Wohlfarth in a long and scholarly paper examines a topic to which allusion is often made, but which is none the less rarely discussed; namely the Jewish motifs in Benjamin's writings. Wohlfarth's paper is an important reminder both of the importance of Judaism within Benjamin's work, as well as the critical function of Judaism itself.

The value of all of these papers is twofold. On the one hand they allow for a deeper understanding of the work of Adorno and Benjamin. On the other hand they are each a significant advance in our understanding both of modernity and the philosophical tasks to which that understanding gives rise.

Finally I must thank Heather Jones, the secretary of the Centre for Research in Philosophy and Literature, for the many hours of work she put in helping in the preparation of this volume. I would also like to acknowledge the continued encouragement of David Wood, the General Editor of the Series, and the assistance by Peter Osborne.

NOTES

1 T. Adorno, *Aesthetic Theory*, trans. C. Lenhardt, London, Routledge & Kegan Paul 1984.
2 An earlier version of this paper was published in *New Left Review*, 157, May/June 1986.
3 An earlier version of this paper appeared in *Theory, Culture and Society*, vol. 2, no. 3, 1985.

Chapter One

ADORNO, POST-STRUCTURALISM, AND THE CRITIQUE OF IDENTITY

PETER DEWS

Over the past few years an awareness has begun to develop of the thematic affinities between the work of those recent French thinkers commonly grouped together under the label of 'poststructuralism', and the thought of the first-generation Frankfurt School, particularly that of Adorno. Indeed, what is perhaps most surprising is that it should have taken so long for the interlocking of concerns between these two philosophical currents to be properly appreciated. Among the most prominent of such common preoccupations are: the illusory autonomy of the bourgeois subject, as exposed pre-eminently in the writings of Freud and Nietzsche; the oppressive functioning of scientific and technological reason, not least in its application to the social domain; the radicalizing potential of modernist aesthetic experience; and – in the case of Adorno at least – the manner in which what are apparently the most marginal and fortuitous features of cultural artefacts reveal their most profound, and often unacknowledged truths. Furthermore, these affinities have not merely been observed by outsiders, but are beginning to become part of the self-consciousness of participants in the two traditions themselves. Towards the end of his life, Michel Foucault admitted that he could have avoided many mistakes through an earlier reading of Critical Theory, and – in the last of several retrospective reconstructions of his intellectual itinerary – placed his own thought in a tradition concerned with the 'ontology of actuality', running from Kant and Hegel, via Nietzsche and Weber, to the Frankfurt School.[1] Similarly, Jean-François Lyotard has employed Adorno's account of the decline of metaphysics and the turn to 'micrology' in order to illuminate – partly by parallel and partly by contrast – his own interpretation of postmodernity,[2] while even Jacques Derrida, the least eclectic of recent French

1

thinkers, has written appreciatively on Walter Benjamin, whose borderline position between the political and the mystical he clearly finds sympathetic.[3] On the other side, contemporary German inheritors of the Frankfurt School, including Habermas himself, have begun to explore the internal landscape of poststructuralism, and to assess the points of intersection and divergence with their own tradition.[4]

In the English-speaking world, it is the relation between the characteristic procedures of deconstruction developed by Derrida and the 'negative dialectics' of Adorno which has attracted the most attention: a common concern with the lability and historicity of language, a repudiation of foundationalism in philosophy, an awareness of the subterranean links between the metaphysics and identity and structures of domination, and a shared, tortuous love-hate relation to Hegel, seem to mark out these two thinkers as unwitting philosophical comrades-in-arms. However, up till now, the predominant tendency of such comparisons has been to present Adorno as a kind of deconstructionist *avant la lettre*.[5] The assumption has been that a more consistent pursuit of anti-metaphysical themes, and by implication a more politically radical approach, can be found in the French Heideggerian than in the Frankfurt Marxist. It will be the fundamental contention of this essay that, for several interconnected reasons, this is a serious misunderstanding. First, although there are undoubtedly elements in Adorno's thought which anticipate Derridean themes, he has in many ways equally strong affinities with that mode of recent French thought which is usually known as the 'philosophy of desire'. It is only the exaggeration of the constitutive role of language in poststructuralism, it could be argued, and a corresponding antipathy – even on the intellectual Left – to the materialist emphases of Marxism, which have led to this aspect of Adorno's work being overlooked or underplayed. Second, from an Adornian perspective, it is precisely this lack of a materialist counterweight in Derrida's thought, the absence of any account of the interrelation of consciousness and nature, particularly 'inner nature', which can be seen to have brought forth the equally one-sided reaction of the philosophy of desire. From such a standpoint, different poststructuralist thinkers appear as dealing, in an inevitably distorting isolation, with what are in fact aspects of a single complex of problems. Finally, Adorno's concept of reconciliation, while far from immune to criticism, cannot be regarded as a simple 'failure of nerve' on his part, even less as an invitation to 'totalitarianism', to be contrasted with the harsher, less compromising vision of post-structuralism. It is rather the logical consequence of the attempt to think beyond a set of oppositions which – in their Nietzschean provenance – remain vulnerably brittle and abstract. In short, I hope to show, through an exploration of the central common theme of the critique of identity, that far from being merely a harbinger of poststructuralist and postmodernist styles of thought, Adorno offers us some of the conceptual tools with which to move beyond what is increasingly coming to appear, not least in France itself, as a self-destructively indiscriminate, and politically ambiguous, assault on the structures of rationality and modernity *in toto*.

In his 1973 essay on the painter Jacques Monory, Jean-François Lyotard makes significant use of the following tale from Borges's *Book of Imaginary Beings*:

> In one of the volumes of the *Lettres édifiantes et curieuses* that appeared in Paris during the first half of the eighteenth century, Father Fontecchio of the Society of Jesus planned a study of the superstitions and misinformation of the common people of Canton; in the preliminary outline he noted that the Fish was a shifting and shining creature that nobody had ever caught but that many said they had glimpsed in the depths of mirrors. Father Fontecchio died in 1736, and the work begun by his pen remained unfinished; some 150 years later Herbert Allen Giles took up the interrupted task. According to Giles, belief in the Fish is part of a larger myth that goes back to the legendary times of the Yellow Emperor.
>
> In those days the world of mirrors and the world of men were not, as they are now, cut off from each other. They were, besides, quite different; neither beings, nor colours nor shapes were the same. Both kingdoms, the specular and the human, lived in harmony; you could come and go through mirrors. One night the mirror people invaded the earth. Their power was great, but at the end of bloody warfare the magic arts of the Yellow Emperor prevailed. He repulsed the invaders, imprisoned them in their mirrors, and forced on them the task of repeating, as though in a kind of dream, all the actions of men. He stripped them of their power and of their forms and reduced them to mere slavish reflections. None the less, a day will come when the magic spell will be shaken off.

The first to awaken will be the Fish. Deep in the mirror we will perceive a very faint line and the colour of this line will be like no other colour. Later on, other shapes will begin to stir. Little by little they will differ from us; little by little they will not imitate us. They will break through the barriers of glass or metal, and this time will not be defeated. Side by side with these mirror creatures, the creatures of water will join battle.

In Yunnan, they do not speak of the Fish but of the Tiger of the Mirror. Others believe that in advance of the invasion we will hear from the depths of mirrors the clatter of weapons.[6]

For Lyotard this story condenses a critique of the modern subject which he shares with the majority of poststructuralist thinkers. Subjectivity presupposes reflection, a representation of experience as that of an experiencing self. But through such representation, which depends upon the synthesizing function of concepts, the original fluidity of intuition, the communication between the human and the specular worlds, is lost. Consciousness becomes a kind of self-contained theatre, divided between stage and auditorium: energy is transformed into the thought of energy, intensity into intentionality. Thus Lyotard writes that

> Borges imagines these beings as forces, and this bar [the bar between representation and the represented] as a barrier; he imagines that the Emperor, the Despot in general, can only maintain his position on condition that he represses the monsters and keeps them on the other side of the transparent wall. The existence of the subject depends on this wall, on the enslavement of the fluid and lethal powers repressed on the other side, on the function of representing them.[7]

This protest at the coercive unification implied by the notion of a self-conscious, self-identical subject is – of course – one of the central themes of poststructuralism. It occurs, in works such as the *Anti-Oedipus* of Deleuze and Guattari, in which the schizophrenic fragmentation of experience and loss of identity is celebrated as a liberation from the self forged by the Oedipus complex. But it can also be found, in a more oblique form, in the work of Michel Foucault. The models of enclosure and observation which Foucault explored throughout his career are, in a sense, historically specific, institutional embodiments of this conception of a consciousness imposing its order upon the disorderly manifold of impulse. This is clearest in the case of the Panopticon which Foucault describes in *Discipline and Punish*; but, in fact, as far back as *Madness and Civilization*, Foucault had analysed what he terms 'the elaboration around and above madness of a kind of absolute subject which is wholly gaze, and which confers upon it and status of a pure object'.[8] Throughout his work the omnipresent look reduces alterity to identity.

Traditionally, within the sphere of philosophy, it is perhaps the stream of dialectical thought derived from Hegel which has most persistently opposed this rigidity of the classifying gaze. Hegel's critique of the 'philosophy of reflection' is based on the view that any assumption abstracted from experience and taken to be fundamental must necessarily enter into contradiction with itself, including the assumption that subjectivity itself is something self-contained, isolated from and standing over against the object of knowledge. In Hegel's conception experience consists in the shifting reciprocal determinations of subject and object, and culminates in an awareness that the very distinction between the two is valid only from a restricted standpoint. As early as his essay on the difference between the systems of Fichte and Schelling, Hegel had established this fundamental principle of his philosophizing. 'The need of philosophy can satisfy itself', he writes, 'by simply penetrating to the principle of nullifying all fixed oppositions and connecting the limited to the Absolute. This satisfaction found in the principle of absolute identity is characteristic of philosophy as such.'[9] However, as this quotation makes clear, the dialectical mobilization of the relation between subject and object in Hegel does not entail the abandonment of the principle of identity. Hence, for poststructuralist thought, the reliance on an Absolute which relativizes and reveals the 'reifying' character of conceptual dissection results in an even more ineluctable form of coercion, since the movement from standpoint to standpoint is oriented towards a predetermined goal. The voyage of consciousness is undertaken only with a view to the treasure of experience which can be accumulated and brought home: the individual moments of the voyage are not enjoyed simply for themselves. This critique of Hegel is also, of course, implicitly or explicitly, a critique of Marxism, which is seen as attempting to coerce the plurality of social and political movements into a single unswerving dialectic of history.

One of the fundamental problems confronting poststructuralist thought, therefore – a problem which accounts for many of its distinctive features – is how to reject simultaneously both the repressive rigidities of self-consciousness and conceptual thought, *and* the available dialectical alternatives. In the quest for a solution to this difficulty, it is Nietzsche who plays the most important role. The central imaginative polarity in Nietzsche's work between the fluidity of the ultimate world of becoming, and the static systems of concepts laid over this fluidity, allows him to reveal the deceptiveness of all partial perspectives on reality, while also blocking the possibility of an historical totality of perspectives, which reveals what cannot be known through any one alone. Nietzsche's characteristic verbal compounds (*hineinlegen, hinzulügen* . . .) render unmistakable his view that all meaning, coherence and teleological movement is projected on to a world which, in itself, is blank, purposeless, indifferent, chaotic. This is a conception of the relation between thought and reality which is common to much of the Nietzsche-influenced philosophy of the 1960s and 1970s in France. Its most striking and systematically elaborated exemplification is perhaps to be found in Lyotard's *Economie libidinale*, which is centred on the notion of a 'grand ephemeral pellicule' constituted by the deployed surfaces of the body, which are swept by an incessantly mobile libidinal cathexis generating points of pure sensation or 'intensity'. This description of the libidinal band is perhaps best considered as a philosophical experiment, a paradoxical attempt to explore what experience would be like before the emergence of a self-conscious subject of experience. In Lyotard's view, this emergence can only take place through a cooling of intensity, a transformation of energy. Rendering more explicit the assumptions of his commentary on Borges, he writes that

> Theatricality and representation, far from being something one should take as a libidinal given, *a fortiori* as a metaphysical given, results from a certain kind of work on the labyrinthine and moebian band, an operation which imprints these special folds and creases whose effect is a box closed in on itself, and allowing to appear on the stage only those impulses which, coming from what will from now on be called the exterior, satisfy the conditions of interiority.[10]

Once the representational chamber of consciousness is constituted, then the libidinal band is inevitably occluded; *all* representation is misrepresentation. For Lyotard each segment of the band is 'absolutely singular', so that the attempt to divide it up into conceptual identities 'implies the denial of disparities, of heterogeneities, of transits and stages of energy, it implies the denial of polymorphy'.[11] This ontological affirmation of an irreducible plurality – in more or less sophisticated versions – has been one of the most influential themes of poststructuralism, and has had widespread political repercussions. It is, however, fraught with difficulties, which I would like to explore by looking a little more closely at the Nietzschean thought by which it is inspired.

From the very beginning of his work, Nietzsche is concerned to combat the notion of knowledge as the mere reproduction of an objective reality, believing that forms of knowledge necessarily are – and should be – in the service of and shaped by human interests. The argument is already central to *The Birth of Tragedy*, where Nietzsche draws an unfavourable contrast between Greek tragedy at the height of its powers – a form of artistic creation which, through its blending of Dionysiac insight and Apollonian order, was able to confront the horror and chaos of existence, and yet draw an affirmative conclusion from this confrontation – and the naively optimistic assumption of Socratic dialectic that reality can be exhaustively grasped in concepts. *The Birth of Tragedy* is directed against 'the illusion that thought, guided by the thread of causation, might plumb the furthest abysses of being, and even correct it'.[12] Throughout his work Nietzsche will stress the aversion of the human mind to chaos, its fear of unmediated intuition, and its resultant attempts to simplify the world by reducing diversity to identity. There is, however, an equally strong pragmatic tendency in Nietzsche, which suggests that this process of ordering and simplification takes place not simply because of an 'existential' need for security, but in the interests of sheer survival:

> In order for a particular species to maintain itself and increase its power, its conception of reality must comprehend enough of the calculable and constant for it to base a scheme of behaviour on it. The utility of perservation – not some abstract-theoretical need not to be deceived – stands as the motive behind the development of the organs of knowledge.[13]

It is on such considerations that Nietzsche bases his many paradoxical pronouncements on the nature of knowledge and truth; his statement – for example – that 'Truth is the kind of error without which a certain species of life cannot live.'[14]

A number of commentators have attempted to moderate the

perplexing and scandalous effect of these formulations by suggesting that Nietzsche draws a distinction, implicitly at least, between two kinds of truth. His attack is directed against correspondence theories of truth, against the failure to consider the extent to which our language and our concepts shape the world, but does not exclude a deeper insight into the nature of reality which would merit the title 'truth'. Such attempts to render Nietzsche's position coherent are not entirely without textual support, but they also have a tendency to underplay the extent to which Nietzsche's paradoxical formulations betray a genuine dilemma. The Kantian element in Nietzsche's thought pushes him towards a thorough-going idealist epistemology, since – like Kant's immediate successors – he rejects the doctrine of the 'thing-in-itself' as incoherent. Thus, in *The Will to Power* he writes:

> The intellect cannot criticise itself, simply because it cannot be compared with other species of intellect and because its capacity to know would be revealed only in the presence of 'true reality'. . . . This presupposes that, distinct from every perspective kind of outlook or sensual-spiritual appropriation, something exists, an "in-itself". – But the psychological derivation of the belief in things forbids us to speak of 'things-in-themselves'.[15]

Yet, despite his strictures, from *The Birth of Tragedy* onward, where he contrasts the shallow optimism of science to an alternative Dionysiac insight into the nature of things, Nietzsche will repeatedly oppose a vision of ultimate reality to accepted truths. Indeed, in *The Birth of Tragedy*, he employs the Kantian concept of the noumenal to illustrate precisely this opposition: 'The contrast of this authentic nature-truth and the lies of culture which present themselves as the sole reality is similar to that between the eternal core of things, the thing in itself, and the entire world of appearance.'[16] In general, Nietzsche's critique of metaphysics, and his denial of the ability of philosophy to establish epistemological criteria, drives him towards an idealism which argues that the structures of knowledge are constitutive of the object, while his insistence that all consciousness should comprehend itself as perspectival pushes him back towards a reinstatement of the distinction between appearance and reality.

I would argue that a similar dilemma, encapsulated in Nietzsche's dictum that 'Knowledge and Becoming exclude on another',[17] pervades the work of those poststructuralist thinkers who have been most directly influenced by Nietzschean schemas. We have already examined how Lyotard's motif of the libidinal band, which fuses a Freudian–inspired theory of cathexis with the doctrine of the Eternal Return, makes possible a denunciation of all theoretical discourses as 'apparatuses for the fixation and draining away of intensity'.[18] Lyotard, however, is too conscientious – and too restless – a figure to be satisfied for long with the monistic metaphysics of libido on which *Economie libidinale* relied. It can be no accident that, shortly after the publication of this work, he began to set off in a new direction, replacing the description of forms of discourse as '*dispositifs pulsionels*' with the less ontologically loaded notion of 'language-games', borrowed from Wittgenstein. In Lyotard's case, the attempt to develop a critique of objectifying theory from the standpoint of an ontology of flux represents an explicit, but only temporary, phase of his thought. With Foucault, however, the tension which this attempt implies is both a more covert, but also a more persistent, feature of his work. It is already apparent in *Madness and Civilization*, where Foucault wishes to develop a critique of the objectifying and alienating nature of modern psychiatric treatment and its theorizations, while also being conscious of the difficulty of appealing to the 'rudimentary movements of an experience' which would be 'madness itself'.[19] In *The Archaeology of Knowledge* Foucault renounces this approach: 'We are not trying to reconstitute what madness itself might be . . . in the form in which it was later organized (translated, deformed, travestied, perhaps even repressed) by discourses, and the oblique, often twisted play of their operations.'[20] He ostensibly adopts a position in which discourses are entirely constitutive of their objects. And yet the contradiction persists, since it is inherent in his attempt to develop a non-dialectical form of critique. In the first volume of *The History of Sexuality*, for example, the oscillation between the epistemological and the ontological occurs in the form of an opposition between the apparatuses of sexuality and a tentatively – but persistently – evoked prediscursive 'body and its pleasures'.[21] Foucault is only able to avoid this dilemma in his final publications by returning to a notion of self-constitution and self-reflection which he had denounced up until this point as illicitly Hegelian. One of the fundamental tenets of poststructuralist thought is tacitly abandoned when Foucault reinstates the relation between knowledge and its object as internal to consciousness; when he enquires:

By means of what play of truth does man offer himself to be thought in his own being when he perceives himself as mad, when he considers himself as ill, when he reflects on himself as a living, speaking and labouring being, when he judges and punishes himself as a criminal?[22]

This is an unmistakably 'revisionist' retrospective.

Having explored this fundamental difficulty of the poststructuralist position, I would now like to introduce the comparison with Adorno. One obvious point of entry would be the fact that both the post-structuralists and Adorno owe an enormous debt to Nietzsche, and in particular to his sense of the cost imposed by the forging of a self-identical, morally responsible subject, perhaps most vividly conveyed in the second essay of *On the Genealogy of Morals*. However, as I have already suggested, the full import of these parallels has been mis-understood, because of a failure to appreciate the gap between the general philosophical projects within which they occur. One of the most important distinctions in this respect is that Adorno is not content with a Nietzschean-Freudian, naturalist critique of con-sciousness, but takes up the discovery of the early German romantics that the philosophy of pure consciousness is internally incoherent. In an illuminating article, Jochen Hörisch has shown that the original antecedents for Adorno's acute awareness of the loss of spontaneity imposed by the formation of the modern autonomous individual, his sense that the identity of the self must be coercively maintained against the centrifugal tendencies of impulse, can be traced back beyond Nietzsche to the critical engagement with Fichte's philo-sophers of Schlegel and Novalis. It is here, in thought partly inspired – like Adorno's own – by dismay at the failure of an attempted political realization of reason, that Adorno discovers a hidden history of subjectivity, an evocation of the pain of the process of individuation which is betrayed by logical incoherence. 'Early romanticism', Hörisch argues, 'discovers suffering as the *principium individuationis* and as the "secret of individuality", which transcendental philosophy can only conceal at the cost of becoming entangled in unavowed contradictions. The pain of individuation derives from the inscription of a compulsory identity which passes itself off as an a priori structure of reason.'[23] Both aspects of this critique will be of crucial importance for Adorno: the demonstration of the structure of contradiction which *both* splits and constitutes the subject, and the sensitivity to the repression of inner nature which is demanded by the forging of such a subject. Adorno's critique of the modern subject, therefore, is as implacable as that of the poststructuralists, and is based on not dissimilar grounds: yet – in contrast to Foucault, Deleuze or Lyotard – it does not culminate in a call for the abolition of the subjective principle. Rather, Adorno always insists that our only option is to 'use the force of the subject to break through the deception of constitutive subjectivity'.[24] In order fully to understand the reasons for this difference of conclusion, we must turn to Adorno's account of the relation between concept and object, universality and particularity, and its opposition to that of Nietzsche.

From the very beginning, Nietzsche's work is haunted by a sense of the inherent fictionalizing and fetishizing tendencies of language and conceptual thought. In his early essay 'On Truth and Lies in an Extra-Moral Sense' Nietzsche remarks that

> Every word becomes immediately a concept through the fact that it must not serve simply for the absolutely individualized original experience, to which it owes its birth, that is to say as a reminder, but must straightaway serve for countless more or less similar cases, and that means must be matched to purely dissimilar cases. Every concept arises through the equating of what is not the same. (*Jeder Begriff entsteht durch Gleichsetzung des Nichtgleichen.*) [25]

Throughout Nietzsche's work such remarks on the 'coarseness' of language, on the indifference to differences entailed by the use of concepts, are to be found. 'Just as it is certain', Nietzsche continues,

> that one leaf is never quite like another, so it is certain that the concept leaf is constructed by an arbitrary dropping of individual differences, through a forgetting of what differentiates; and this awakens the idea that there is something in nature besides leaves which would be "leaf", that is to say an original form, according to which all leaves are woven, drawn, circumscribed, coloured, curled, painted, but by clumsy hands, so that no example emerges correctly and reliably as a true copy of the original form. . . . The overlooking of the individual gives us the form, whereas nature knows no forms and no concepts, and also no species, but only an X, which is unaccessible and indefinable to us.[26]

It is precisely such a view of the deceptive identity forged by concepts, as we have seen, which motivates Lyotard's evocation of the ineffably

11

singular points of intensity which constitute the libidinal band, or Foucault's reluctant but repeated recourse to an uncapturable prediscursive spontaneity – whether under the title of 'madness', 'resistance', or 'the body and its pleasures'.

Nietzsche's account of the manner in which real, particular leaves come to be seen as poor imitations of the concept 'leaf', captures precisely that process which Adorno refers to as 'identity-thinking'. 'The immanent claim of the concept', Adorno writes, 'is its order-creating invariance over against the variation of what is grasped under it. This is denied by the form of the concept, which is "false" in that respect.'[27] However, Adorno does not believe that this situation can be remedied simply by counterposing the contingent and particular to the universality of concepts. Rather, he argues, the assumption that what he terms the 'non-identical', what is left behind by the concept, is merely an inaccessible and undefinable X, the belief that 'nature knows no forms and no concepts', is itself the result of the primacy of the universal in identity-thinking. Adorno's philosophical effort is directed towards moving beyond the split between bare facticity and conceptual determination, through an experience of the contradiction which that split itself implies. Non-identity, Adorno suggests, 'is opaque only for identity's claim to be total'.[28] Thus, in the Introduction to *Against Epistemology (Zur Metakritik der Erkenntnistheorie)*, a series of critical essays on Husserlian phenomenology, Adorno employs the following passage from *The Twilight of the Idols* to demonstrate that Nietzsche 'undervalued what he saw through':

> formerly, alteration, change, any becoming at all, were taken as proof of mere appearance, as an indication that there must be something which led us astray. Today, conversely, precisely in so far as the prejudice of reason forces us to posit unity, identity, permanence, substance, cause, thinghood, being, we see ourselves caught in error, compelled into error.[29]

Against the bent of this text, which is characteristic both of Nietzsche and his poststructuralist followers, Adorno insists that

> The opposition of the stable to the chaotic, and the domination of nature, would never have succeeded without an element of stability in the dominated, which would otherwise incessantly give the lie to the subject. Completely casting away that element

and localizing it solely in the subject is no less *hubris* than absolutizing the schemata of conceptual order . . . sheer chaos, to which reflective spirit downgrades the world for the sake of its own total power, is just as much the product of spirit as the cosmos it sets up as an object of reverence.[30]

Adorno's argument is that pure singularity is itself an abstraction, the waste-product of identity-thinking.

Two major implications of this position are that the attempt by poststructuralist thought to isolate singularity will simply boomerang into another form of abstraction; and that what it mistakes for immediacy will in fact be highly mediated. These pitfalls are clearly exemplified by Lyotard's working through of the 'philosophy of desire' in *Economie libidinale*. The notion of a libidinal band composed of ephemeral intensities is an attempt to envisage a condition in which, as Nietzsche puts it, 'no moment would be for the sake of another'. But if every moment is prized purely for its uniqueness, without reference to a purpose or a meaning, to a before or an after, without reference to anything which goes beyond itself, then what is enjoyed in each moment becomes paradoxically and monotonously the same: in Lyotard's work of the mid-seventies any action, discourse, or aesthetic structure becomes an equally good – or equally bad – conveyor of intensity. Furthermore, Lyotard's own evocations betray his ostensible intention, since they make clear that such 'intensities' cannot be reduced to pure cathexis, but are symbolically structured, coloured by remarkably determinate situations:

> the slow, light, intent gaze of an eye, then suddenly the head turns so that there is nothing left but a profile, Egypt. The silence which settles around her extends to great expanses of the libidinal band which, it seems, belongs to her body. Those zones also are silent, which means that dense, inundating surges move noiselessly and continually towards 'her' regions, or come from these regions, down the length of slopes.[31]

It is important to note that Adorno does not avoid these difficulties by espousing a Hegelian position. He agrees with Hegel that, as a unity *imposed* on particulars, the abstract universal enters into contradiction with its own concept – becomes itself something arbitrary and particular. But he argues that even Hegel's solution – an immanent, self-realizing universal – fails to challenge the primacy of

13

the universal as such. Identity-thinking, even in its Hegelian form, defeats its own purpose, since by reducing what is non-identical in the object to itself, it ultimately comes away empty-handed. For Adorno, the experience of this contradiction sparks off a further movement of reflection, to a position in which the non-identical is no longer viewed as the isolated particular which it is forced back into being by identity-thinking. The particular is now seen as standing in a pattern of relations to other particulars, a historically sedimented 'constellation' which defines its identity. 'What is internal to the non-identical', Adorno writes, 'is its relation to what it is not itself, and which its instituted, frozen identity withholds from it. . . . The object opens itself to a monadological insistence, which is a consciousness of the constellation in which it stands.'[32] This consciousness, in its turn, can only be expressed through a 'constellation' – as opposed to a hierarchical ordering – of concepts, which are able to generate out of the tension between them an openness to that non-identity of the thing itself, which would be 'the thing's own identity against its identifications'.[33] There is for Adorno, in other words, no necessary antagonism between conceptual thought and reality, no inevitable mutual exclusion of Knowledge and Becoming. The problem is posed not by conceptual thought as such, but by the assumption of the primacy of the concept, the delusion that mind lies beyond the total process in which it finds itself as a moment. The characteristics of reality which poststructuralist thought ontologizes are in fact merely the reflection of an historically obsolete imperiousness of consciousness, a lack of equilibrium between subject and object. 'What we differentiate', Adorno writes, 'will appear divergent, dissonant, negative for just as long as the structure of our consciousness obliges it to strive for unity: as long as its demand for totality will be its measure of whatever is not identical with it.'[34]

One way of summarizing the argument so far would be to say that, for Adorno, the compulsive features of identity are inseparable from its internal contradictions: identity can only become adequate to its concept by acknowledging its own moment of non-identity. In the more naturalistic of the French thinkers influenced by Nietzsche, however, this logical dimension of the critique of consciousness is entirely absent. The ego is portrayed unproblematically as the internally consistent excluder of the spontaneity and particularity of impulse, with the consequence that opposition can only take the form of a self-defeating jump from the 'unity' of self-consciousness to the dispersal of intensities, or from the Oedipalized subject to a metaphysics of 'desiring machines'. In the work of Jacques Derrida, by contrast, a complementary one-sidedness occurs: the naturalistic dimension of Nietzsche's thought is almost entirely excluded in favour of an exploration of the contradictions implicit in the notion of pure self-identity. Derrida, in other words, shares a penchant for dialectics with Adorno, is sensitive to the unexpected ways in which philosophical opposites slide into one another, but is unable to link this concern with an account of the natural-historical genesis of the self.

The implications of this failure can perhaps best be highlighted by comparing Adorno's and Derrida's critiques of Husserlian phenomenology. Like Merleau-Ponty, whose account of the relation between consciousness and nature bears many affinities to his own, Adorno contests the very possibility of Husserl's transcendental reduction:

> the idealist may well call the conditions of possibility of the life of consciousness which have been abstracted out transcendental – they refer back to a determinate, to some "factual" conscious life. They are not valid "in themselves". . . . The strictest concept of the transcendental cannot release itself from its interdependence with the *factum*.[35]

It is important to note, however, that Adorno speaks of 'interdependence': he by no means wishes to effect an empiricist or naturalistic reduction of consciousness. Rather, his argument is simply that 'The mind's moment of non-being is so intertwined with existence that to pick it out neatly would be the same as to objectify and falsify it.'[36] Adorno, as a materialist, argues for the anchoring of consciousness in nature, while resisting any attempt to collapse the dialectic of subject and object into a metaphysical monism.

In Derrida's thought, however, the possibility of the transcendental reduction is never questioned as such. Rather, deconstruction incorporates the transcendental perspective, in an operation which Derrida terms 'erasure', but which – in its simultaneous cancellation and conservation – is close to a Hegelian *Anfhebung*. Thus, in *Of Grammatology* Derrida suggests that there is a 'short-of and a beyond of transcendental criticism', and that therefore 'the value of the transcendental arche must make its necessity felt before letting itself be erased'.[37] What this erasure consists in for Derrida is not the insistence on an irreducible break between facticity and the transcendental, which metaphysics has always dreamed of over-coming, but rather a 'reduction of the reduction', an appeal to what he explicitly terms an 'ultra-transcendental text'. For Derrida the incoherence of the concept of self-presence on which Husserl's theory of transcendental subjectivity is based reveals that the transcendental subject and its objects, along with the other characteristic oppositions of metaphysical thought, are in some sense – which he finds rather uncomfortable to expound – the 'effects' of a higher principle of non-identity for which his most common name is *différance*. The result is a final philosophical position remarkably reminiscent of pre-Hegelian idealism. Since absolute difference, lacking all determinacy, is indistinguishable from absolute identity, Derrida's evocations of a trace which is 'origin of all repetition, origin of ideality . . . not more ideal than real, not more intelligible than sensible, not more a transparent signification than an opaque energy',[38] provide perhaps the closest twentieth-century parallel to the *Identitätsphilosophie* of the younger Schelling.

It appears, therefore, that Derrida's attempt to develop a critique of the self-identical subject which eschews any naturalistic moment, results in a position no more plausible than Lyotard's monistic metaphysics of libido. Although Adorno did not live long enough to confront Derrida's position directly, his likely response to current comparisons and interassimilations of deconstruction and negative dialectics can be deduced from the critique of Heidegger's thought – undoubtedly the central influence on Derrida – which threads its way through his work. Heidegger is correct to suggest that there is 'more' to entities than simply their status as objects of consciousness, but – in Adorno's view – by treating this 'more' under the heading of 'Being' he transforms it into a self-defeating hypostatization:

> By making what philosophy cannot express an immediate theme, Heidegger dams philosophy up, to the point of a revocation of consciousness. By way of punishment, the spring which, according to his conception, is buried, and which he would like to uncover, dries up far more pitifully than the insight of philosophy, which was destroyed in vain, and which inclined towards the inexpressible through its mediations.[39]

For Adorno, whatever experience the word 'Being' may convey can only be expressed by a constellation of entities, whereas, in Heidegger's philosophy, the irreducibility of a relation is itself transformed into an ultimate. In the evocation of a Being which transcends the subject-object distinction 'the moment of mediation becomes isolated and thereby immediate. However, mediation can be hypostatized just as little as the subject and object poles; it is only valid in their constellation. Mediation is mediated by what it mediates.'[40] *Mutatis mutandis*, one could also argue that Derridean *différance* is in fact differentiated by what it differentiates. While it is true that nature and culture, signified and signifier, object and subject would be nothing without the difference between them, this is not sufficient to ensure the *logical priority* of non-identity over identity which is crucial to Derrida's whole philosophical stance. The distinction between his position, according to which 'subjectivity – like objectivity – is an effect of *différance*, an effect inscribed in a system of *différance*',[41] and that of Adorno, is clearly revealed by the following passage from *Negative Dialectics*:

> The polarity of subject and object can easily be taken, for its part, as an undialectical structure within which all dialectics take place. But both concepts are categories which originate in reflection, formulas for something which is not to be unified; nothing positive, not primary states of affairs, but negative throughout. Nonetheless, the difference of subject and object is not to be negated in its turn. They are neither an ultimate duality, nor is an ultimate unity hidden behind them. They constitute each other as much as – through such constitution – they separate out from each other.[42]

By this point it will be clear that the frequent attempt of post-structuralist thinkers, and of literary and political commentators influenced by poststructuralism, to oppose the Nietzschean critique of identity to the coercive totalizations of dialectical thought, is beset with intractable difficulties. Adorno, no less than recent French thought, criticizes Hegel's dialectic as being in many ways the most insidious, most ineluctable form of identity-thinking. Yet, at the same time, his deeply dialectical sensibility perceives the self-defeating dynamic of a blunt prioritization of particularity, diversity, and non-identity. The dissolution of the reflective unity of the self in Deleuze or Lyotard leads only to the indifference of boundless flux, or to the monotonous repetition of intensity; while in Derrida's work the jettisoning of the materialist ballast of the Nietzschean and Freudian critique of consciousness, results in the installation of difference as the principle of a new kind of 'first philosophy'. For Adorno, by contrast, non-identity cannot be respected by abandoning completely the principle of identity. 'To define identity as the correspondence of the thing-in-itself to its concept', he writes,

> is *hubris*; but the ideal of identity must not simply be discarded. Living in the rebuke that the thing is not identical with the concept is the concept's longing to become identical with the thing. This is how the sense of non-identity contains identity. The supposition of identity is indeed the ideological element of pure thought, all the way through to formal logic; but hidden in it is also the truth moment of ideology, the pledge that there should be no contradiction, no antagonism.[43]

Bearing this argument in mind, we are now perhaps in a position to return with more insight to the Borges story with which we began. It will already be apparent that the tale of the subduing of the mirror animals can be interpreted in terms not only of the libidinal critique of consciousness, but also of the 'Dialectic of Enlightenment' which was first formulated by Horkheimer and Adorno during the early 1940s, and which continues to underpin *Negative Dialectics* and *Aesthetic Theory*. The humanization of the drives, represented by the transformation of the animals into reflections, does indeed result in a kind of mastery by the ego. But this mastery is bought at the price of a terrible isolation: in *Negative Dialectics* Adorno returns repeatedly to the pathos of a self helplessly confined within the circle of its own immanence, unable to make contact with anything external which does not turn out to be simply its own reflection. The need to break out of this isolation generates a tension at the heart of subjectivity itself, which poststructuralism, in general, is reluctant or unable to recognize. This inadequacy suggests that there might be substantive aspects of the story which Lyotard has failed to account for in his interpretation.

First, Lyotard describes the banishment and punishment of the animals as a simple act of force, of repression and containment, whereas Borges describes the Emperor as employing his 'magic arts', as putting the animals under a spell. Significantly, the concept of a spell plays an important role in Adorno's philosophy; since enchantment can constitute a peculiarly intangible and non-apparent form of coercion, to speak of a spell suggests a state of compulsive selfhood in which actions are simultaneously autonomous and heteronomous, accompanied by an exaggerated subjective illusion of autonomy, but carried out by subjects nevertheless. The metaphor of the spell, in other words, captures both the repressive and enabling features of processes of socialization, which are portrayed as an aspect of the human conquest of nature in the interests of self-preservation. As Adorno writes in *Negative Dialectics*, 'The spell is the subjective form of the world spirit, the internal reinforcement of its primacy over the external processes of life.'[44] In the later *Critical Theory of Habermas*, this parallelism of the instrumental domination of outer nature and the repression of inner nature will be contested. Habermas will avoid Adorno's implication that emancipation from nature entails the closing-down of all communicative sensitivity by attributing socialization and instrumental action to categorially distinct dimensions of historical development. Nevertheless, already, in its Adornian version, the Critical Theory position has a distinct advantage over that of the poststructuralists; for while figures such as Lyotard force themselves into a corner, where they can only denounce the dominance of the ego as an arbitrary coercion which should be abolished (whether it could is somewhat more problematic), Adorno perceives that compulsive identity, the sacrifice of the moment for the future, was necessary at a certain stage of history, in order for human beings to liberate themselves from blind subjugation to nature. To this extent such identity already contains a moment of freedom. Accordingly, the 'spell of selfhood' cannot be seen simply as an extension of natural coercion; rather it is an illusion which could, in principle, be reflectively broken through by the subject which it generates – although the full realization of this process would be inseparable from a transformation of social relations. Furthermore, the result of such a breakthrough would not be the self-defeating inrush of the 'fluid and lethal powers' which Lyotard describes, but rather a true identity – one which would be permeable to its own non-identical moment. One of the major differences between poststructuralism and Critical Theory is summarized in Adorno's contention that 'even when we merely limit the subject, we put an end to its power'.[45]

This brings us to a second point. Lyotard describes the mirror animals as 'monsters', but Borges specifies that the people of Canton believe the creature of the mirror to be a fish, 'a shifting and shining creature that nobody has ever caught', while in Yunnan it is believed to be a tiger. In Adorno's thought it is under this double aspect that the non-identical appears to identity-thinking: on the one hand as something of tantalizing beauty which perpetually eludes our grasp, on the other as something menacing and uncontrollable, menacing precisely because of our inordinate need to control it. Yet we cannot enter into relation with this creature either by smashing the mirror (the solution of the 'philosophers of desire'), or by claiming – as does Derrida – that both the true world and the reflected world are merely effects generated by its invisible surface. Rather, the only way to achieve this relation is to revoke the spell cast by the Emperor on the animals, and which is also – as we have seen – a spell cast on himself.

It would not do to conclude, however, without stressing an important distinction between the lesson of Borges's tale and the philosophical position of Adorno. The story does contain an evocation of utopia, but Borges sets this in a distant, irrecoverable past. 'In legendary times', he tells us, 'the world of mirrors and the world of men were not . . . cut off from each other. They were, besides, quite different, neither beings, nor colours, nor shapes were the same. Both kingdoms, the specular and the human, lived in harmony; you could come and go through mirrors.' In Borges's version this initial accord is broken by an unexplained onslaught of nature, temporarily repulsed by humankind, but destined to triumph in the end: 'a day will come when the magic spell will be shaken off', and this time the animals 'will not be defeated'. Adorno does not deny the possibility of such a calamitous conclusion to history: the 'clatter of weapons' from 'the depths of mirrors', which some believe will precede the final invasion, will undoubtedly sound, to our late twentieth-century ears, like a three-minute nuclear warning. But Adorno does contest that such a terminus is inevitable. Our historical dilemma consists in the fact that the essential material preconditions for a reconciliation between human beings, and between humanity and nature, could only have been installed by a history of domination and self-coercion which has now built up an almost unstoppable momentum. As Adorno writes in *Negative Dialectics*, 'since self-preservation has been precarious and difficult for eons, the power of its instrument, the ego drives, remains all but irresistible even after technology has virtually made self-preservation easy'.[46] To suggest a prelapsarian harmony, in the face of this dilemma, is merely to fall resignedly into conservative illusion. Nevertheless, Borges's evocation of a state of peaceful interchange between the human and the mirror worlds provides a fitting image for that affinity without identity, and difference without domination – rather than coercive unity – which Adorno believes to be implied by the pledge that there should be 'no contradiction, no antagonism'.

NOTES

1 See 'Structuralism and Post-Structuralism: an Interview with Michel Foucault', *Telos* 55, Spring 1983, p. 200, and 'Un cours inédit', in *Magazine littéraire*, no. 207, May 1984.
2 See Jean-François Lyotard, 'Presentations', in Alan Montefiore (ed.) *Philosophy in France Today*, Cambridge 1983, pp. 201–4.
3 See Jacques Derrida, *La Verité en peinture*, Paris 1978, pp. 200–9.
4 Axel Honneth, *Kritik der Macht*, Frankfurt 1982; Albrecht Wellmer, *Zur Dialektik von Moderne und Postmoderne*, Frankfurt 1985; Jürgen Habermas, *Der philosophische Diskurs der Moderne*, Frankfurt 1985.
5 See, for example, Rainer Nägele, 'The Scene of the Other: Theodor W. Adorno's Negative Dialectic in the Context of Post-structuralism', *Boundary 2*, Fall–Winter 1982–3; Martin Jay, *Adorno*, London 1984, pp. 21–2; and, above all, Michael Ryan, *Marxism and Deconstruction*, Baltimore 1982, pp. 73–81.
6 Jorge Luis Borges, 'The Fauna of Mirrors', in *The Book of Imaginary Beings*, Harmondsworth 1974, pp. 67–8.
7 Jean-François Lyotard, 'Contribution des tableaux de Jacques Monory', in Gérald Gassiot-Talabot *et al*, *Figurations 1960/1973*, Paris 1973, pp. 155–6.
8 Michel Foucault, *Histoire de la folie à l'âge classique*, collection TEL edn, Paris 1976, p. 479.
9 G.W.F. Hegel, *The Difference Between Fichte's and Schelling's Systems of Philosophy*, Albany 1977, p. 112.
10 Jean-François Lyotard, *Economie libidinale*, Paris 1974, p. 11.
11 ibid., p. 294.
12 Friedrich Nietzsche, *Die Geburt der Tragödie aus dem Geiste der Musik*, in G. Colli and M. Montinari (eds) *Sämtiche Werke, Kritische Studienausgabe*, Berlin/New York 1980, vol. 1, p. 99.
13 Fredrich Nietzsche, Walter Kaufman (ed.) *The Will to Power*, New York, 1967, pp. 266–7.
14 ibid., p. 272.
15 ibid., p. 263.
16 *Die Geburt der Tragödie*, pp. 58–9.
17 *The Will to Power*, p. 280.
18 *Economie libidinale*, p. 295.
19 Michel Foucault, 'Preface', in *Histoire de la folie à l'âge classique*, original edn, Paris 1961, p. vii.
20 Michel Foucault, *The Archaeology of Knowledge*, London 1972, p. 47.
21 See, in particular, Michel Foucault, *The History of Sexuality*, Harmondsworth 1981, pp. 150–9.
22 Michel Foucault, *L'Usage des plaisirs*, Paris 1984, p. 13.
23 Jochen Hörisch, 'Herrscherwort, Gott und Geltende Sätze', in Burkhardt Lindner

and W. Martin Lüdke (eds) *Materialien zur ästhetischen Theorie: Th. W. Adornos Konstruktion der Moderne*, Frankfurt 1980, p. 406.

24 Theodor W. Adorno, *Negative Dialectics*, London 1973, p. xx. In quotations from this text the translation has frequently been altered.

25 Friedrich Nietzsche, 'Ueber Wahrheit und Lüge im äussermoralische Sinne', in *Sämtliche Werke, Kritische Studienausgabe*, vol. 1, pp. 879–80.

26 ibid., p. 880.

27 *Negative Dialectics*, p. 153.

28 ibid., p. 163.

29 Friedrich Nietzsche, *Götzendammerung*, in *Sämtliche Werke, Kritische Studienausgabe*, vol. 6, p. 77, cited in Theodor W. Adorno, *Zur Metakritik der Erkenntnistheorie*, Frankfurt 1970, p. 26.

30 ibid., p. 27.

31 *Economie libidinale*, p. 40.

32 *Negative Dialectics*, p. 163.

33 ibid., p. 161.

34 ibid., pp. 5–6.

35 *Zur Metakritik der Erkenntnistheorie*, pp. 227–8.

36 *Negative Dialectics*, pp. 201–2.

37 Jacques Derrida, *Of Grammatology*, London 1976, p. 61.

38 ibid., p. 65.

39 *Negative Dialectics*, p. 110.

40 ibid., p. 99 (translation altered).

41 Jacques Derrida, *Positions*, Paris 1972, p. 40.

42 *Negative Dialectics*, p. 176.

43 ibid., p. 149.

44 ibid., p. 344.

45 ibid., p. 183. It is worth noting that the poststructuralist critique of consciousness, while exploiting Nietzsche's abstract opposition of particularity and conceptual identity, is in other respects extremely unfaithful to Nietzsche. Far from advocating a dissolution into impulse, Nietzsche is fully aware that the painfully acquired strength of self-discipline is a precondition for the liberation from discipline.

46 *Negative Dialectics*, p. 349.

Chapter 2

ADORNO AND THE METAPHYSICS OF MODERNISM: THE PROBLEM OF A 'POSTMODERN' ART

PETER OSBORNE

Aesthetic questions always boil down to
this: is the objective spirit in a specific
art work true?
(Adorno (draft introduction) *Aesthetic Theory*)

INTRODUCTION

The starting-point of Adorno's philosophical project was the rejection of idealism: 'the illusion . . . that the power of thought is sufficient to grasp the totality of the real'.[1] Its rationale, however, was always the redemption of the metaphysical or 'emphatic' concept of truth as the self-presentation of actuality ('the whole') from the context of idealist ontology. That the course of history has 'shattered the basis on which speculative metaphysical thought could be reconciled with experience', Adorno argued in *Negative Dialectics*, does not abolish the problem – the problem of truth – to which such thought was addressed. Rather, it 'forces materialism upon metaphysics': 'Kant's epistemological question "How is metaphysics possible?" yields to a question from the philosophy of history: "Is it still possible to have a metaphysical experience?"'.[2] The whole of Adorno's work revolves, in one way or another around this question. And it is by virtue of the ultimately affirmative character of the response to it that it offers (however qualified or paradoxical the character of this affirmation may be) that it is best understood as the elaboration of a modern metaphysics in the form of a *materialist metaphysic of modernity*; rather than, for example, either a negative *theology* or a mere *sociology* of illusion.[3] Nowhere is this clearer than in *Aesthetic Theory*, Adorno's monument to the critical metaphysics of the modernist aesthetic.

It is argued in *Negative Dialectics* that 'metaphysics cannot rise again', but that it may none the less '*originate* . . . with the realisation of what has been thought in its sign'.[4] Art, Adorno suggests, 'anticipates some of this'. *Aesthetic Theory* is an attempt to establish

23

the character and possibilities of this anticipation. It sets out a philosophical interpretation of the 'truth' of art which is at once essentially *historical*, in being located within the general terms of a philosophy of history (the dialectic of enlightenment), and avowedly *concrete*, in being oriented towards and guided by the experience of specific works of art. Its primary preoccupation is with modern art, and more specifically, with modernism. But if it is in this sense a vindication of modernism from the standpoint of metaphysics, *Aesthetic Theory* also involves a further questioning of the possibility of metaphysical experience (of the possibility of truth) from the standpoint of the crisis of modernism. Aesthetics, Adorno points out, 'can no longer rely on art as a fact'. 'Whether art will survive . . . is anybody's guess'. Aesthetics, in any case, 'is powerless to avert its becoming a necrologue of art'.[5] Its role for Adorno, one might say, following Hegel, is simply 'to comprehend what is'. And what is at present is a situation in which the 'affirmative essence' of art as an autonomous sphere of value has become so 'insufferable' in the context of an unfree society that 'true' art (an art which is true to the idea of truth) has been forced to 'challenge its own essence' and to revolt against itself. It does this, according to Adorno, 'by developing the aesthetic concept of anti-art'. From now on, he argues, 'no art will be conceivable without the moment of anti-art'.[6]

But if art has reached a point at which it must 'revolt against its essential concepts' in order to survive, it none the less remains inconceivable without them. All modern art, according to Adorno, is inscribed within the terms of this contradiction. Under such conditions, aesthetics can have only one goal: 'to foster the rational and concrete dissolution of conventional aesthetic categories' in such a way as to 'release new truth content into these categories', by confronting them with the most recent forms of artistic experience.[7] This, in a nutshell, is the project of *Aesthetic Theory*, undertaken in full awareness of the uncertainty and precariousness of its object. For while aesthetics may be powerless to combat the basic social determinants underlying what Adorno calls the 'desubstantialisation' (*Entkunstung*) of art (the loss of its capacity to act as a medium for the expression of historical possibilities),[8] it may none the less contribute, within the terms of these determinations, to its resistance to them.

It is on account of his awareness, first, of the fundamentally problematic status of modern art, and second, of the consequent increased need for theoretical reflection upon its meaning and possibilities, that Adorno's work bears on the problem of the 'post-modern'; both in its narrow sense as the problem of the possibility and meaning of a postmodern art, and in its extended and still far from clear sense as the problem of the fate of the whole enlightenment project of 'modernity' – assuming, for the moment, that it is possible to speak of some such unitary project. Precisely how it does so however, remains obscure. This is not just because of the loss of clarity suffered by the idea of the postmodern on its journey from the architectural realm, through the general aesthetic, to the socio-historical – a loss which has been both obscured, and to some extent compensated, by a corresponding increase in its suggestiveness and ideological force. It is also, and perhaps even primarily, because of certain ambiguities, or at least certain difficulties, within Adorno's work itself. Thus, some like Martin Jay, have pointed to the proto-deconstructionist tendencies in Adorno's work.[9] Others have stressed his refusal to give up the emphatic concept of truth.[10] While Wellmer, starting out from Habermas's critique of Adorno, has suggested the possibility of a synthesis of these opposing tendencies within his work on the basis of a reconstruction of its metaphysical premises.[11] In this respect, Adorno's work would appear to be as much a symptom of the intractability of the problem of the postmodern as a possible basis for its resolution.

But if the dispute over the meaning of Adorno's work may be understood as a sign of the intractability of the problem of the postmodern, the work itself also offers, within the account of modernism it contains, a diagnosis of this condition. It is in this respect, I want to suggest, that it has most to contribute to the furthering of current debates. In the first place, its interpretation of the crisis of modernism from the standpoint of a basically classical conception of the metaphysical significance of aesthetic experience *problematizes* our understanding of the latest aesthetic phenomena; rather than, like certain proponents of the idea of postmodernism, either merely celebrating their self-understanding, or alternatively, precipitately imposing tendentiously deconstructive interpretations upon them. Second, it provides us with a determinate set of historically grounded aesthetic categories of modernism through which to approach the question of the possibility and possible meaning of a postmodern art. It thus avoids the twin and convergent dangers of a pre-emptive theoretical closure of the issue (that would deny both the relative historical openness and the genuinely problematic character of the current aesthetic conjuncture), on the one hand, and a regression to a self-defeating descriptivism (that would surrender the task of interpretation to the art market), on the other.

There are four main elements to Adorno's diagnosis of the crisis of modernism:

1 the thesis of the tendential elimination of the autonomy of art under the conditions of the progressive commodification of culture;
2 the thesis of the inherently degenerative character of the dialectic of aesthetic modernism that is generated in defensive reaction to the erosion of the autonomy of art;
3 an insistence upon the autonomy of art as a condition of the possibility of authentic aesthetic experience;
4 an interpretation of authentic aesthetic experience as the bearer of the promise of the idea of truth and a prefigurative anticipation of a state of reconciliation and a transformed subjectivity.

Of these four elements, it is the way in which the historical process represented by the first two, erodes the conditions for the possibility of the form of experience specified by the second two, that produces the historical blockage that simultaneously gives rise to the idea of the necessity for, but denies the actual possibility of, a postmodern art. It is the dual and contradictory status of the autonomy of art that underlies this process. For art gains its autonomy as 'an entity unto itself', an independent sphere of value, only through its commodification. Commodification, however, simultaneously provides the conditions for the subversion of this autonomy by the values of the market – the progressive domination of use-value by exchange-value characteristic of the development of capitalism as a whole. In this respect, art may be understood, as Terry Eagleton has put it, as 'the commodity as fetish resisting the commodity as exchange, its solution to reification part of that very problem'.[12]

Postmodernism, in its epochal interpretation, appears from within this perspective as a problem essentially to do with the *commodity status* of art. More specifically, it appears as a result of an erosion of the traditional distinction between 'high' art and mass culture – a separation referred to by Adorno as the 'torn halves of an integral freedom, to which however they do not add up'. Adorno, however, considered it *romantic* to attempt to overcome this opposition within the framework of a society dominated by capitalist relations of production.[13]

It is for its account of the progressive 'neutralization' of culture by commodification, and of modernism as an aesthetic response to this situation which nevertheless remains trapped within its terms, that Adorno's aesthetics is best known. Within this account, it is its descriptive aspect that critics have generally been most prepared to accept. What has provoked more resistance has been Adorno's continued defence of the project of furthering the dialectic of aesthetic modernism as the sole hope of authentic aesthetic experience within a commodified culture, despite his recognition (indeed, his theorization) of its essentially degenerative character. As in his epistemology (negative dialectic), so too in his aesthetics (modernism), it is increasingly suggested that Adorno has argued himself into a dead-end.[14] What is at issue here is the inherent traditionalism of Adorno's concept of aesthetic experience (however modified this may be by his account of modernism); and correspondingly, the underlying metaphysical basis of his understanding of art. It is with this metaphysical ground of Adorno's aesthetics that the rest of this essay is primarily concerned in its presentation of *Aesthetic Theory* as a *materialist metaphysic of modernism*. For only through a detailed consideration of the metaphysical substance of Adorno's aesthetics is it possible to comprehend, and thus to criticize, his intransigent modernism.

TRUTH AND RECONCILIATION

The first problem that arises in the consideration of the metaphysical ground of Adorno's aesthetics concerns its explicit dependence upon an 'emphatic' concept of truth as the self-presentation of actuality. It is the maintenance of this idea that differentiates Adorno both from the poststructuralists, on the one hand, who reject the concept of truth altogether, and from his Habermasian critics on the other hand, who are prepared only to maintain a 'discursive' or 'consensual' conception – a conception which, from Adorno's standpoint, falls prey to 'the all but universal compulsion to confuse the communication of knowledge with knowledge itself'.[15] From each of these two standpoints, Adorno's work can only appear as a form of negative theology, flawed irredeemably by its implicit commitment to a quasi-Hegelian telos of reconciliation. To represent Adorno in this way, however, is to misrepresent him. For it is to neglect the argument by which Adorno *derives* his concept of truth through the immanent critique of the inherently identificatory character of all conceptual thought – what Adorno calls 'identity-thinking'. It is out of this critique of identity-thinking that Adorno's basic conception of aesthetic experience, as the experience of the 'non-identical', arises.

Adorno's critique of identity-thinking is based, first, upon Nietzsche's idea of the inherently identificatory (because pragmatic) character of all conceptual thought, and second, upon the association of the possibility of metaphysical experience (the possibility of truth) with the possibility of freedom. In the first place, Adorno argues, 'we cannot think without identifying. Any definition is identification'.[16] To think simply is for a subject to identify a concept with an object. The cognitive ideal of identity is inherent in the very form of thought. It cannot be given up without regression to an irrationalism which is in principle indefensible. Such an ideal, however, is also unrealizable – at least, within the parameters of conceptual thought. For the splitting of objectivity into the dichotomy of subject and object out of which the possibility of thought arises (the formation of subjectivity) creates an irreducible epistemological gap between subject and object that thought alone can never, in principle, overcome. The critique of thought's inherent claim to identity with its objects is thus a 'Sisyphean labour' for the modern subject, a task to be endlessly reiterated, since it acquires critical force only in relation to an ideal to which it must always aspire but which it can never meet.[17] This is the Kantian, tragic element in Adorno's thought. For Adorno however, unlike Kant, such a critique is always two-sided. It is not just a critique of the untruth of conceptual thought. It is also, and equally, a critique of *objectivity* in so far as it remains irreconcilable to thought; a critique of the irreconcilability of objectivity to the needs and desires from which the identificatory impulse of thought springs. For, Adorno argues, 'need is what we think from'.[18] This is simultaneously the *materialist* and the *utopian* moment in Adorno's thought: the critique of the irreconcilability of subjectivity to its own epistemic goals as the critique of the unfreedom of the existing state of things. 'The supposition of identity', Adorno argues, 'is indeed the ideological element of pure thought . . . but hidden in it is also the truth moment of ideology, the pledge that there should be no contradiction, no antagonism. In the simple identifying judgment the pragmatist nature-controlling element already joins with a utopian element': 'Living in the rebuke that the thing is not identical with the concept is *the concept's longing to become identical with the thing*'.[19]

28

Only in a world in which the structural opposition of objectivity to the needs and desires of the subject has been overcome – a reconciled society – will the idea of truth be realized. It will be realized there, however, not merely in some form of 'rational identity-thinking', some new form of '*thought*' premised upon the existing subject-object dichotomy, but more fundamentally as 'rational identity': a new ontological configuration of subject and object, a transformed subjectivity, the precise character of which is by definition 'unthinkable' from the standpoint of the present.[20] In the meantime, the possibilities for metaphysical experience, for the apprehension of truth, are restricted to those modes of experience which, first, register such a situation, and second and consequently, in some way anticipate a state of reconciliation (rational identity). For Adorno, there are two such modes of experience: the reflective experience of non-identity thinking (negative dialectics), and 'authentic' or philosophically reflective aesthetic experience. Of the two, it is the latter, philosophically reflective aesthetic experience, that is taken by Adorno to be the more metaphysically substantive. As one commentator has put it: for Adorno, 'where theory ends, there art begins'.[21] It is this massive philosophical investment in aesthetics in Adorno's work which is primarily responsible for its heightened sensitivity to the crisis of modernism.

AESTHETIC EXPERIENCE: THE DIALECTIC OF MIMESIS AND RATIONALITY

Aesthetic experience is characterized by Adorno, as it is by Kant, by two main distinguishing features: the non-subsumptive character of its apprehension of objects, and its 'disinterestedness', its disengagement from the realm of instrumentality: its *autonomy*.[22] It is produced, not by the subjective unification of a manifold of intuitions according to the rules of the schematism of the understanding (the subsumption of the object under a concept – identity-thinking), but by the reflective intuition of the 'togetherness in diversity' of the elements of the manifold: a reflective intuition of the unity of the 'one and the many'. It is the form of experience closest to the utopian idea of metaphysical experience, of reconciliation, because it is governed not by the logic of identity, but by that of *affinity*: the mutual affinity of the elements of objectivity. Its basic epistemological category is not subsumption but *reflection*.

Non-identity-thinking (negative dialectic) resists the compulsion to identification inherent in all conceptual thought by continual self-reflection upon the inadequacy of such thought. It thus approaches truth only negatively. Aesthetic experience, on the other hand, (for which the institutional autonomy of art as a distinct sphere of value is an historical precondition) resists identification through withdrawal, withdrawal from practical interests and thus from cognitive judgment. 'Disinterestedness', in other words, is a condition for the non-subsumptive character of aesthetic experience. At the same time, however, it opens up the possibility of art's acting as a medium of truth; not directly, but indirectly, through a 'second reflection' upon its cognitive status. For Adorno then, unlike Kant: 'Art *is* mediated conceptually, but in a qualitatively different way than thought. What is already mediated in art – i.e. the fact that art works are more than mere thisness – has to be mediated by reflection a second time, namely through the medium of concepts'.[23] It is this full, doubly reflective, form of experience that is for Adorno 'authentic' aesthetic experience, or what he sometimes refers to as 'artistic cognition' or 'artistic experience'. *Philosophical or 'second' reflection is constitutive of authentic aesthetic experience.* Aesthetic experience, more-over, is not for Adorno, as it was for Kant, primarily a generic category of experience, and only secondarily a category of art. Rather, it is primarily an artistic category and only secondarily, and *by analogy*, a generic one.

The reason for this is that the non-identitarian character of aesthetic experience derives not from the subject, but from the specific character of its object: the autonomous work of art. The definitive characteristic of such objects is their quality as self-contained *illusions* (*Scheinen*). Art is illusion, mere appearance, the self-conscious presentation of an illusory reality. But its illusion, the irresistible part of it, 'is given to it by what is not illusion': the process of its production. As such, it is both a medium for the expression of truth and, through its self-sufficient positivity, its integral unity, 'a promise of non-illusion', of reconciliation, of the non-identical, of all that falls outside the net of identifying judgements.[24] Furthermore, through its promise of non-illusion, its *promise de bonheur*, art is able to act as a criticism of the existing state of affairs. In comparison with reality, it reveals all apparent fulfilment in the present to be but 'a broken promise'.[25]

There is, of course, a form of identity at work in aesthetic experience, as there must be in all experience, in so far as 'every work of art spontaneously aims at being identical with itself'.[26] Indeed, this identity is essential to its cognitive status. But this 'aesthetic identity' is of a qualitatively different order to the repressive identification inherent in conceptual thought, since it derives not from the subject, but from the art work itself as a self-contained reality, an 'entity unto itself'. Such an identity originates in the unity of the process of the work's production. This is a process governed by the logic not of identification but rather, primarily, by that of *mimesis*. It is through mimesis that works of art become a possible site for the 'experience of the non-identical'.

Adorno defines mimesis as 'the non-conceptual affinity of a subjective creation with its objective and unposited other'.[27] It is this non-conceptual character that is crucial to art's metaphysical role as a 'spokesman for repressed nature' (the non-identical). It plays this role by expressing, in the form of a trace, that material unity of subjectivity with nature (objectivity) that is denied by the reified opposition of subject and object in conceptual thought, and which exists and is reproduced only through *practice*. Art, in this sense, is 'an after-image of praxis'.[28] As such, it conveys a truth to which philosophy aspires but which it can never reach. 'Philosophy', Adorno remarks, 'says what art cannot say, but it is art alone which is able to say it: by not saying it'.[29] But art is not just the product of mimetic behaviour. It is also instrumental, subjective, the result of an imposition of form. As such, it is a product of *rationality*, of *construction*. It is in the precise way in which mimesis and rationality, mimesis and construction, dialectically combine in the production of a work that, for Adorno, the truth content of the work resides.

The problem with purely mimetic behaviour is that it does not so much 'imitate' something as, in its 'endeavour to recover the bliss of a world that is gone', to reunite the subject with nature, 'assimilate itself to that something'.[30] It requires rationality, the imposition of form, the activity of a subject, in order to become genuinely imitative. Rationality is the organizing and unity-constitutive moment of a work. It is through the combination of mimesis and rationality that art is produced. And it is through the apprehension of their dialectical interplay within the work that, for Adorno, art is to be understood. The dialectic of mimesis and rationality thus stands at the very centre of Adorno's aesthetics. Two things about it in particular need to be stressed. The first is that ultimately, for Adorno, its two moments are *irreconcilable*. The second is that in so far as they do dialectically combine in the production of a work, they do so in such a way that they are realized only *through each other*. Thus Adorno argues: 'Construction is not a corrective of expression, nor is it a shoring-up of expression by means of objectification, but is something that has to emerge in an unplanned way from the mimetic impulse'. Mimesis 'only goes on living through its antithesis' (rationality). The rationality of works of art, on the other hand, 'becomes spiritual only when it has been immersed in its opposite' (mimesis). Art thus 'absorbs both the mimetic impulse and the critique of that impulse (rationality – P.O.) by objectifying it'. The objectification of mimesis is 'the constitutive act of spiritualisation in art'. It is through it that works of art become, paradoxically, 'free objects'.[31]

In a work of art, the mimetic moment dialectically interpenetrates the rational, constructive moment (without ultimately being reconciled with it) in such a way that it is expressed through it, while none the less, through its difference from it, acting as a criticism of it. In an authentic work, the domination of the natural-material (i.e. the mimetic) moment by the rational, subjective moment 'is mitigated by the fact that, through the principle of domination, the repressed finds a way of expressing itself'. The subjective moment is essential to expression. But the form in which it appears in art is that of self-criticism, since it is dependent upon its opposite, the natural-material, mimetic moment, for its aesthetic rationality. Art is thus 'rationality criticising itself without being able to overcome itself'. The configuration of mimesis and rationality is the essence of the work. It is 'the enigmatic image of art'.[32] It is through this idea of the work of art as an enigma that Adorno develops his account of the significance of the ultimate irreconcilability of mimesis and rationality for art's critical function.

ENIGMA: DETERMINATE IRRECONCILABILITY

Art, for Adorno, is constitutively enigmatic, in the sense of being a riddle or a puzzle (a *Vexierbild* – a picture-puzzle) which, while it has no explicit or objective solution, none the less contains potential solutions, the endless search for which provides the rationale of the object. The complete or final interpretation of a work is thus impossible. The reason for this is that, because of the ultimate irreconcilability of its basic moments, no work of art can be completely successful. In this sense, works of art *always* fail: 'Art cannot live up to its concept'. The classical ideal of organic unity or the harmony of the elements of a work is unattainable. 'The assertion made by the official curators of culture that there is an undifferentiated unity in classical-traditional works of art', Adorno argues, 'can be refuted by looking more closely at any single one of them: they all reveal the illusion of unity to be the result of conceptual mediation', of the imposition by the viewer of a will to unity. This 'failure', however, is not, according to Adorno, a deficiency. Rather, it is only because of it that art is able to function as a medium of truth. It is through the dialectic of reconciliation and irreconcilability that is generated within every work by the ultimate irreconcilability of its mimetic and rational moments that the configuration of these two moments within the work produces an image of truth.[33]

The idea that mimesis and rationality are ultimately irreconcilable, at least in an unreconciled society, would appear to conflict with the idea of art as an 'image of reconciliation'. It is however, in Adorno's view, essential to it. For it is Adorno's argument that it is precisely *through* the irreconcilability of their basic moments that works of art become images of reconciliation. The way in which this works is through what Adorno calls 'the setting free of the powers of art'. The constitutive failure of the work to achieve organic unity produces an interpretative indeterminacy that sets the work free from the determining intentions of its producer. It thereby achieves an autonomy as an apparently *self*-determining object that is 'akin to reconciliation' in its realization of the idea of freedom. In this respect, art is 'what metaphysics always wanted to be . . . an empirical existent determining itself as spirit'. It achieves that toward which philosophy can only aspire. Indeed, Adorno argues, tacitly in all idealism it is art that has been the model for philosophy all along, rather than *vice versa*.[34]

It is as 'images of reconciliation' in the sense of being free objects that art works are irreconcilable to, and critical of, the lack of freedom in reality. The irreconcilability of art's two basic moments to each other is thus the basis for its irreconcilability to reality. In this sense, *all* art is critical, simply as art. Art criticizes society just by being there.[35] The relative success or failure of individual works in expressing the truth about the society in which they are produced, on the other hand, will depend upon the precise way in which the irreconcilability of their mimetic and rational moments is expressed through the formal properties of the work. For, Adorno argues, the unresolved antagonisms of reality (the basic form of which is that

33

between nature and subjectivity, mimesis and rationality) 'reappear in art in the guise of immanent problems of aesthetic form'. The criterion of success in handling these problems is twofold. First, 'works of art must be able to integrate materials and details into their immanent law of form'. This is the moment of the interpenetration of mimesis and rationality, of unity, out of which the classical aesthetic conception of form as 'the non-repressive synthesis of diffuse particulars' arose. Second, however, this integration must not take place in such a way as to conceal the inevitability of its ultimate failure. Works of art, in other words, 'must not erase the fractures left by the process of integration, preserving instead in the aesthetic whole the traces of those elements which resisted integration'. For 'a work of art is as much a sum total of relations of *tension* as it is an attempt to resolve them'. It is an articulated 'system of contradictions', an 'antagonistic totality'. Indeed, Adorno argues against the classical ideal of harmony, it is precisely the *independence* of details that 'distinguishes art from a merely schematic activity'. Art transcends the antagonisms between its elements not by 'resolving' them, but by mediating them through expression, through their technical articulation.[36]

Art, then, is 'true to the extent to which it is discordant and antagonistic in its language and in its whole essence, provided that it synthesises those diremptions, thus making them *determinate in their irreconcilability*'. It is true to the extent to which it succeeds in the '*figuration*' or formed presentation of antagonism. It is untrue to the extent to which it either represses the expression of antagonism through the imposition of an 'organic' unity, or fails adequately to mediate antagonism to produce a coherent work. Art must 'hold fast to the idea of reconciliation in an antagonistic world', while 'firmly rejecting the appearance of reconciliation'.[37] The immanent, aesthetic rationale for the rejection of the appearance of reconciliation is that a reconciled, harmonious work would effectively deny the reality of the basic antagonism between mimesis and rationality through which art gains its autonomy at the level of its production of meaning. As such, it would cease to be an autonomous aesthetic object at all. Such a work though, is impossible to produce, since the irreconcilability of mimesis and rationality is an *ontological*, if historically specific, condition: the condition of the alienated subject of a reified society. There is though, another, more directly social, reason for Adorno's ban on the attempt to produce the appearance of reconciliation. This is that while art's constitutive autonomy as a sphere of value *in itself* cuts it off from the possibility of acting as a medium of *real* reconciliation, the images of reconciliation it produces (through which it asserts its irreconcilability to reality) are in perpetual danger of being mistaken or substituted for real reconciliation. Art, in other words, is in constant danger of becoming complicit with the presentation of the existing world as one in which real reconciliation *is* possible (if only in a restricted domain); of performing what Horkheimer was the first to call the 'affirmative' function of culture in bourgeois societies.[38] To the extent to which works are produced and interpreted in line with the (impossible) ideal of harmony, the *appearance* of reconciliation, art will continue to play an essentially ideological role which, if it can never completely escape, it can nevertheless resist and reflect upon, if it embraces the idea of determinate irreconcilability.

The inherent danger of art's being co-opted into the production of a false reconciliation is, for Adorno, the main political problem posed for the artist by the autonomy of the art object. And it is on the issue of what constitutes the most effective response to it (the question of how the aesthetic dialectic of reconciliation and irreconcilability may be exploited to counter the possibilities of a false reconciliation) that Adorno's aesthetics differs most sharply from Lukacs's. For it is around this question that Adorno's whole construction, interpretation, and evaluation of modernism revolves. It is the different ways in which art's irreconcilability to reality is expressed in classical and modernist or 'non-organic' works that, for Adorno, both marks the essential difference between them, and demonstrates the decisive superiority of the modernist aesthetic.

Our discussion so far has taken place at the level of abstraction of the work of art as such. It must now descend to a level appropriate to the theorization of the constitutive effect upon art of more specific socio-historical processes. For it is primarily as a reflective response to the effect of such processes upon art that Adorno understands the modernist aesthetic.

MODERNISM: ABSTRACTION, DISSONANCE AND 'THE NEW'

Two apparently conflicting points have emerged so far from our discussion of Adorno's aesthetics: his adoption of a classical conception of aesthetic experience as the 'togetherness in diversity' or mutual affinity of the elements of objectivity'; and his rejection of the appearance of reconciliation, organic unity, or harmony as a realizable aesthetic ideal. The conflict between them, however, has been shown to be mediated by the essentially historical character of Adorno's aesthetic perspective. None the less, the idea of determinate irreconcilability around which Adorno's aesthetics revolves remains so far in our account both abstract and essentially negative, since it gains its rationale only from the recognition of the structural impossibility of the realization of the classical aesthetic ideal of organic unity in an unreconciled society. Organic unity, in other words, would appear to remain Adorno's aesthetic ideal *in so far as it is possible without the enforced reconciliation of a work's basic elements.* Modernism though, is understood and valued by Adorno, as it is by many others, as 'the historical emancipation from harmony as an ideal'. It is *dissonance,* the precise opposite of harmony, that is, according to Adorno, the 'trademark' of modernism.[39] How is this transition within the logic of Adorno's thought from a recognition of the essential limitations of the classical aesthetic ideal to the affirmation of its opposite as a principle for the construction of a work to be explained?

The answer lies in Adorno's sociological theory; specifically, in his accounts of reification and the neutralization of culture through its progressive commodification. In order to explore this connection, it is necessary to distinguish between three distinct elements of Adorno's conception of modernism: *abstraction, dissonance* and '*the new*'. For although they are obviously closely connected, each of these three principles has a distinct place in the categorial structure of Adorno's work. Indeed, it is one of the great virtues of Adorno's work on modernism that (unlike for example that of Clement Greenberg) it makes these categorial distinctions.

The categorial distinctions between the principles of abstraction, dissonance, and 'the new' which are implicit in Adorno's treatment of them in *Aesthetic Theory* derive from the different roles played by the three principles within the productive rationale of modern works. These different roles, in turn, derive from the effect upon art of the social determinants underlying the development of the aesthetic dialectic. Thus, the general tendency towards abstraction in modern art is explained and understood by Adorno primarily with reference to the tendential reification of all social relations corresponding to the generalization of capitalist relations of production. The effect of this process is the reification or 'rationalization' of the mimetic moment in art. The modernity of art is thus seen by Adorno to derive from the fact that its mimetic relation to reality has become a mimetic relation to 'a petrified and alienated reality'. Modern art, he argues, is 'as abstract as the real relations among men'.[40] It is in this sense that Beckett is a realist. The principle of *dissonance*, on the other hand, is to be explained and understood as a critical reaction within art to this reification of the mimetic. It is the basic principle of modernism.

The principle of dissonance is derived by Adorno from the fact that if, on the one hand, all genuinely 'modern' works must of necessity be characterized by a certain level of abstraction, they must also, if they are to remain authentic works (media for the expression of philosophical truth), not simply reproduce the abstract character of modern social life, but *express* it, via their subjective, constructive moment (as outlined above) *as an alienated reality*. It is in order to achieve this that they must embrace the principle of dissonance. For the reification of the mimetic undermines the tension, the basic irreconcilability, between art's mimetic and rational moments, out of which springs its capacity to function critically as an image of reconciliation. To regenerate this tension, and thereby to maintain art's irreconcilability to reality, irreconcilability must be consciously introduced into the work by the artist as a constructive principle, that is, as dissonance. A far greater weight, in other words, must be placed upon the subjective, constructive moment with the productive rationale of the work if it is to remain critical. Its critical character must be self-consciously produced by the artist. Modern art is thus *radically nominalistic*, and consequently of necessity far more complexly *conceptually* mediated than its classical predecessor. This means that criticism (reflection upon the truth content of specific works), which was always for Adorno 'an essential and necessary complement of art works', becomes of increasing importance. As we shall see in a moment, however, it is precisely the radical nominalism of modern art that leads to its increasingly problematic status.[41]

The importance of the principle of '*the new*' to Adorno's idea of modernism (modernism as a dialectic of the new) is twofold. On the one hand, it can be derived directly from the principle of dissonance. On the other hand, its centrality to modernism is increased enormously by the exigencies involved in realizing the principle of dissonance under the conditions of the increasing commodification of aesthetic form through its appropriation for directly commercial purposes by the culture and advertising industries. In the first place, Adorno argues, whereas 'previously, styles and artistic practices were negated by new styles and practices', modernism (as an aesthetic of dissonance) 'negates tradition itself'. Through the idea of dissonance the modernist aesthetic defines itself in terms of 'the new' in a completely abstract, and consequently radically open, way which undermines the temporality of classical aesthetic development. For to the extent to which 'the new' in modernism is, as a general principle, a 'longing for the new' rather than 'the new' itself in a determinate form, it is the 'curse' of anything *actually* new – since this immediately becomes the present (a new tradition) against which the *idea* of the new is once more to be measured, by its distance from it. Modernism is thus not strictly a *temporal* phenomenon at all, but actually *represses* duration. 'The new', in other words, 'is an invariant'. It generates a restless dialectic of formal innovation directed toward the continual re-newal of dissonance: an art 'groping for objectivity in a framework of open-endedness and insecurity'.[42]

That dissonance is something that must be continually re-newed is something that stems from its inherently negative essence: the in-built tendency of the dissonance of any actual work to turn into its opposite through familiarization. This inherent tendency towards re-newal, however, is reinforced, both externally and immanently to the aesthetic dialectic, by two closely related social developments: the progressive commodification of culture, and the aestheticization of the commodity-form itself. First, there is the commodity character of the art work itself, the art market, within which the general tendency within commodity markets toward incessant innovation is manifest in an exaggerated form because of its inherently speculative and manipulative character. For the use-value of the autonomous art object derives, paradoxically, only from the fact that it has no use-value. There is thus an inherent tendency for use-value to become reduced to exchange-value. To the extent to which artists are to live off the sale of their works, such a tendency will tend to be internalized by them at the point of production; both in the general form of an imperative to innovate, and in the specific form of a demand by agents and dealers for particular forms of innovation at particular times. This reinforcement of the dialectic of new is *external* to the aesthetic dialectic itself and, to the extent to which market demand (created and manipulated by the institutionalized network of critics, agents, dealers, owners and curators) conflicts with the demand of aesthetic form, it distorts it.

Second, there is the more general aestheticization of the commodity form in the culture and advertising industries. What is involved here is the neutralization of the critical capacity of particular forms and techniques through their instrumental use. Thus Adorno argues: 'To paint *à la cubiste* in the year 1970 is like making advertising posters. And the originals are not immune, either, to this kind of sell out'.[43] This tendency reinforces the dynamic of the dialectic of the new *internally*, for it strengthens and quickens the inherent tendency of dissonance to become harmony through familiarization. At the same time, it leads to the increasing forced marginalization of authentic art, since the capacity of a work to resist this kind of assimilation – its constitutive *un*intelligibility – becomes a critical principle. This further strengthens the increased domination of the mimetic by the rational within modern works to the extent that it is precisely the mimetic aspect of works which is the more immediately intelligible.

Adorno's modernism, then, is a restless aesthetic dialectic of the new, driven on by the principle of dissonance, in the context of an inherent tendency toward abstraction, which gains its aesthetic rationale from its immanent resistance to the reification of both social life in general, and the cultural sphere in particular. It is 'the new' through which 'the old' (the idea of art as an autonomous sphere of value and a medium of philosophical truth) continues to be possible. The immanent dynamic of autonomous works under the conditions of the rationalization of the mimetic and 'the growing power of external reality over the subject' *converge* in dissonance. The metaphysics of classical aesthetics lives on, negatively, as the metaphysics of modernism. Modernism, however, as we noted at the outset, has become problematic. To see how and why this is so, it is necessary to return to the question of modern art's inherent nominalism. For it is the nominalistic aspect of modernism that is, according to Adorno, undermining art from within.

THE CRISIS OF MODERNISM: DESUBSTANTIALIZATION AND CONCEPTUALITY

The crisis of modernism, and thereby of art, is the direct result, for Adorno, of the rationalization of the mimetic and the correspondingly increased significance and role of the subjective, constructive moment with the productive rationale of the work. For, as was argued above, art's capacity to express critically the truth of the present is dependent, first, upon the ultimately irreconcilable *difference* between the rational and the mimetic, and second, originally at least, upon the *structural priority* of the latter within the work, since it is the principle of subjective rationality that it is one of the main functions of art to criticize. From the standpoint of philosophical aesthetics, there is thus a deepening contradiction at the heart of the radical nominalism of modern art. For it is increasingly forced to rely, as the tool of its critical function, upon precisely that which it is its function to criticize: 'The new wills non-identity but, by willing, inevitably wills identity'. Modern art is 'constantly practicing the impossible trick of trying to identify the non-identical'.[44] Its increased self-consciousness is not so much an advantage as a curse. Yet it is inescapable. Art's 'elective affinity' to conceptuality is in danger of being dissolved into equivalence.

Two things should be noted about this process. One is the idea of 'desubstantialization' (*Entkunstung*) – the loss of art's capacity to act as a medium of historical possibilities. The other concerns the concrete aesthetic ground of this process: the erosion of the aesthetic significance of sensuousness. *Sensuousness* is an essential aspect of mimesis and thereby of art. More specifically, it is through the 'spiritualization' of the sensuous (which is the product of the expression of the mimetic through the rational) that art takes on the appearance of being a free object, and is thereby able to become, simultaneously, an image of reconciliation and a medium of truth. There is an essential non-sensuous moment within the sensuous structure of all works which cannot appear except through that structure. It is through this dialectic of the sensuous and non-sensuous that art acquires its peculiar ontological status as something that is simultaneously conceptual and sensuous: 'a vision of the non-visual . . . similar to a concept without being one'.[45] The promise of the reality of content, which makes that content true, Adorno argues, is tied up with its sensuousness. The socially determined, declining

40

aesthetic significance of mimesis, however, appears as *a proscription against sensuousness*. This is the real crisis of art: 'Art will not survive if it forgets sensuousness, just as it will not survive if it gives itself over to an external sensuousness that is divorced from its real structure'.[46]

This is a 'desubstantialization' of art in two senses. First, in the immediate sense of the erosion of art's materiality. Second, in the mediated sense of the loss of the possibilities for the expression of truth associated with this materiality. Such a loss is endemic to modernism because, in its increasing nominalism, it is increasingly capable of expressing truth only *negatively* and abstractly, as a *will* to irreconcilability, rather than concretely, through its classical, integrative moment. This is maintained as a condition of the possibility of art in even the most modernist work, but it declines in aesthetic significance proportionally to the rationalization of the mimetic. The desubstantialization of art is thus both 'a stage in the liquidation of art' and an essential part of its 'logical development'.[47] Modernism, for Adorno, has turned out to be a dead-end street; not so much for intra-aesthetic reasons, as because of objective social determinants. Is there then nothing left for Adorno's aesthetics to contribute to current debates about the possibility of going beyond this destructive dialectic, to the idea of a postmodern art, except for a knowing reiteration of its impossibility?

POSTMODERNISM AND THE THESIS OF THE MOST ADVANCED ARTISTIC MATERIAL

Two things, at least, are clear. The first is that in so far as it is Adorno's social theory (specifically, his theory of reification) that underlies his account of how it is that 'everything about art has become problematic: its inner life, its relation to society, even its right to exist',[48] then it is in the first place within the domain of social theory that the reconstruction of Adorno's perspective on current aesthetic possibilities must begin. Secondly, however, it is clear that from the standpoint of Adorno's conception of modernism, the idea of a postmodern art (although not that of a postmodernist culture) is, strictly speaking, self-contradictory. For if postmodernism is to be understood, as it is for example by Jameson, from within the broad terms of Adorno's sociology of art, as an expression of the *dissolution* of the autonomy of the cultural sphere, then its products simply do not have the status of works of art in the classical sense.

They lack the capacity to act as media for the expression of philo-sophical truth. Terry Eagleton is quite right, in this respect, to characterize postmodernist culture as a *parody* of the aspirations of the historical, revolutionary avant garde to reintegrate aesthetic experience into life-praxis through the politicization of art: a 'sick joke' at their expense.[49] Proponents of the project of a critical appropriation and transformation of the postmodern have yet to take this fundamental facet of its existence sufficiently seriously. Postmodernism, however, is not just the parodic inverse of revolutionary avant gardism in art. It is also a timely reminder of the absolute dependence of aesthetic revolutions upon the success of the broader social and political movements of which they are a part.

Contrary to the increasingly common accusation that *Aesthetic Theory* 'was obsolete to begin with because its concept of modern art is too closely welded to artistic tendencies which came to an end with the first half of this century, if not earlier',[50] Adorno was in fact acutely aware of the aesthetic developments which have more recently come to be understood through the idea of postmodernism. Indeed, it was precisely these developments, understood by him as a kind of '*hyper-modernism*', that fuelled his sensitivity to the crisis of art. Hyper-modernism, he argued, 'prefers to join forces with reified conscious-ness rather than stay on the side of an ideology of illusory humanness. Dissonance . . . congeals into an indifferent material, a kind of new immediacy without memory trace of its past, without feeling, without essence'.[51] It is the product of a wariness of dissonance because of its proximity to consonance: the ultimate outcome of 'the taboo on sensuality' in art. At the same time however, Adorno was far from conceiving of this development, and the consequent dissolution of autonomous art, as inevitable, in the way that Jameson has a tendency to do. Indeed, he explicitly remarks that it is 'difficult to say whether this most recent taboo on sensuousness is grounded in the inner logic of form or whether it merely reflects artistic incompetence – a moot problem, incidentally, the likes of which turn up more and more frequently in debates about modern art'.[52] The destruction of tradition is at the same time a destruction of the stability of the interpretive community which weakens its resistance to purely commercial criteria of evaluation – a process which reinforces the need for informed criticism as an essential part of a work's reception.

For Adorno, then, postmodernism can only be understood first, as 'hyper-modernism' – the final, dissolutive stage in the degenerate dialectic of modernism, the last, and most futile avant garde[53] – and second, and consequently upon the dissolution of autonomous art, as a new 'cultural dominant' (Jameson) *without any critical potential*: a manifestation of the onset of total reification. But what of *other* aesthetic possibilities, other emergent tendencies, both social and artistic? In what way can Adorno's aesthetics help us to understand these? The basic problem here stems from the *unilinearity* of Adorno's orientation to history: the one-dimensionality of his conception of the tendency towards the reification of all social relations inherent in the development of capitalism. This conception is notoriously undialectical: at least, it *marginalizes* dialectics, restricting their play to the sphere of the remnants of autonomy capable of motivating the resistance of individual subjects (the avant garde artist and enlightened viewer). Once this unilinearity is recognized as an inadequate representation of the complexity and essential *unevenness* of the process of historical development, however, a whole series of aesthetic possibilities begin to emerge centred upon the 'non-contemporaneous' moment of the dialectics of development.

Such a perspective is in fact immanent in Adorno's own accounts both of the development of modernism ('Only where the development towards the administered world and social modernity has not yet asserted itself so successfully – in France and Austria, for example – did the aesthetically modern – the avant garde – thrive.'[54]) and of current political possibilities ('It is only where that which was is still strong enough to form the forces within the subject and at the same time to oppose them that the production of that which has not yet been seems possible.'[55]). Yet it is consistently marginalized. Two things in particular suggest the necessity for it to play a far greater role in all aesthetic debate than it has done up until now: 1. the structurally contradictory character of all reification in the continued if distorted reproduction of that which is suppressed – the subject; 2. the explosively contradictory character of the way in which non-capitalist societies have been and continue to be integrated into the accumulative regimes of trans-national capital. Of particular importance from the standpoint of the renewal of the aesthetic dialectic of modernism, in this regard, has been the importation into European modernism of the cultural manifestations of the latter phenomenon. Jameson, in fact, has himself recently suggested that 'magic realism' be considered 'a possible alternative to the narrative logic of contemporary postmodernism'.[56] Whatever one may think of this suggestion (and there are clearly complexities at issue here of an unparalleled kind, both theoretically and politically), there is obviously a dynamic at work here that questions the unilinearity of Adorno's conception of the dialectic of modernism as a progressive erosion of the concrete aesthetic significance of the mimetic, towards the self-destructive triumph of nominalism in meaninglessness.[57] More specifically, what is in question here is the formalism of Adorno's conception of 'the most advanced artistic material'.

Peter Burger has described the idea of artistic material as 'the central category of Adorno's aesthetics'.[58] All of the main themes of Adorno's aesthetics are refracted through it in condensed form. For it is the basic category through which the aesthetic and social dialectics are mediated. It is through it, as the historically given, sedimented content of a work, that Adorno attempts to demonstrate that in art 'social antinomies turn into the dialectic of forms'.[59] Adorno's concept of artistic material refers to 'all that is being formed'. It is 'the stuff the artist controls and manipulates: words, colours, sounds – all the way up to connections of any kind and to the highly developed methods of integration he might use': 'all that the artist is confronted by, all that he must make a decision about, and that includes forms as well'. As such, it is 'always historical, never natural, irrespective of what artists themselves might think' and 'just as dependent on technical changes as technique is on materials worked upon by it'.[60] The loss of the historical dimension of the material of recent works is, in this respect, itself a historical trend – the aesthetic reflection of reification. It is the way in which the material of any specific work is treated by the artist that determines its critical effectivity. At the same time, however, for Adorno, the critical potentiality of a work is determined by the materials out of which it is produced. For it is via its materials that a work acquires its historical content. More specifically, it is the progressive (socially determined) redundancy of particular materials as possible media for the expression of truth that drives on the dialectic of modernism. This is the thesis of the most advanced artistic material: the idea that at any one time there will be some particular set of artistic materials optimally suited to the aesthetic expression of the truth of the present. As Burger has put it: 'Holding firmly to the idea that artistic material reflects the total social development without the consciousness of the producer being able to see this connection, (Adorno) can recognise only *one* material in a given epoch'.[61]

The problem with this idea, as Burger goes on to point out, is that: 'Whether recourse to past formal schemata merely reproduces them or they are made into a convincing means of expression for a current expressive need cannot be decided by theory, but only by meticulous, detailed analysis of individual works'. I think that Adorno would have agreed.[62] The trouble is, though, that the unilinearity of his *social* theory led him to prejudge the aesthetic issue. The rejection of this unilinearity, however, need not lead to aesthetic pluralism: an arbitrary and eclectic coexistence of forms. Rather, it suggests instead simply a 'richer, more variegated' modernism, the course of which cannot be *pre*judged, but the state of which may none the less be judged historically according to the broad philosophical criteria of Adorno's aesthetics: the dialectic of mimesis and rationality (expression and form) and the ideal of determinate irreconcilability.

In an age of such artistic uncertainty, artistic experimentation is both increasingly essential and yet increasingly difficult. To the extent to which some of the works included within the increasingly amorphous canon of postmodernism may be viewed as 'authentic' (that is to say, socially determined yet *'autonomous'*) works, they may well represent not, as Wellmer has suggested, 'the still unclear consciousness of the *end* of the transition',[63] but the emergent consciousness of the *beginning* of a transition – a transition beyond neither modernity nor modernism (in its philosophico-aesthetic interpretation), but rather to a new stage in the dialectic of modernism; a stage determined less by the experience of 'late capitalism' as such, than by the increasing experience of the contradictoriness, complexity, and unevenness, of global social development.

A theory of contemporary aesthetics, Burger has suggested, 'has the task of conceptualising a dialectical continuity of modernism'.[64] It can have no better starting-point than the attempt to work out the concrete aesthetic implications of the effect upon Adorno's aesthetics of the dialectical reformulation of his social theory.[65]

NOTES

1 Theodor W. Adorno, 'The Actuality of Philosophy' (1931), *Telos* 31, 1977.
2 Theodor W. Adorno, *Negative Dialectics* (1986), tr. E.B. Ashton, Routledge & Kegan Paul, London 1973 (ND), pp. 362, 365, 372.
3 For the attribution to Adorno of a negative theology, see Jean-François Lyotard, 'Adorno as the Devil', *Telos* 19, and Albrecht Wellmer, 'Truth, Semblance, Reconciliation: Adorno's Aesthetic Redemption of Modernity', *Telos* 61, 1984/85,

pp. 8–9. A reading of Adorno's work as a sociology of illusion is given in Gillian Rose, *The Melancholy Science. An Introduction to the Thought of Theodor W. Adorno*, Macmillan, London 1978.

4 ND, p. 404, emphasis added.

5 T.W. Adorno, *Aesthetic Theory* (1970), tr. C. Lenhardt, ed. Gretel Adorno and Rolf Tiedemann, Routledge & Kegan Paul, London 1984, (AT), pp. 464/5.

6 ibid, pp. 2, 43.

7 ibid., p. 468.

8 ibid., p. 368.

9 Martin Jay, *Adorno*, Fontana, London 1984.

10 Peter Osborne, review of Jay, op. cit., *Radical Philosophy* 42, Winter/Spring 1986, p. 45; Peter Dews, 'Adorno, Poststructuralism, and the Critique of Identity', above pp. 1–22.

11 Albrecht Wellmer, 'Truth, Semblance, Reconciliation', op. cit.

12 Terry Eagleton, 'Capitalism, Modernism and Postmodernism', *New Left Review* 152, July/August 1985, p. 67. Cf. AT, pp. 320–6.

13 Adorno to Benjamin, 18/3/36, *Aesthetics and Politics*, New Left Books, London 1977, p. 123. For an epochal conception of postmodernism centred upon the commodity status of culture, see Frederic Jameson, 'Postmodernism, or the Cultural Logic of Late Capitalism', *New Left Review* 146, July/August 1984.

14 See, for example, Fredric Jameson, 'Reification and Utopia in Mass Culture', *Social Text*, vol. 1, no. 1, Winter 1979, p. 130.

15 ND, p. 41.

16 ibid., p. 149.

17 AT, p. 365.

18 ND, p. 408.

19 ibid., p. 149.

20 The attribution to Adorno of an idea of 'rational identity-thinking' is to be found in Gillian Rose, *The Melancholy Science*, op. cit., chapter 4.

21 Rudiger Bubner, *Modern German Philosophy*, Cambridge University Press, Cambridge 1981, p. 181.

22 For Kant's conception of aesthetic experience, see Immanuel Kant, *The Critique of Judgement*, tr. James Creed Meredith, Clarendon Press, Oxford: 1952, Part One, 'Critique of Aesthetic Judgement'.

23 AT, p. 490, emphasis added.

24 ND, pp. 404, 405. Translations altered.

25 Theodor Adorno and Max Horkheimer, *Dialectic of Enlightenment* (1944), trans. John Cumming, Verso, London 1979, p. 140.

26 AT, p. 113.

27 ibid., p. 80.

28 ibid., p. 439.

29 ibid., p. 107.

30 ibid., pp. 465, 162.

31 ibid., pp. 65, 141, 174, 162, 165.

32 ibid., pp. 398, 81, 185.

33 ibid., pp. 178, 80, 161, 143.

34 ibid., pp. 81, 471, 114.

35 ibid., p. 321.

36 ibid., pp. 8–10, 207, 407, 263, 446, 420.

37 ibid., pp. 241, 48.

38 Max Horkheimer, 'Egoism and the Freedom Movement: On the Anthropology of the Bourgeois Era' (1936), *Telos* 54, 1982/83, p. 51. The classic exposition of the idea of affirmative culture is Marcuse's 1937 essay 'The Affirmative Character of

Culture', in Herbert Marcuse, *Negations, Essays in Critical Theory*, trans. Jeremy
Schapiro, Beacon Press, Boston 1968. Marcuse defines affirmative culture there
as:

> that culture of the bourgeois epoch which led in the course of its own development
> to the segregation from civilisation of the mental and spiritual world as an
> independent realm of value that is also considered superior to civilisation. Its
> decisive characteristic is the assertion of a universally obligatory, eternally
> better and more valuable world that must be unconditionally affirmed: a world
> essentially different from the factual world of the daily struggle for existence, yet
> realisable by every individual for himself 'from within', without transformation
> of the state of fact. It is only in this culture that cultural activities and objects
> gain that value that elevates them above the everyday sphere. Their reception
> becomes an act of celebration and exaltation' (p. 95)

While Adorno accepts Marcuse's account of the affirmative essence of
autonomous art, he none the less considers his critique of it to be one-sided. Cf.
AT, pp. 332–3, 357.

39 AT, pp. 161, 221.
40 AT, pp. 31, 45.
41 ibid., pp. 50, 51, 131.
42 ibid., pp. 31, 47, 383, 470.
43 ibid., p. 417.
44 ibid., p. 31.
45 ibid., p. 142. Cf. Adorno's description of reading as 'simultaneously sensual and
    non-sensual vision', ibid., p. 391.
46 ibid., p. 389.
47 ibid., p. 117.
48 ibid., p. 1.
49 Terry Eagleton, '*Capitalism, Modernism and Postmodernism*', op. cit., p. 60.
50 Christian Lenhardt (the translator of the English edition of *Aesthetic Theory*),
    'Reply to Hullot-Kentor', *Telos* 65, Fall 1985.
51 AT, p. 22.
52 ibid. The term 'hyper-modernism', it should be noted, is an invention of Adorno's
    English translator. I am grateful to Neil Roughley for pointing this out to me.
53 For a criticism of postmodernism for its avant-gardism, see John Tagg,
    'Postmodernism and the Born-Again Avant-Garde', *Block* 11, Winter 1985/6.
54 Theodor W. Adorno, 'Culture and Administration' (196), *Telos* 37, p. 103.
55 ibid.
56 Frederick Jameson, 'On Magic Realism in Film', *Critical Inquiry* 12, p. 302. See
    also his 'Third World Literature in the Era of Multi-national Capitalism', *Social
    Text* 15 (Fall 1986), pp. 65–88.
57 Cf. AT, p. 412: 'The crisis of meaning in art is the immanent outcome of the
    irresistible moving force of nominalism'.
58 Peter Burger, 'The Decline of the Modern Age', *Telos* 62, Winter 1984/85, p. 122.
59 AT, p. 330.
60 ibid., pp. 213, 214.
61 Peter Burger, op. cit., p. 120.
62 Because of his reliance for his account of Adorno's position upon his concrete
    aesthetic studies, rather than *Aesthetic Theory*, and the inevitable disparity that at
    times arises between Adorno's concrete aesthetic judgments and the interpretive
    possibilities suggested by his theory, Burger tends to *oppose* his position to
    Adorno's when in fact he is often merely playing off one element of Adorno's work
    against another.

63 Albrecht Wellmer. 'On the Dialectic of Modernism and Postmodernism', *Praxis International*, vol. 4, no. 4 January 1985, p. 343.
64 Peter Burger, op. cit., p. 127.
65 An earlier version of this paper was presented to a conference on 'Problems of Postmodernism: Adorno and Benjamin' at the Centre for Research in Philosophy and Literature, University of Warwick, November 1985. I would like to thank those present on that occasion, and Peter Dews and John Kraniauskas, for their comments on the draft version.

Chapter 3

ART AGAINST ENLIGHTENMENT: ADORNO'S CRITIQUE OF HABERMAS

JAY BERNSTEIN

Cultural modernity, Habermas claims, can be characterized

> as the separation of the substantive reason expressed in religion
> and metaphysics into three autonomous spheres. They are:
> science, morality and art. These came to be differentiated because
> the unified world conceptions of religion and metaphysics fell
> apart. Since the 18th century, the problems inherited from these
> older world-views could be rearranged so as to fall under specific
> aspects of validity: truth, normative rightness, authenticity and
> beauty. They could then be handled as questions of knowledge, or
> of justice and morality, or of taste. (MvP, p. 8)[1]

Habermas regards these achievements of modernity to be its non-
reversible, and greatest accomplishments. Each autonomous domain
can now be institutionalized and developed according to its own
inner logic. These logics, as pursued by their respective experts,
constitute the objectivity, the forms and conditions for objectivity of
each separate domain. For Habermas the possibility of dedifferenti-
ation, of the lapsing or fusing of these autonomous forms of discourse
can only be conceived of as a regression, a re-enchantment of the
world, as a re-fusing of nature and culture in such a manner that
knowledge and power would again become coeval.

The first sentence of Adorno's *Aesthetic Theory* reads: 'Today it goes
without saying that nothing concerning art goes without saying,
much less without thinking. Everything about art has become
problematic: its inner life, its relation to society, even its right to
exist.' The art which Adorno contends has become problematic is
the very same autonomous art which Habermas regards as an

unassailable accomplishment of modernity. Worse still, as Adorno's threefold delimitation of the problematic character of art makes evident, art has become problematic *because* it has become autonomous. Autonomous art, art whose forms are no longer underwritten by or derived from myth or religion, metaphysics or tradition, whose forms are internal to each artistic domain itself (literary forms, musical forms, etc), this art has become problematic because autonomization makes the question of its sense, meaning, point, *telos* without any but an external, relative and contingent answer. And this answer inevitably tends to contradict art's own inner logic. Art can answer to society only by abrogating its own internal standards of validity. To be true to itself, then, art must turn against itself, against its autonomy, and hence against the processes of societal differentiation which have deprived it of substantiality. But this it can do only through its forms, by the urging of those forms to the limit until the limit itself begins to tremble so that both limit and what transcends it are revealed in their disfigured duality. For Adorno, the cognitive import of the autonomous art is its testimony against differentiation, against formal reason, against modernity.

Habermas's various critiques of Adorno focus on the question of whether critique can be sustained independently of the possession of a normative foundation. Habermas's insistence on the necessity of such a foundation for critique is, however, question-begging, since it short-circuits the anterior question of modernity. Adorno's lack of a rational foundation for critique cannot be used as a reason for or criteria of unacceptability if that lack is a consequence of the processes against which the testimony of art inveighs. In order, then, to justify his contention that critique can be founded, and that the differentiation of spheres produced through the rationalization process should be regarded as a *non-reversible* cognitive achievement – I do not wish to deny differentation *was* a form of cognitive progress – Habermas must demonstrate the inadequacy of Adorno's analysis of art without presupposing these points. This, I shall contend, he does not and cannot do.

My paper will fall into two parts. The first will outline briefly the central argument of Adorno and Horkheimer's *Dialectic of Enlightenment,* and explicate how the status of art becomes a test case for their theory. The second part engages Albrecht Wellmer's Habermas-inspired critique of Adorno's *Aesthetic Theory* in his 'Truth, Semblance, Reconciliation: Adorno's Aesthetic Redemption of Modernity'.

I

According to Adorno and Horkheimer, enlightenment is from the very beginning anti-enlightenment; indeed, even prior to the commencement of the overt strategies of enlightenment, the myths against which enlightened thinking comported itself were themselves implicated in the strategies of identity and repetition, mastery and domination (DoE, p. 8): 'Myth intended report, naming, the narration of the Beginning; but also presentation, confirmation, explanation.' Myth succumbs to enlightenment, while enlightenment inevitably reverts to myth. This reversion or engulfment of enlightenment in myth, enlightenment's becoming 'animistic magic' (DoE, p. 11), is consequent upon its adoption of the 'principle of immanence, the explanation of every event as repetition,' (DoE, p. 12), which is the principle of myth itself. What allows this dialectic to escape the charge of factitiousness, the charge of being premised upon a fragile and simplistic rhetoric of inversion, is Adorno's and Horkheimer's contention that the fatalities of reason are premised upon and are to be explained by the drive for self-preservation, a drive for mastery and control which governs, in differential ways and to different degrees, with greater or lesser effectivity, the logics of myths and reason. What has come to be called instrumental reason, the reduction of cognition to means-ends calculation and hence to instrumentality, is grounded in the anthropological foundations of the history of the species. Hence what might appear at first as a rhetorical strategy is in fact a work of detection, the glimpsing of the rough contours of mastery and domination beneath the glimmering surface of mythic play and epic wanderings.

The major instance of dialectical reversal presented by Adorno and Horkheimer is instrumental reason's revenge upon the reasoner. They contend that a condition for subjugating external nature by reason is the repression of internal nature, that is, roughly, the inhibition and domination of drives and desires is a condition for the employment of discursive reason. Further this same repression of inner nature precipitates the formation of the individualized self or subject, so each victory over external nature is paid for by a defeat for inner nature and a strengthening of the self as subject, a strengthening which is, of course, also a defeat. The sacrifice of the self for its own sake is quixotic since the repression of inner nature entails the distortion and eventual occlusion of the purposes for the

51

sake of which the domination of external nature is undertaken. What in capitalism is exemplified by the domination of exchange value over use value, a domination which systematically voids the teleological rationality of our productive activity, is, Adorno says, 'already preceptible in the pre-history of subjectivity' (DoE, p. 52).[2] He continues:

> Man's domination over himself, which grounds his selfhood, is almost always the destruction of the subject in whose service it is undertaken; for the substance which is dominated, suppressed, and dissolved by virtue of self-preservation is none other than that very life as functions of which the achievements of self-preservation find their sole definition and determination: it is, in fact, what is to be preserved. The irrationalism of totalitarian capitalism, whose way of satisfying needs has an objectified form determined by domination which makes the satisfaction of needs impossible and tends toward the extermination of mankind, has its prototype in the hero who escapes from sacrifice by sacrificing himself. The history of civilization is the history of the introversion of sacrifice. In other words: the history of renunciation. Everyone who practises renunciation gives away more of his life than is given back to him: and more than the life he vindicates.

Now this argument would be enough to invalidate the self-sufficiency of instrumental reason since it would demonstrate that the reason which is and ought to be the slave of the passions enslaves its master through its subservience. However, the purpose of Adorno and Horkheimer's genealogy of reason was to throw into question the rationality of reason as such, to critique the idea that enlightened reason is reasonable or rational, the bearer of a progressive disenchantment of the world. For this, something more is needed; something like a demonstration of the growing hegemony of formal, instrumental rationality over other forms of rationality, or the collapse of the distinction between reason (*Vernunft*) and understanding (*Verstand*). And, indeed, demonstrations of this sort are found in the second 'Excursus' on morality, and in the chapter on the culture industry. These demonstrations, however, draw their force from a more direct line of argument which seeks to show that the logic of reversals which beget instrumental rationality is not a contingent feature of what we call reason, but its essence; discursive rationality and instrumental reason are one. If so, then the identitarian logic of exchange value, the equivalencing of use values under homogeneous units of labour-time, would not be a distortion of enlightened reason, temporarily halting its progress, but a triumphal realization of it.

This direct argument figures early on in *Dialectic of Enlightenment*; it states: the minimal unit of rational thought, the concept or, what is the same, the sign-unit, is itself an instigator, bearer, and product of this repressive logic. Concepts *subsume* particulars under themselves; they insist that one (unique) thing is the *same* as another. But only so, says Kant, for example, can we *think*; thinking is the recognition of individuals in accordance with what they are not *qua* individuals, namely, the same as other things, and hence different from themselves. To be sure, there is no surprise in this since the concept in its purity, expresses nothing but a rejection of immediacy, a rejection which makes possible the separation of the actual, the given, and the possible, the given in terms of its characteristics. None the less, despite the potentialities built into the negativity of the concept, its origin marked it off for a different destiny:

> The universality of ideas as developed by discursive logic,
> domination in the conceptual sphere, is raised up on the basis of
> actual domination. The dissolution of the magical heritage, of the
> old diffuse ideas, by conceptual unity, expresses the hierarchical
> constitution of life determined by those who are free. The
> individuality that learned order and subordination in the
> subjection of the world, soon wholly equated truth with the
> regulative thought without whose fixed distinctions universal
> truth cannot exist. (DoE, p. 14)

Adorno's target here is not conceptual thought as such, but the regimentation of it into system, correspondence and universality; in other words, those features of our conceptual system that spell out its eventual rejection of historicality. As Adorno clearly states some pages later:

> what is abandoned (by subjective or formal rationality) is the
> whole claim and approach of knowledge: to comprehend the given
> as such; not merely to determine the abstract spatio-temporal
> relations of the facts which allow them just to be grasped, but on
> the contrary to conceive them as the superficies, as mediated
> conceptual moments which come to fulfilment only in the

development of their social, historical, and human significance.
(DoE, pp. 26–7)

Conceptual thought *qua* subjective reason betrays the mediational
powers of the concept because it institutes an immediacy as its goal,
a making present of the world in universal truth, and hence forfeits
the inner impulse of cognition to know what is other as such, in its
alterity. And this goal, clearly now, for Adorno is conceivable only in
terms of a substantive concept of reason or truth as historicality.
Truth becomes.

It is of course true that the subsumptive employment of concepts
is not the only use to which they can be put, concept and sign have
expressive, performative, communicative and akin uses. Discursive
logic, the only logic available in which we can consider the world,
including the expressive, performative and kindred portions of it, is
governed by the presuppositions concerning identity, difference and
sameness which govern the subsumptive employment of reason and
its truth-concept. Hence, even if it were to be granted that there
were portions of the world that escape the dominion of reason, we
could not – rationally – understand them. *We* have no other notion of
truth.

A totalizing critique of this sort deprives critique of any vantage
point from which, or normative guideline in accordance with which,
it could validate its claims. Further, reason's turning upon itself in
this way does involve it in a performative contradiction: it is by
reason that the critique of reason is carried out. These facts do not
invalidate the analysis; on the contrary, we could only regard the
failure to apply reason to itself as blindness or dogmatism. What the
critique reveals is not the lack of a foundation, the search for such
was (is), after all, part of the logic of domination – certainty precision,
foundations being both corollaries and figures of mastery – but the
opacity of reason to itself, the entrapment of conceptual mediation in
the clutches of an impossible immediacy. From this vantage point
Adorno's later programme of negative dialectic, his strategy of
continually reapplying determinate negations to the matter to hand,
can be seen as possessing a threefold significance.

1 First, and most evidently, it is a strategy for avoiding the determinations of subjective reason. The procedure of determinate
   negation denies, even to the accomplishments of critique, the

status of being – universally – true, for such a being true as being present institutes an immediacy which both dominates, through its representational character, its objects, and hence represses the historical trajectory, the historicality of representation and object.

2 Second, then, determinate negation attempts to preserve a faithfulness to the inner possibilities of conceptual thought by preserving a sense of the concept as a negation of particularity that can be employed for the sake of particularity.

3 And this, finally, prefigures a substantive reason, an historical reason which while employing concepts (what else?), is none the less not governed by the truth-concept of immanence.

So, although Adorno does equate instrumental reason with conceptual thought, he does *not* think this entails a denial of conceptuality *as such*; it is rather the regimentation of conceptual thought by the principle of immanence which is the culprit. None the less, because that regimentation of conceptuality by the principle of immanence is now operative, in force, then determinate negation's faithfulness and prefigurative power are inadequate to the task assigned it. Determinate negation is too implicated in the regime of enlightened reason to be trusted.

Now while art too is, inevitably, implicated in domination and enlightenment, it is not implicated in the same way or to the same degree. And this for a very precise reason, namely, that art does engage the particular *qua* particular, and does so according to forms which are determined by there being the remnant or remainder of conceptual activity once the forms of conceptual reason in its practical and theoretical aspects are established. However, art forms are not just remnants: aesthetic synthesis evokes and echoes conceptual synthesis since it seeks to establish a non-conceptual unity of its elements (AT, p. 180), and further, evoking and echoing practical reason, aesthetic judgment, judgments of taste, aspire to universality (AT, p. 190). Art practices, productive and receptive, are modelled on and drawn from theoretical and ethical cognition. Art seeks cognition: to be really true and really purposive, but is only semblance. Art's semblance is a semblance of the overcoming of the differentiation of reason into the isolated spheres of truth, normative rightness and beauty. Art practices are a model for an alternative form of praxis, and art products are images of things as they could be for an objective reason, an historical reason. This is the nerve of Adorno's aesthetics. Appropriations of Adorno which centrally seek to elude the hardness of his theory are less transformations of it than acts of instrumental cannibalism.

II

'Aesthetics cannot hope to grasp works of art if it treats them as hermeneutical objects. What at present needs to be grasped is their unintelligibility.' (AT, p. 173) The unintelligibility of works of art is consequent upon a double exclusion, their exclusion from the domain of conceptual understanding as it is accomplished by theoretical reason – science, social science, philosophy, *et al.*; and their exclusion from the accomplishments of practical reason. Adorno characterizes the first exclusion in a variety of ways; for example, he contends that in art spirit, i.e. objective reason, discards its natural medium and becomes manifest in its opposite – materiality (AT, p. 173). Or, he claims, in art the logicality, the kind of conceptual consistency exemplified in works, is not a true logicality; art's logic still harbours 'an archaic unity of logic and causality' (AT, p. 199); which is to say, that in art the difference between purely logical forms, and empirical forms does not exist. For unproblematic examples of this consider the temporality, the temporal structures and modes of temporalization in modernist novels or music; or, more directly still, the spatializing features in the work of a sculptor like David Smith. Art's rejection of abstract conceptuality, or better, art's being abandoned to aconceptuality engenders art's concern for visuality, a concern for particularity and the non-identical. But the incommensurability of art with the demands of conceptuality must not be understood as positing art in a relation of brute externality with respect to conceptual understanding.

> Art is no more a concept than it is intuition (*Anschauung* – vision, immediacy). By its very existence, art protests against the dichotomy. Moreover the visual aspect of art differs from the empirical perception because it always points beyond empirical perception to spirit. Art is a vision of the non-visual; it is similar to a concept without actually being one. (AT, pp. 141–2)

Adorno explicates art's exclusion from the domain of practical reason through a socio-historical generalization of Kant's characterization of works of art as being internally purposive, marked, that is, by an intentional ordering, while externally purposeless, not actually *for* anything. Archaic art participated in magical and cult practices which sought to affect nature; later, religious and political art was given a purpose by the wholes of which it was a part. Once these purposes had evaporated, art had to go its own way; its own, immanent way involves acquiring meaning 'by giving expression to its glaring lack of meaning' (AT, p. 185). This expression, however, should not be construed as providing art with an *easy* social purpose; for this end is realized not directly, but indirectly by means of art's cognitive claims and achievements, that is, through art's truth potential.

> No longer do art works face the viewer's repetitive question, "What are you for?" Instead they asked "Are you telling the truth?", which is a question concerning the absolute. Art works respond to it by giving an answer that is non-discursive because discursive thought is unable to reply. Art seeks to give an answer, but since that answer is mimetic rather than judgmental it is in a sense a non-answer. This accounts for art's becoming enigmatic. (AT, p. 185)

We shall return to the question of aesthetic truth shortly. What is important to note here is Adorno's claim that autonomous art is problematic, 'enigmatic' is his preferred term, in virtue of its diremption from practical and theoretical reason; and further, that nonetheless art can only proceed by operating with forms which approximate to the work of these others: art works are transformations of their elements in accordance with unifying procedures and forms. Art is troubled because its transformations are not real, i.e. they do not effect an empirical purpose, nor do they establish any conceptual truth. If modern art is antinomic and in this way, then what art questions is theoretical and practical reason as differentiated from it and from one another. Art's enforced marginality hence becomes the condition for its questioning of the centre, but equally constrains it from providing an answer.

Further evidence of this construal of Adorno's diagnosis of autonomous art is to be found in his analysis of the dialectical interaction and mutual interdependency of art and philosophy. One tempting way to state the relationship, employed by Wellmer (TSR, p. 92), is to conceive of art works as intuitions in need of the conceptual illumination which philosophy alone can provide. Art's way of saying by not saying is enjoined by its sensuality, particularity, and aconceptuality; because of its non-discursive mode of presentation it is in danger of collapsing into immediacy, of becoming just another fact or experience. Philosophy, for its part, even in its authentic mode in which it attempts to 'open up the non-conceptual by means of concepts, without making it equivalent to these concepts' (ND, p. 10), is consigned to conceptuality, and is hence threatened by abstractness. Art without philosophy is blind, and philosophy without art is empty. As stated, this fails to carry conviction because even if we grant that aesthetic particulars as particulars are in need of conceptual mediation, it does not follow that this mediation needs to be philsophical. In order for this latter to be the case a further thesis is required, namely, that the truth content of works of art is categorical and not empirical, it concerns the categories of truth, meaning, space, time, identity, art, etc. 'Philosophy and art overlap in the idea of truth content. The progressively unfolding truth of a work of art is none other than the truth of the philosophical content' (AT, p. 189). Adorno continues several lines later

> Truth content is *not* what art works denote (i.e. the truth content of a work of art is not representational), but the *criterion* which decides if they are true or false in themselves. It is this variant of truth content in art, and this variant alone which is susceptible of philosophical interpretation, because it corresponds to an adequate concept of philosophical truth. (AT, p. 190)

The truth content of works of art is the criterion of truth invoked by the work, a criterion which is true if the work is true. Because this criterion questions the truth of non-art bound concepts of truth, art requires philosophy, and aesthetic experience is genuine only if it leads to philosophical reflection. But philosophy, because of its immersion in instrumental reason, cannot validate the claims of art works; rather, philosophy can only raise our comprehension of works to the point at which their claim can come into view. For the rest we must return to the work.[3]

The hyperbole and apparent tendentiousness of this claim is mitigated if we recall that according to Adorno 'Art works are true in the medium of determinate negation only' (AT, p. 187), or 'Actually, only what does not fit into this world is true' (AT, p. 86), that is, the inner authenticity, truth, validity of art works, provides testimony against the universality of instrumental reason and hence testifies to the possibility of an alternative truth concept (AT, p. 79). However, this clearly falls a good deal short of claiming actually to provide such an alternative. On the contrary, Adorno emphasizes how the semblantic character of art infects its meaning *and* being.

> Every artefact works against itself. But especially art is such that it is deliberately designed as a *tour de force* or balancing act in which the impossible is realized. Even the simplest work is a *tour de force*, for it is defined by the realization of the impossible. . . . Works which are from the outset deliberately conceived as *tour de force* are illusions because they pretend to have an essence they cannot have. They correct themselves by stressing their own impossibility. (AT, pp. 155–6)

In order to suggest that what appears as meaning outside art is non-meaning, art must risk meaning; the risk is real, but its accomplishment illusory. To be *only* art is the condition for works exemplifying an alternative mode of synthesis; but because works are art, the synthesis is not real. It is for this reason that Adorno claims that 'Illusion is not a formal but a substantive characteristic of works of art. It is the vestige of an injury that art seeks to undo' (AT, p. 157). Art seeks to be purposive and true, but it can so seek only in the mode of semblance; art desires non-art, but only as art can it authenticate that desire. This is the antinomy of art. For Adorno, it is an historically engendered and historically soluble antinomy. The antinomy of art, the antinomic structure of authentic, autonomous works is a figure of differentiated reason *as* differentiated, divided, torn, sundered; that differentiation can only be critiqued, determinately negated, figuratively is so because differentiation is categorical, it determines the meaning of truth in general, and hence cannot be critiqued internally without contradiction. Art cannot *simply* navigate its way through this impasse; rather, its truth claim as expressed in authentic works is of a repressed truth potential; only as injured, as unable to be really true does art attain cognitive import. Elsewhere I have denominated this thesis 'aesthetic alienation'.[4]

Now the Habermasian critique of Adorno's aesthetics, as worked through by Wellmer, is oblique rather than direct. Wellmer attempts a decoding or appropriation of Adorno's theory in terms of the Habermasian communication theory which escapes the former's aporias and antinomies. This is problematic because Adorno's theory is aporetic and antinomic, and he does not conceive of the aporias and antinomies of his theory as *his*; they are the antinomies of bourgeois thought. None the less, the *places* of confrontation are readily detectible.

1 Wellmer questions the apparently utopian character of Adorno's theory generally and the apparently ecstatic character of Adorno's conception of aesthetic awareness in particular.
2 Both Habermas and Wellmer question the status of Adorno's conception of the mimetic element in art; an element which figures art's relation to particularity, the non-identical, without passing over into a truth theory proper.
3 Wellmer claims that Adorno remains trapped within the philosophy of consciousness, and as a consequence overemphasizes the figure of reconciliation, and underemphasizes, indeed fails to account for, the communicative and receptive aspects of aesthetic cognition.
4 Finally, Wellmer contends that aesthetic validity entails nothing about truth. Truth and truthfulness in art are metaphorical. Hence, *pace* Adorno, art may require criticism but does not require philosophical criticism.

In Wellmer, these criticisms are less discrete, more tightly interwoven in that they all presume the validity of Habermasian communicative theory which is revealed to be preferable to Adorno *because* it can undo the aporias and antinomies of his *Aesthetic Theory*. If, however, the acknowledgement of the autonomous structure of art works is the goal of Adorno's theory, then this line of questioning must be handled circumspectly.

Wellmer argues that the Adornoesque paradigm of reconciliation ought to be replaced by the Habermasian vision of dialogical relationships between human individuals in a liberal society (RUE, p. 48), that is, the image of the non-violent togetherness of the manifold imaged in authentic artworks properly pre-figures an uncorrupted intersubjectivity, a 'mutual and constraint-free understanding among individuals in their dealings with one another, as well as the identity of individuals who come to a compulsion-free understanding with themselves – sociation without repression' (TCA, p. 391). The reason proffered as to why we ought to make this substitution is that the philosophy of consciousness within which Adorno works restricts the comprehension of rationality to instrumental rationality; as a consequence it cannot actually name or analyse *what* is destroyed through instrumental reason. Mimesis as a *figure* of what is lost suggests 'a relation between persons in which one accommodates to the other, identifies with the other, empathizes with the other' (TCA, p. 390), but can do no more. Hence what is other than instrumental reason remains opaque to rationality, and a liberated society becomes simply the other of this society. The alteration to a communication based theory, on the other hand, allows the rational core of the mimetic achievements of art to be unlocked in terms of communicative rationality. 'This utopian projection', Wellmer says, 'does not describe the "Other" of discursive reason, but its own idea of itself. Because this utopian projection remains attached to the conditions of language, what is at issue here is an inner-worldly – in this sense a "materialist" – utopia' (TSR, p. 99). Therefore what is significant about autonomous art is its functional capacity for altering intersubjective relations and releasing the communicative potential repressed by capital's intrusion into artistic distribution and reception. (Since Habermas and Wellmer regard autonomous art as an achievement, they cannot legitimately claim that artistic *production* is distorted in its capitalist setting, which, of course, is the core of Adorno's analysis. We shall return to this question subsequently.)

Now in fact Adorno does think art prefigures liberated communicative relations, and recognizes as well that art has a communicative function. Thus, 'the process enacted by every artwork – as a model for a kind of praxis wherein a collective subject is constituted – has repercussions on society' (AT, p. 343). And a few pages earlier:

> Enshrined in artistic-objectification is a collective We. This We is not radically different from the external We of society. It is more like a residue of an actually existing society of the past. The fact that art addresses a collectivity is not a cardinal sin; it is the corollary of the law of form. (AT, p. 339)

Wellmer, ignoring the 'repercussions on society', chides Adorno for conflating art as a model of reconciliation with art as a medium for transcending reification; and further contends that Adorno's 'we' speaks with one voice, speaking to itself as it were, while the Habermasian norms of intersubjective communication apply to an open dialogue with many voices (RUE, p. 49). What is at stake between Adorno's 'we' and Wellmer's 'many voices'?

It would appear to be this: while no one is more alert to the reification of subjectivity under capital than Adorno, he regards solidarity as a condition for substantive reason; since such a we does not at present exist, then there is no extant alternative to instrumental reason. The law of form in autonomous art addresses us because in it empirical form and logical form are not differentiated; a *form* that is quasi-empirical is precisely one which is *not* universal, hence if true and purposive such a form could only be *our* form, the form of the praxis of a substantially joined collectivity. The 'repercussions on society' of the law of form is just the reiterated desire of radical aesthetic culture to have its autonomy superseded, to overcome the differentiation between aesthetic culture and political culture. If Adorno was pessimistic about the capacity of aesthetic culture itself to engineer this overcoming – the programmes of surrealism and dadaism – this is because he recognized that art's critical strength is bought at the price of praxial powerlessness. None the less, Adorno's conception of a radical aesthetic culture is surely *as* immanent, indeed more immanent and concrete than anything Habermas can offer. Habermas's theory has consistently been bedevilled by the lack of a volitional component, that is, by the lack of a point of entry into social practice where his communicative norms might matter. In his perspicacious reply to Axel Honneth's analysis of Habermas's advance over Adorno, James Schmidt concluded, 'In the end, Habermas's reconstruction of universal pragmatics seems to maintain the same distance from the practical domain of communicative inter-action as Adorno's resigned stance before "the debris of language!"'[5] While I would want to complain about Adorno's lack of an adequate conceptualization of the political sphere, I would none the less suggest that this statement is, if anything, unjust to Adorno.

As for Wellmer's 'many voices', either it is an *empty* reminder of the fact that any workable socialism will have to leave room for some pluralism, which none the less leaves the question of solidarity unanswered, hence the emptiness of the reminder; or it is a quiet defence of liberalism – which should be rejected outright.

Of course, the question of immanence might be conceived as pulling in other directions. For Habermas and Wellmer immanence entails the *continuity* of historical progress; while Adorno's rejection of immanence in this sense instantiates his claim that socialism will be radically discontinuous with capitalism. Indeed, in Adorno 'utopia' figures only as a *marker* for discontinuity and clearly contains none of the assumptions about transparency, homogeneity, abundance, reason, what have you, that has made some Marxist theory, including some of Marx's own writings, the focus of deconstructive type critiques by writers like Castoriadis, Lefort and Baudrillard. On the contrary, Adorno's conception of substantive reason entails a conception of historicality which rules out, in principle, any but a trivial utopianism. In straightforward practical terms, Adorno's discontinuity thesis is in no worse shape than Habermas and Wellmer's continuity thesis, given the latter's silence on the issues of motivation and agency. Theoretically, the question can be decided in only one way, namely, by deciding whether autonomous art is problematic in itself because of differentiation, as Adorno argues; or whether the critique of autonomous art is a misplaced critique of art as a bourgeois institution, with the weight of argument posed 'against art as commodity and as a part of mass culture, and against art as a self-contained sphere of ideological consolations' (RUE, p. 63), as Wellmer and Habermas contend. That in the case of autonomous art, but not in the case of mass art, Wellmer and Habermas are willing to rescind the conditions of production from the conditions of distribution and consumption, certainly appears prima facie insupportable; it is incompatible with Marxist theory generally, and most evidently bypasses Adorno's analysis of the separation of autonomous and mass art as representing two halves of an integral freedom, to which however they do not add up. For the sake of argument, let us ignore these points, and focus on the question of truth in art, a question which turns, in the final analysis, on diverging views of autonomous art itself.

Wellmer argues, and my own analysis concurs with this, that Adorno's theory attempts dialectically to link two notions of truth: truth one is aesthetic validity, or what I have called authenticity, and refers to works matching internally generated formal and technical norms; truth two is cognitive truth, which I have already suggested refers not to a representational truth a work might possess, but rather to the *question* of truth, the truth of truth as we now have it. It is important to remember that this theory of truth in art is not intended as a general theory, but *only* as an account of truth for autonomous works of art, with Beckett serving as Adorno's paradigm case.[6] Overlooking which artworks Adorno is analysing, or perhaps merely overlooking Adorno's restriction of his theory to this range of objects, Wellmer claims that because art is the – semblantic – other of unreconciled reality,

> it can only be true in the sense of being faithful to reality to the extent that it makes reality appear as unreconciled, antagonistic,

fragmented. But it can only do this by letting reality appear in the light of reconciliation. This means, however, that an antinomy is carried into the very interior of aesthetic synthesis: aesthetic synthesis can, by definition, only succeed by turning against itself and calling its own principle into question – it must do this for the sake of truth which may not be had except by means of this principle. (TSR, p. 95)

It follows, Wellmer argues, that Adorno is forced to read reconciliation into the work's truth content; reconciliation is the idealization of the work's truth content. And this idealization as something knowable turns into a truth *about* art, and thus not the truth content of the particular work of art at all (TSR, p. 106). It is this to which Wellmer objects, and to which he counterposes a functionalist theory in which the transformation of the subjectivity of the audience becomes the primary focus.

To be sure, it sounds odd, especially if one is thinking of traditional art works, to claim that the truth content of a work should end up being a truth about art. Yet this claim is not odd with respect to autonomous works for they are, almost be definition, works in which the question of autonomy and hence of art itself is posed. As Stanley Cavell has recently stated it:

In modernist arts the achievement of the autonomy of the object is a problem – the artistic problem. Autonomy is no longer provided by the conventions of an art, for the modernist artist has continuously to question the conventions upon which his art has depended; nor is it furthered by any position the artist can adopt towards anything but his art.[7]

By turning away from production to the question of reception, Habermas and Wellmer abandon the modernist arts to their problem, which is to say, they attempt to bracket the problem as one for the producers but not for the receivers. Yet modernist art is the sort of art for which the existence, the meaning of art is a question, and that question is posed by art's autonomy.

Because he fails to take adequate account of the sort of art which forms the focal point of Adorno's concern, Wellmer tends to over-substantialize the image of reconciliation presented by art works. The non-violent synthesis of modernist works is not an image of reconciliation, but rather an image of the *form* of praxis appropriate to a reconciled society.

In the eyes of the existing rationality, aesthetic behaviour is irrational because it castigates the particularity of this rationality in its pursuit not of ends but of means. Art keeps alive the memory of ends-oriented reason. It also keeps alive the memory of a kind of objectivity which lies beyond conceptual frameworks. That is why art is rational, cognitive. Aesthetic behaviour is the ability to see more in things than they are. (AT, p. 453)

More briefly: 'The falsehood opposed by art is not rationality *per se*, but the rigid juxtaposition of rationality and particularity (AT, p. 144).

Governed, I suspect, by the undoubted success of modern science, Habermas and Wellmer have been led to an acceptance of instrumental reason's conception of truth, and hence forced to embrace the differentiated forms of normative rightness and aesthetic validity. The latter two, however, have become deeply problematic to us and to themselves, because they have lost the power to speak the truth, to say what is true, to be true. Contra Wellmer, Adorno does not conceive of the transformation to socialism in terms of a sublation of instrumental into aesthetic rationality; rather, aesthetic rationality *images* the idea of an objective, substantive reason, a reason premised on solidarity, which fuses universal and particular, empirical form and conceptual form, and hence can acknowledge alterity and difference. For Adorno, post-modernity is just modernity at the limit. Because that limit has still to be trespassed beyond, and yet we are unable to rest within modernity, we balance at the limit. In balancing this performance one can but use reason against reason. The result, however, is neither consolation nor a universal truth, some cognitive commodity to be exchanged at some later date. It is rather an address, a call, not to assent, but to solidarity.

NOTES

1 The following abbreviations and editions have been used throughout this chapter:
T. W. Adorno, *Aesthetic Theory* (London 1983) – 'AT'; Adorno, *Negative Dialects* (New York 1973) – 'ND'; Adorno and Max Horkheimer, *Dialectic of Enlightenment* (New York 1972) – 'DoE'; Jurgen Habermas, 'Modern *versus* Postmodernity,' *New German Critique*, 22 (Winter 1981) – 'MvP'; Habermas, *The Theory of Communicative Action*, vol. I (London 1984) – 'TCA'; Albrecht Wellmer, 'Reason Utopia, and the Dialectic of Enlightenment,' in R. J. Bernstein (ed.) *Habermas and Modernity* (Cambridge 1985) – 'RUE'; Wellmer, 'Truth, Semblance, Reconciliation: Adorno's Aesthetic Redemption of Modernity,' *Telos* 62 (Winter 1985) – 'TSR'.

2 See also Aristotle's *Politics*, Book II, chapter 9.
3 See my 'Philosophy's Refuge; Adorno in Beckett,' in David Wood (ed.), *Philosophers' Writers*, London: Routledge (forthcoming).
4 'Aesthetic Alienation: Heidegger, Gadamer, and Truth at the End of Art,' in John Fekete (ed.), *Life After Deconstruction: Essays on the Post-Modern Contents of Value*, (forthcoming).
5 'Offensive Critical Theory? Reply to Honneth,' *Telos* 39, (1979).
6 See my 'Philosophy's Refuge', op. cit.
7 Stanley Cavell, *Must We Mean What We Say*, Cambridge 1976, p. 116.

Chapter 4

MUSIC, LANGUAGE AND MODERNITY

ANDREW BOWIE

The present intensive discussion of the question of modernity and post-modernity has tended to give music a rather subordinate role. I want to suggest in the following that this is a significant mistake. In *The Order of Things* Michel Foucault, who, like Habermas, has little time for the idea of post-modernity, gives the following account of the emergence of a modernity of which we are still a part:

> The threshold between Classicism and modernity (though the terms themselves have no importance – let us say between our prehistory and what is still contemporary) has been definitely crossed when words cease to intersect with representations and to provide a spontaneous grid for the knowledge of things. At the beginning of the nineteenth century they rediscovered their ancient enigmatic clarity.[1]

With the divorce of language and representations – to which I shall return in a different but related context – it becomes possible that 'language may sometimes arise for its own sake in an act of writing that designates nothing other than itself'.[2] Foucault makes the obvious link to a later manifestation of this in the work of Mallarmé:

> To the Nietzschean question: "Who is speaking?" Mallarmé replies – and constantly reverts to that reply – by saying that what is speaking is, in its solitude, in its fragile vibration, in its nothingness, the word itself – not the meaning of the word but its enigmatic and precarious being.[3]

Such a conception of the word has no essential difference from a conception of a note in music. Lévi-Strauss has defined musicality as 'Language minus meaning'. Foucault, though, makes no substantial mention of music in *The Order of Things*. Such an omission is the rule rather than the exception in most accounts of modernity and post-modernity. The most obvious example of a conception of modernity where this is not the case is the work of Adorno. This essay also wants to suggest a new direction from which some of Adorno's more hyperbolic claims could be re-examined.

The first oddity is, then, in a debate which is substantially concerned with questioning the nature of language's referentiality and its relationship to concepts, that music does not play a larger role. This is even more surprising, given the massive public importance of music of all kinds in the modern period. One might, indeed, almost be able to define the modern period in terms of the increasing public availability of all forms of music. It is surprising that Benjamin spends so little time talking about the gramophone and privileging, in the manner of the dominant western philosophical tradition, the visual media.

It is somewhat intriguing to find Hegel in the *Aesthetics* suggesting a view of music which is not very far from Foucault's 'act of writing that designates nothing other than itself'. Hegel, of course, sees this less positively. Hegel's text refers to what he calls 'independent music', music without a verbal text, and relates it to a specific view of consciousness:

> Subjective inwardness constitutes the principle of music. But the most inward part of the concrete self is subjectivity as such, not determined by any firm content and for this reason not compelled to move in this or that direction, rather resting in unbounded freedom solely upon itself.[4]

On the one hand one has, in Foucault's case, language resting upon itself in a state of semantic indeterminacy; on the other, in Hegel's case, subjectivity resting upon itself with an indeterminate relationship to its other. The negative relationship to concepts is the same, albeit from opposing directions. (One can note in passing the structural relationship of this to the debate between a rigidly language-based structuralism and a rigidly consciousness-based hermeneutics: both are confronted with the problem of just how meaning can then be constituted in a determinate fashion.) Hegel's account of the note as 'an expression which precisely by the fact that it is externality immediately makes itself disappear again'[5] has the same features as Mallarmé's view of the word's 'fragile vibration' and transience.

Hegel, as is well known, sets up a positive view of the way which subjectivity develops via its increasing self determination via the concept; Foucault subordinates subjectivity to the happening of language, largely in the manner of Heidegger. Despite this diametrical opposition, the analogies in the characterization of music on Hegel's part and language's divorce from representations on Foucault's part seem to me worth pursuing.

Foucault's essential event in language takes place at the beginning of the nineteenth century. Hegel's account of music is not much later and largely refers to music prior to Beethoven. It is important to see Hegel's view of music in the context of his larger argument about art. As is well known Hegel gives art a subordinate place in his system. For Hegel 'Thought and reflection have outstripped art' in his period; whether because 'passions and selfish interests' have pushed art out of the way or because the 'complicated state of civil and political life' no longer allows time and energy for substantial attention to the 'higher purposes of art', the 'particular nature of artistic production and of its works no longer fulfils our highest need'. Furthermore, 'the present is in its general state not favourable to art'[6] and the 'science of art' is now most appropriate because art alone no longer satisfies the demands of the mind for analysis and reflection. Art is the lowest, sensuous form of reconciliation between 'Nature and finite reality, and the infinite freedom of comprehending thought'[7]: the highest form is, of course, philosophy, Hegel's philosophy.

There is evidently something rather odd to us about Hegel's assessment. The least knowledge of music history makes it clear that at this time unfavourable to art arguably the greatest music of western civilization is being produced: one is more likely to say 'Hegel is the Beethoven of philosophy' than vice versa. However ambiguously, the continuing public importance of music in our historical present tends to suggest a profound misunderstanding in Hegel's statement that his present was not favourable to art. The test of actuality is one still effortlessly passed by the music of Schubert, Beethoven and others. The reason for Hegel's judgment is initially obvious: he doesn't regard music as particularly important. By the time he is giving lectures on aesthetics this is, though, hardly the dominant view. At much the same time Schopenhauer was giving music the highest philosophical status: that of being a direct image of the Will. In fact this is the time of an epochal shift in the status of music, initially in Germany, but the implications will be felt elsewhere. This shift has been splendidly described by Carl Dahlhaus in *Die Idee der absoluten Musik*.

Until quite late in the eighteenth century the essential view of music was that music with a verbal text was a higher form. At the end of the eighteenth century this view changes and 'conceptless instrumental music – and precisely because of and not despite its lack of concepts – was elevated to a language above verbal language'.[8] The concept of music that is replaced is essentially Platonic, consisting of Harmonia, Rhythmos and Logos: 'By Harmonia one understood regulated, rational relations of notes brought into a system, by Rhythmos the temporal order of music . . . and by Logos language as expression of human reason'.[9] At the very moment when Foucault sees the intersection of words and representations as ceasing music becomes a privileged form of art if it is *not* accompanied by a text. Furthermore a dynamic of development in music itself takes place whose products are central to any view of modern art. One cannot pursue all the implications of this here: they seem to me vital in a reconsideration of the history of modernity. One can, though, suggest some new ways of telling the story.

Key figures in Foucault's account of modernity and language are Mallarmé and Nietzsche, both of whom were very involved in music, though Foucault never mentions the fact. Their involvement can best be seen in the light of Dahlhaus' account of 'absolute music'. In a complex interaction of musical, literary and philosophical developments what Dahlhaus calls a 'topos of Unsayability'[10] emerges. What is not available to discursive language is articulated in a privileged sphere of its own by music. One can trace this in part to a misunderstanding of Kant's remarks about 'intellectual intuition' in the *Critique of Judgement*. Intellectual intuition, a contradiction in Kantian terms because all intuitions are sensuous and ordered by concepts of the understanding, would be a transcending of the divide between the ordering of intuitions by the understanding and the supersensuous idea of freedom. Because this cannot be articulated in concepts it would have to be made available in some other way, for instance in conceptless music. E. T. A. Hoffmann's famous review of Beethoven's fifth suggests this:

> Music opens up an unknown realm to man; a world that has
> nothing in common with the surrounding external world of the

70

senses and in which he leaves behind all feelings which are determinable by concepts in order to devote himself to the unsayable.[11]

Importantly for my argument this idea becomes transferred also to poetic language and Novalis and others ponder the idea of a 'purely poetic language'. Dahlhaus points out a significant link:

One can admire the boldness with which the idea of *poésie absolue* was sketched seventy years before Mallarmé – so to speak in a vacuum – but should not fail to recognise that it was first of all music, classical instrumental music which gave a theory of absolute art real historical substance.[12]

Foucault's inability in *The Order of Things* to give anything but a tired Heideggerian account of how such shifts take place can in this account be related to music and conceptions of subjectivity of a kind Foucault thinks, like Heidegger, he can subordinate to the words of Being, or whatever. This point will be explained more fully later: what is clear is that Foucault's argument is linked to music.

Given the importance of music in suggesting a re-orientation in Foucault's account of modernity it is worth now taking a closer look at what Hegel has to say about music. Habermas's most recent analysis of modernity sees it as the problem of an age which, without theological constraints, seeks to ground its own relationship to things in the principle of subjectivity, thus, so to speak, in itself. Hegel

posits the absolute self-relationship of a subject which attains self-consciousness out of its substance, which carries the unity and the difference of finite and infinite *in itself*. . . . The Absolute is conceived of neither as substance nor as subject but solely as the mediating process of self-relationship which produces itself without conditions.[13]

The point of Hegel's philosophy is to demonstrate the ultimate transparency of Being to itself by seeing the dynamic process of its development as the process of reason. Hegel's *Logic* therefore begins with a concept of Being which is, as Dieter Henrich says, the 'simply immediate, unfulfilled, the anticipation of concrete significance'.[14] Only in the process of *determination*, of the continual concretization of the nature of Being does it come to itself. Being is thus, in fact, as Manfred Frank says, 'a mode of reflection which has not yet been comprehended'[15] and which therefore awaits its conceptual realization and has no transcendent basis. This can be perhaps more easily understood via Hegel's earlier notion of 'Life' which 'one can only understand if the opposition of living beings among each other and the organic unity in each of them is conceived via the generality of an organisation which nevertheless does not exist prior to and outside of the process of living beings'.[16] The movement of thought as negation and the successive negation of forms in a living organism have the same principle. In this way the concepts of reflection will grasp the real process of Being, the two being identical. Only via the process of reflection does Being come to its truth.

What has this to do with music? When Hegel discusses the 'material' of music he contrasts the note with the material of plastic arts: whereas the latter 'take up the forms of a broad, multiple world of objects into themselves' the note is 'completely abstract'. For this reason 'Musical expression is only appropriate . . . for completely objectless inwardness, abstract subjectivity as such. This is our completely empty ego, the self without further content.'[17] The beginning of the Logic, Hegel states 'as the beginning of *thought*, is supposed to be quite abstract, quite general, wholly form without any content'.[18] There is, then, a structural similarity. The movement of the *Logic* is then that of Becoming and of the increasing determination of Being by the concept. The note is 'an independent, completed existence in itself' but only its relationship to other notes 'gives it its own real determinacy and with it the difference, opposition to other notes or unity with them'.[19] Hegel explicitly relates this view of the note to the *Logic*:

> In my logic I developed the concept as subjectivity but this
> subjectivity as ideal transparent unity sublates itself to what is
> opposed to it, to objectivity; indeed it is as the simply ideal itself
> only a one-sidedness and particularity . . . and only truly
> subjectivity when it goes into this opposition and overcomes and
> dissolves it.[20]

The same applies to the movement of a musical piece: the resolution (the German word for dissolution and resolution is the same, *Auflösung*) of dissonance into harmony in notes parallels that in the logic of the concept. This is impressive stuff and, as I shall suggest later, can tell us about, say, Beethoven's music. However, Hegel does have his doubts about music in broader terms.

This brings us into the centre of the argument. Hegel's objections to music are based on its lack of a specific *content*. It is not conceptual: 'however much music also takes up a content of mind into itself . . . this content, precisely because it is grasped according to inwardness remains . . . more indeterminate and more vague'.[21] It is obvious that real determinacy is thus linked to *verbal* language. Hegel conceives of music in terms of Logos: the text which accompanies music or which music accompanies 'gives certain ideas (*Vorstellungen*) and thereby tears away consciousness from that more dreamy element of feeling without ideas'.[22] This might sound somewhat intolerant, but compared to Kant's view of music it is positively enthusiastic. For Kant music was a 'language of the emotions' but as the aesthetic ideas involved were not 'concepts and definite thoughts' all they did was give, via their mathematical proportions, the 'aesthetic idea of a coherent whole'.[23] Because, unlike literature, music did not leave any space for reflection it was 'more pleasure than culture'[24] and was the lowest form of art, not bearing repeated listening and being rather like the smell produced by someone who takes out a perfumed handkerchief in company. The reasons for these judgments have much to do with dominant ideas of the time about doctrines of emotion, but they point to more significant issues.

One reason music is seen as simply the language of the emotions is obviously its relation to 'primitive' expressions such as wordless cries or bird-song. These neither have the status of art nor of determinate conceptual language. In this view consciousness transmutes them into a higher form. Behind this view is, though, a specific conception of language. Derrida makes some remarks in relation to this topic in his Hegel essay 'The Well and the Pyramid'; my view will be somewhat different. As Derrida suggests, Hegel has a 'representational' model of language in which words express inner states. For Hegel the voice is the most immediate means of communication in music, it makes us hear 'the sounding of the soul itself, as the sound which inwardness (*das Innere*) by its nature has to express inwardness'.[25] A musical instrument is seen as a 'distant body'. As I have suggested, this is at precisely the time that instrumental music is taking on prior importance, both theoretically and practically, because it is not attached to words and concepts. I suggested above that this was in part for philosophical reasons; it is also, though, for musical reasons: Haydn's and Beethoven's symphonies made the 'paradigm shift' to absolute music possible.

The historical explanation of a shift away from determinate conceptuality should not assume that determinate conceptual reasons are necessarily prior. The historical complexities of explaining such a shift are too great to be gone into here: the essential point is to be aware that the factors involved are not reducible to what is most easily discursively formulated.

If we follow a further aspect of Hegel's argument this constellation leads one to certain important contemporary considerations. Hegel sees music as having to bring 'feelings into determinate relations of notes' and 'to take the natural expression out of its wildness, its raw state and moderate it': the roots of music are, then, in nature. The natural material is transformed by its being technically reordered in the organization of notes in a tonal system. (The tonal system in question has been tempered, a regularization whose parallels to the Galilean mathematicization of the cosmos need more investigation – Galileo's father was, of course, a musician.) Hegel describes the system in question as follows: 'the notes are in themselves a totality of differences, which can divide themselves and combine themselves into the most multiple kinds of direct consonances, essential oppositions, contradictions and mediations'; these give the 'inspired expression of that which is present as the determinate content of mind'.[26] Now it can hardly have escaped anyone's attention by now that views of language and expression have, especially in the wake of structuralism, come radically to question the view I have suggested that Hegel holds. It is therefore interesting to see that Hegel's notion of a totality of differences, the tonal system, is not so far from Saussure's 'langue', which is a system of differences with no positive terms via which meaning is constituted. In this theory supersensuous ideas result from the articulation of the *material* of the signifier, a complete reversal from the notion that ideas are 'represented' in language. In this perspective it is not perhaps so easy to write off otherwise admittedly wildly metaphysical Romantic theories of music such as those of Hoffmann and others which see it as articulating a sphere not otherwise available to us. In an early essay Nietzsche suggests: 'But how should the image, the idea (*Vorstellung*) produce music out of itself? Let alone the concept or, as has been said, the "poetic idea" being able to do so'.[27] The point in relation to Hegel's view of music is that if determinate content, with all that implies in terms of the *Logic*, is as closely linked to language as Hegel suggests and if language itself is no longer dependent upon the movement of the concept, indeed in some way determines the concept, then a whole new series of questions arises.

What I want to suggest now is that considerations of structuralist and poststructuralist views of language for the debate over modernity and postmodernity cannot, as I have already indicated in the case of Foucault, ignore the issue of music. This will lead to a brief consideration of why Adorno's contributions in this area might be more central than they have sometimes looked, despite their obvious limitations. Manfred Frank, to whose version of many of these issues I am much indebted, sees the structuralist re-orientation of language theory as having essentially two components. The first is an anti-metaphysical view, stated above, of language's relationship to concepts; the second is a metaphysical view which, despite its decentring of consciousness via consciousness's need for the system of articulation of the 'langue', is concerned to find 'general principles of order and universal regularities, the knowledge of which makes the social world controllable via technology and science'.[28] This is in line with the foundational project of a modernity in which Hegel evidently belongs. Poststructuralism's claims to 'postmodernity' are based on the attempt to rid structuralism and other modes of thought of the last traces of such metaphysical thinking. This requires an attack on the '(metaphysical) concept of controllability and of the system'.[29] Thus there can, for example, be no Searlean rules of meaning as contexts in which meaning arises are boundless. There is evidently much more to be said about this but it is clear that systems of musical articulation are similarly open-ended and contextual and it is these which in the nineteenth century are often central in the opposition to Hegelian and other forms of self-grounding rationality. The putatively 'postmodern' tends on certain levels to look very closely related to debates that, albeit otherwise riddled with meta-physics, open up a related space of argument in the nineteenth century.

Hegel's project was based on the proving of Being's transparency to itself via the concept. The main impetus of much poststructuralism can be seen as directed against all views with a similarly foundational character. Much depends, though, upon how the questioning of Being's transparency to subjectivity is actually formulated. There seem to me to be at present three basic positions involved in the debate that interests me here. These can, very reductively, be seen as follows. An essentially poststructuralist line which relates closely to Heidegger sees consciousness as subsequent to the happening of language, so that the subject is 'subverted' by the 'symbolic order' (Lacan) or is an 'effect' of the 'general text' which is constituted by the movement of 'différance', the continual deferral of any possible full coincidence of signifier and signified (Derrida). Alternatively there is Habermas's line which wishes to renounce the paradigm of constitutive subjectivity for 'the paradigm of communication and understanding between subjects which are capable of language and action',[30] which results in a sophisticated form of transcendental pragmatism. The third position, that of Manfred Frank, wishes to sustain a view of the subject but not in Hegel's sense. It is this view which I want to link to the question of music and modernity.

Frank shares one side of poststructuralism's Heideggerian suspicion of an instrumentalized or simply pragmatic view of language's relation to Being but does not wish to surrender the notion of the subject. Now the issues involved here are too large and important to be dealt with fairly in the space available. The arguments offered here will, I hope, be expanded in a larger context later. The immediate link of my account so far to Frank's position becomes clear when he links a version of the 'topos of Unsayability' to aspects of Derrida's theory, suggesting that the 'musicality' of 'poetic' language – those aspects which depend upon repetition and unexpected departure from repetition – cannot be adequately explained by assuming there are two separate dimensions of language, the poetic and the referential: 'For if – according to Saussure – a language only consists of differences, and if, furthermore, the differences are unsayable, then one can justifiably claim that the unsayable is the ground of the sayable'.[31] What makes a differential system signify cannot itself be subsumed within the system: the 'poetic', in the strong sense of the creative, must somehow be accounted for, as otherwise the 'marks' that enable signification remain inert. Seen like this, what is wholly accessible to agreed rules of interpretation in language cannot be primary; the same applies, though in many ways more obviously, to the differential structure of music. An analysis of the place of every note in a Bruckner symphony within a conception of the harmonic, rhythmic and contrapuntal systems involved in such music does not tell us about the foundation of those systems themselves. Neither does an account in terms of acoustics, physics or any other discourse of science.

Habermas is, in some ways rightly, worried that one version of a related view of language in Derrida 'makes the problem-solving capacity of language disappear behind its world-creating capacity',[32] thereby involving an aestheticizing lack of attention to the normal agreed language of the everyday 'life-world'. This, though, does assume that one *can* draw a clear boundary between the varying kinds of language. It is not clear to me that the 'world-creating' aspect even of forms of articulation like music cannot have problem-solving capacities in the life-world. (Speaking briefly as a musician, I know they can.) There is a sense in which Habermas at certain points is not too far from Hegel's position (as, I will suggest, is Peter Bürger whose position is often very close to that of Habermas). The advantage of Frank's view is that it enables one to take on board the idea that language could not be self-grounding and amenable to total interpretation without drawing the poststructuralist consequence that you can essentially forget subjectivity.

The key figures in Frank's argument are, importantly, Hegel's room-mates at the Tübingen seminary, Hölderlin and Schelling. Frank's point is that there is a counter-discourse of modernity which emerges parallel with Hegel's self-grounding system. This counter-discourse can be clearly linked to Adorno and thus to the question of music; it also arises, of course, parallel to the idea of absolute music. We must, then, briefly return to the more abstract metaphysical debate before coming back to music. As we have seen, Hegel regards the Absolute as a two-way process of reflection in which Being comes to itself via the determination of the concept. Hölderlin and Schelling hold a view that suggests that this conception is deficient. For them Being cannot be reduced to that which takes place in the reflection process of subject and object. Instead of being the subject that can come to the point of comprehending nature and itself as part of the same process, humankind is always subsequent to its foundation. Hölderlin states:

> the art and activity of men, even though it has already done so much, cannot produce something living, cannot itself create the original material which it changes, works upon, it can develop the creative force, but the creative force itself is eternal and not the product of human hands.[33]

Hölderlin therefore sees the need to recognize the limitation of subject and object. As Dieter Henrich says: 'Hölderlin thinks that both can only be made comprehensible on the basis of a pre-condition which neither functions as ego nor as object. Hölderlin calls it "Being"'.[34] In this way reflexive self-identification is always on the basis of a ground which cannot be subsumed within the reflection itself. (I have described the consequences of such a view for a critique of poststructuralism in more detail elsewhere.[35]) Frank explains the point via the metaphor of the mirror: looking at oneself in the mirror – as a metaphor of mind and nature as Hegel sees it, for example – cannot be a process of self-*identification*: 'For looking at something (even if it is *myself*) will never tell me about the particular quality of my object that it is *I* that I am looking at. I must already have had this insight'.[36] This insight cannot, then, have come about by a conceptual identification. Schelling puts it as follows in one of his later formulations:

> The subject can never possess itself as that which it is, for even as it attracts itself to itself it becomes something else, this is the basic-contradiction, we can say the misfortune in all Being – for it either leaves itself, so it is as nothing, or it attracts itself, so it is something else and not the same as itself. . . . Note that correspondingly the first beginning is expressly thought as something contingent (*Zufälliges*). . . . This whole construction . . . begins with a dissonance and has to begin that way.[37]

One notes the opposition to Hegel's view of the *Logic* as ultimately harmonious resolution, the revelation of ultimate identity. Now obviously one way in which the subject attempts to possess itself is via language. This brings us again to the questions outlined above.

Schelling's view of the subject prefigures in certain ways Lacan's notion of the 'real subject' which is 'subverted' by the 'symbolic order'. As Frank suggests, though, the question is whether the assumption of its subversion is all there is to it, whether language, without which consciousness cannot articulate itself, actually explains the fact of consciousness itself, its Being. This can never be identical with the marks via which it articulates itself or reflects itself, whether these marks be words or notes or anything else. The importance of this version of the issue of subjectivity for the question of modern aesthetics seems to me vital.

It is hardly coincidental that Schelling should attempt earlier in his career, in the *System of Transcendental Idealism*, to make art the 'organ' of philosophy and not an object of it as it was to become for Hegel. Schelling, like Hölderlin, saw Being as 'endless activity' of which we are a part but which concepts can never fully grasp: as he later says in an almost Marxian criticism of Hegel's *Logic*: 'Concepts as such really only exist in consciousness (*Bewusstseyn*), they are, therefore, taken objectively, *after* nature, not *before* it; Hegel took them from their natural place by putting them at the beginning of philosophy'.[38] Schelling sees art in the *System of Transcendental Idealism* as reflecting the 'identity of conscious and unconscious activity',[39] thereby suggesting that it reflects more than is accessible to categories of reflection and is amenable to endless interpretation. Though Schelling himself does not devote an enormous amount of attention to it, it should by now be obvious that music will play a major role in such a theory: the date of the *System of Transcendental Idealism* coincides exactly with the rise of the idea of absolute music. It is, of course, not long before Schopenhauer will take the step of saying that nature and music are 'different expressions of the same thing',[40] the Will, which is inaccessible to the concepts of reason. Music is a ' "language which reason does not understand" and yet which Schopenhauer claims to have completely deciphered', as Ernst Bloch put it.[41] One does not need to descend into Schopenhauer's irrationalism from the perspective I have been trying to outline. There is no reason to privilege music over language and to make it the sole representative of a metaphysical principle like the Will. One is looking at a specific historical constellation which poses questions which have arisen in a different form in the recent debate over modernity.

It is in this context that I think one can usefully suggest that the work of Adorno may offer resources whose relevance had been obscured by the more questionable aspects of his philosophy. Adorno's concentration on music may have had contingent biographical reasons but what I have said so far will, I hope, indicate that it may tell us more about the debate on modernism and postmodernism than previously suspected. Dahlhaus suggests of the *Aesthetic Theory* that it is probably the 'first – albeit unsystematic – aesthetic in which one as a rule can translate the word "Art" by "Music"'.[42] Peter Bürger's important criticisms of Adorno's conception of art and modernity, whilst making many valid points in relation to such problematic ideas as the 'state of the material', do not deal adequately with music's role in Adorno's thinking. Hence when we read the following remarks of Bürger on the *Aesthetic Theory*, 'the artistic medium that his reflections primarily relate to is music. To the extent that it is not connected to texts, in music the content of the work can only be established via formal characteristics', we are simply confronted with another version of Hegel's view of music and language. The danger of this view is that it cannot deal with a whole dimension of Adorno's reflections on art. Bürger wants in some way to be able to give an adequate account of the social determination of the work of art and rightly sees that Adorno's approach to this question is problematic. The worrying part is that his initial assumption about music and text already prejudges the issue in a way which leaves no space for the issues I have been trying to outline. The desire for a wholly adequate means of conceptual determination of the nature and status of art reduces it to a role much like that which Hegel attributes to it. One does not need to accept the strong version of Adorno's arguments in the *Dialectic of Enlightenment* or *Negative Dialectics* on the totalizing domination of the activity and products of instrumental reason to suggest that Adorno's concentration upon philosophy as the 'effort to say that of which one cannot speak'[43] may have more than some kind of quasi mystical significance when seen in the perspective of the question of music, language and modernity.

As Frank points out, Adorno's *Aesthetic Theory* adopts a position explicitly related to that of Schelling in its criticism of Hegel's conception of art and its relation to the rest of philosophy. Hegel

> hypostasises the ordering of all being (*Seienden*) by subjectivity as the Absolute and the non-identical is only important for him as a fetter on subjectivity instead of him determining its experience as the telos of the aesthetic subject and as its emancipation. The progress of dialectical aesthetics necessarily becomes a critique of the Hegelian dialectic.[44]

As I have already tried to show, a similar criticism is made from a different position in poststructuralism. It takes a largely Heideggerian line and sees Hegel's philosophy as part of the 'subjectification' of Being in western metaphysics, whilst paying no attention to the issue of how one might salvage the subject. Adorno's attention to music relates to a salvaging of at least some aspects of subjectivity in a world increasingly dominated by mechanisms which threaten to abolish it. This domination becomes most apparent in the constellation of Hegel's philosophy and the rise of the world commodity system, which Adorno sees as related: the kernel of truth in Hegel's system is that in the material world the totalizing power of the exchange principle creates a real totality which is figured in a mystified form in Hegel's resolution of the subject-object division: everything is reduced to equivalence.[45] Evidently linked to this is the emergence of a western musical tradition that at a time of such increasing domination uses technical resources to articulate those aspects of the subject's Being that are otherwise being subsumed within systems based on conceptual identification – the natural sciences and their technological products and the world of commodities. Music's *resistance* to wholesale interpretation and conceptual determination thus becomes increasingly important, as is the case in the idea of absolute music.

If one looks at one aspect of Adorno's account of the dialectic involved in this process of musical change one encounters familiar issues to those outlined above. Dahlhaus has very effectively analysed aspects of these issues in his account of Adorno's view of Beethoven. Dahlhaus points to the fact that Adorno links the 'antagonism of "totality and infinity"' in philosophical systems to Beethoven's music. The conflict of totality and infinity is essentially that between Hegel and Schelling suggested above. It can be seen also to be 'valid . . . for the musical contradiction between a reprise form which presents itself as a closed whole with beginning, middle and end and thematic work which has a tendency to progress ad infinitum'.[46] Adorno's objections to those Beethoven sonatas (by no means all, of course, hence his attachment to Opus 111) which end with a triumphal response is linked to their 'complicity with the great idealist systems, with Hegel the dialectician, in whom at the end the epitome of negation and thus of becoming itself results in the theodicy of the existent (*des Seienden*)'.[47] The importance of Mahler to Adorno is that he increasingly liberates music from the static elements of exposition and reprise and gives primary importance to the development section, thereby liberating the potential of the subject via using the potential of the technical means of the music of his time. In Adorno's account this *then* leads to the situation in 12-tone music in which 'the subject rules over music via the rational system, and then itself succumbs to the rational system. . . . Out of the operations which broke the blind dominance of the material of the notes the system of rules brings about a second blind nature':[48] the products of subjectivity lead to its own imprisonment – a version of the dialectic of enlightenment. One does not need to accept the rest of Adorno's arguments on this issue to suggest that this version of the history of one major aspect of western music has important analogies to the debate on modernity and postmodernity suggested above.

I suggested above how Manfred Frank related the structuralist project of establishing the system of the 'langue' to the foundational aims of one discourse of modernity: that project seems to me clearly analogous to Adorno's way of looking at the development of the language of music. As my final point I want to use one of Frank's most emphatic attacks on a dominant view of language and modernity as the link between the two questions. The issue can only be sketched: detailed development of the point will form the substance of subsequent work. In his account of the Searle-Derrida 'debate' Frank centres his argument on the question of the 'code model' of language. Such models are dependent upon the setting up of the kind of rules of usage which would enable the question of language and meaning to be subsumed within the kind of enterprise that has been characteristic of the human sciences since the rise of positivism. In my terms the enterprise can evidently also be linked to music: musical analysis is dependent upon the location of the components of a particular piece in terms of the dominant systems of analysis. In both music and language the systems of analysis can hardly be said to have been stable or to be now in a state of agreed certainty. Both work upon a basic principle of repetition: what is amenable to analysis is that which repeats some component of either agreed rules of usage or known patterns of differentiation. Obviously there is nothing essentially wrong with this in its own terms. Derrida's point is to reveal that the system of the 'langue' can, though, never be closed (for a good analysis of this point see Culler's *On Deconstruction*[49]). At the same time Frank suggests that Derrida shares with Searle a fundamental assumption.

The assumption is that of iterability. Derrida's 'minimal consensus' with Searle is that iterability and conventionality in language are a fact, which they are also, of course, in music. The problem is, Frank argues, that neither Derrida nor Searle can give a satisfactory account of the fact of meaning because neither of them allows for the necessarily individual component in all production of meaning. Frank puts it as follows:

> In the emphatic sense something is only then understood at the
> point where the jump is made from the universal system (from the
> code, from the convention, from the type of language) into the

individual style of a historically situated subject. Only via this jump does the general schema attain its individual sense.[50]

In music in the modern period there is much more clearly a sense in which the importance of the particular mode of articulation in question lies precisely in the way in which it gives both producer and listener an individual role which can never be fully amenable to analysis in terms of identity with dominant rules. Adorno's suggestion that even music in the modern age can end up using the same dominant mode of rational identification which negates individual meaning – as in the view of 12-tone music cited above – has now been overtaken by other historical developments and revealed as an unnecessarily limiting view of music and modernity. The implicit warning it contains is, though, that of the need to sustain means of articulation which enable subjects to assert some kind of freedom against the dominant modes of discourse. Frank's point about Derrida is that despite presenting arguments which, as I tried to show above, can lead to a greater awareness of the way in which the creative is the ground of any possible meaning, Derrida is ultimately in complicitly with much that he appears to oppose because of the manner in which he deals with subjectivity.

The importance of music in the history of modernity seems to me in part at least explained by its role as part of the counter discourse of modernity, that discourse that in the face of the determination to ground the subject in rules, codes and systems always reveals the extent to which these systems cannot be self-grounding. As Frank points out, any model of language based solely on the notion of conventions and rules tends to break down at the point when it is asked to explain what it is that brings about change in meaning. Derrida, by refusing to accept that the transformation might be a result of individual self-consciousness of the kind outlined above in relation to Schelling, ends up with the metaphysical idea of the language which talks itself. As such Frank sees him as still bound up with that which links 'classical reflection theory' (such as in Hegel) and the positivist tradition of rule-bound science. Though Derrida is a master at demonstrating how meaning will always go beyond the rules of any scientific theory of language he uses this to found a 'theoretical antihumanism. It seems to me that with that he reaches the furthest spiral of alienation: instead of becoming aware of a tormented and silent subject beneath the corset of a rationality which has become totalitarian, he finally gives it up'.[51] Derrida achieves from a different direction what the progress of one version of modernity achieved from another: the threat of denying even the idea of freedom. In the attempt to reconsider the history of modernity it seems to me that it is increasingly important to be able to tell the story of those aspects of that history such as music which subvert the dominant story so far: retracing the repressed possibilities of individuality may turn out to be a more valuable enterprise than the celebration of entry into a 'postmodernism' after the death of the subject.

NOTES

1 Michel Foucault, *The Order of Things*, London 1970, p. 304.
2 ibid., p. 304.
3 ibid., p. 305.
4 G. W. F. Hegel, *Vorlesungen über die Asthetik*, Dritter Band Jubiläumsausgabe Band 14 Stuttgart-Bad Cannstatt 1964 (*Asthetik 3*), p. 210.
5 *Asthetik 3*, p. 130.
6 G. W. F. Hegel, *Vorlesungen über die Ästhetik* I/II, ed. Rüdiger Bubner, Stuttgart 1971, pp. 48–9.
7 ibid., p. 45.
8 Ed. Carl Dahlhaus and Michael Zimmermann, *Musik zur Sprache gebracht*, Munich and Kassel 1984, p. 179.
9 Carl Dahlhaus, *Die Idee der absoluten Musik* Munich and Kassel 1978, p. 14.
10 ibid., p. 145.
11 *Musik zur Sprache gebracht*, p. 197.
12 *Idee der absoluten Musik*, p. 145.
13 Jürgen Habermas, *Der philosophische Diskurs der Moderne*, Frankfurt 1985, p. 46.
14 Dieter Henrich, *Hegel im Kontext*, Frankfurt 1967, p. 36.
15 Manfred Frank, *Der unendliche Mangel an Sein*, Frankfurt 1975, p. 33.
16 *Hegel im Kontext*, p. 36.
17 Hegel, *Asthetik 3*, p. 129.
18 Frederick G. Weiss (ed.), *Hegel The Essential Writings*, New York 1974, p. 108.
19 Hegel, *Asthetik 3*, pp. 154–5.
20 ibid., p. 178.
21 ibid., p. 181.
22 ibid., p. 191.
23 Immanuel Kant, *Kritik der Urteilskraft* Werkausgabe Band X Frankfurt 1977, p. 268.
24 ibid., p. 267.
25 Hegel, *Asthetik 3*, p. 170.
26 ibid., p. 145.
27 *Musik zur Sprache gebracht*, p. 326.
28 Manfred Frank, *Was ist Neostrukturalismus?* Frankfurt 1984, p. 36.
29 ibid., p. 37.
30 *Der philosophische Diskurs der Moderne*, p. 345.
31 *Was ist Neostrukturalismus?*, p. 601.
32 *Der philosophische Diskurs der Moderne*, p. 241.

33 *Der unendliche Mangel an Sein*, p. 14.
34 *Hegel im Kontext*, p. 65.
35 See Andrew Bowie, 'Individuality and Différance' in *The Oxford Literary Review* vol. 7, nos 1–2, 1985, pp. 117–30.
36 *Was ist Neostrukturalismus?*, p. 251.
37 F. W. J. Schelling, *Ausgewählte Schriften*, Band 4 Frankfurt 1985, p. 517.
38 ibid., p. 556.
39 Schelling, *Ausgewählte Schriften*, Band 1, p. 687.
40 Arthur Schopenhauer, *Die Welt als Wille und Vorstellung*, Erster Band Leipzig (no date), p. 345.
41 Ernst Bloch, *Geist der Utopie* Frankfurt 1964, p. 195.
42 *Musik zur Sprache gebracht*, p. 130.
43 T. W. Adorno, *Drei Studien zu Hegel*, Frankfurt 1969, p. 119.
44 T. W. Adorno, *Asthetische Theorie*, Frankfurt 1973, p. 119.
45 See *Drei Studien zu Hegel*, p. 103–4.
46 Burkhardt Lindner and W. Martin Lüdke (ed) *Materialien zur ästhetischen Theorie. T. W. Adornos Konstruktion der Moderne*, Frankfurt 1980, p. 498.
47 T. W. Adorno, *Mahler*, Frankfurt 1976, p. 127.
48 T. W. Adorno, *Philosophie der neuen Musik*, Frankfurt, Berlin, Vienna, pp. 64–5.
49 Jonathan Culler, *On Deconstruction*, London 1983, pp. 110–34.
50 Manfred Frank, *Das Sagbare und das Unsagbare*, Frankfurt 1980, p. 202.
51 Manfred Frank, *Das Sagbare und das Unsagbare*, p. 203.

If the reference is not to an English edition the translation is my own.

Chapter 5

FEMINISM AND POST-MODERNISM: MISLEADING DIVISIONS IMPOSED BY THE OPPOSITION BETWEEN MODERNISM AND POST-MODERNISM

JOANNA HODGE

The postmodernist emphasis on the irreducibility of particular interests and on the need for cultural constructs to be 'user friendly' positively invites an explicitly feminist response. This paper addresses the questions posed by Craig Owens in his paper[1] in the collection *Postmodern culture*: is postmodernism especially hospitable to the interests of women and to the claims of feminists? There are three parts to the following discussion the first part introduces a distinction between modernism and postmodernism, and indicates a connection between these two and the so-called epochs of modernity and postmodernity. Since postmodernism is often identified with poststructuralism, the first part will also indicate the connection between these distinctions and the project of poststructuralism. This discussion will introduce one aspect of the main theme: the fragility of the distinction between modernism and postmodernism, as shown in the proximity between the work of Adorno, the bearer of the supposedly modernist project in philosophy, and that of Deleuze, the bearer of the supposedly postmodern project.

The second part of the paper indicates the distinguishing features of a specifically postmodern mode of philosophizing. This part will also suggest a resonance between the ideals of the project of modernity and those attributed to classical antiquity, and the resulting exclusion of women from intellectual life in both epochs. The third part will show the commonality of themes between the supposedly postmodern features of philosophical enquiry and the theoretical orientations of Irigaray and Kristeva. This third section will suggest that Irigaray and Kristeva mobilize the traditional ideals of philosophical enquiry,

86

neutrality and timelessness, in order to identify and criticize the actual partiality of theoretical practices which, while pretending to exemplify those traditional ideals, in fact affirm a male figure at their centre. Kristeva's and Irigaray's endorsement of the partiality privileged by postmodernism is thus inflected by their recognition that this partiality has always operated in the western philosophical tradition to place men at its centre, and to exclude women from engaging in it. Thus some of the supposedly distinctive features of postmodern philosophy can be seen from a feminist angle always to have operated within the western philosophical tradition, classical, modern and postmodern, with the effect, amongst others, of problematizing women's participation in the production of philosophical discourse. This is the second aspect of the main theme: the fragility of the distinction between the modern and the postmodern modes of philosophical practice.

In a number of recent attempts to summarize and package both structuralism and poststructuralism for popular consumption, however, the work of women poststructuralists has been ignored. While the work of some of these women may in no obvious way support a feminist cause and collective project, it is clear that analysing the work of men, and ignoring parallel work done by women, is antifeminist. This ignoring of work done by women has been made all the easier as a result of the construction of a debate between the so-called modern and the so-called postmodern, for which the questions of feminism and the claims of women have been of lesser significance. That division between the so-called modern and the so-called postmodern has the further antifeminist effect of dividing liberal feminism and radical feminism. There is a strong connection between liberal feminism and the project of modernity on the one hand, and a strong connection between radical feminism and the postmodernist eschatological rejections of time, narrativity and historical process on the other. This is the third aspect of the main theme: the fragility of the distinction between modernism and postmodernism, shown in the proximity between liberal feminism, the bearer of the ideals of modernity, and radical feminism, the bearer of the ideals of postmodernity. The suggestion that the supposedly specifically postmodern features of philosophy are in fact characteristic features of philosophy in general generates the suspicion that the Marxian rejection of postmodern theorizing is merely a repetition of Marx's claim that historical materialism has made philosophy redundant.

Significantly Adorno rejects this element in Marxism, since he thinks that the moment for unifying philosophical analysis and political action in a proletarian revolution is not a present possibility. This indicates the revisionist nature of Adorno's Marxism. The dispute between modernist and postmodernist theorists can then be seen as a rehearsal of the dispute between Marx's historical materialism and the claims of philosophy.

MODERNISM, POSTMODERNISM; POSTSTRUCTURALISM: ADORNO AND DELEUZE

Jurgen Habermas, in his 1981 lecture entitled 'Modernity versus post-modernity',[2] argues that declarations of a postmodern age are political interventions designed to disrupt the liberatory project of modernity, launched by the French Revolution and the American Declaration of Independence. Mary Wollstonecraft wrote her *Vindication of the Rights of Women*, published in 1792, in response to, and in the hope of deepening the ideals and achievements of that project. Hers is a classic statement of a liberal feminism, which seeks to imagine how the rights of men might be extended to women, without presupposing unacceptable degrees of disruption in existing social institutions. Habermas seeks to refute the postmodernist claim and to retrieve the project of liberation; however he has nothing at all to say about the way in which that project might have to be reconstructed in order to accommodate feminist claims. In the course of the lecture he accuses Michel Foucault of being a neoconservative, since Foucault does not affirm the enlightenment ideals of progress, universal human rights, and the triumph of reason. Foucault,[3] in turn, interrogates the democratizing ideals of the modern age and its systems of representative government with respect to a moment of coercion built into the practice of political representation, into the practice of speaking on behalf of others. This mutual interrogation concerning political implication makes room for feminist claims, both as the issue of the relatively disadvantaged position of women over against men, and as a social theory, in which the oppression of women by men is a central explanatory feature for the production and reproduction of central features of social organization.

Jurgen Habermas is hailed by the Old New Left as picking up the mantle of the so-called Frankfurt school of critical theory, and especially from Theodore Adorno. Both Habermas and Adorno are hailed as representatives of the European tradition of Marxists, who can show middle-class intellectuals how still to be on the winning side, even after a proletarian revolution. Foucault, and his compatriot the philosopher Gilles Deleuze, on the other hand, are deeply sceptical about the retrievability of a Marxian account of society, and identify both Whig and Marxian accounts of history and reason as reproducing all the indefensible claims to universality and completeness which philosophers have always made. Deleuze in particular is irredeemable, as far as the Old New Left are concerned, since he wrote with Felix Guattari perhaps the quintessential postmodernist theoretical tract: *Anti-Oedipus: on Capitalism and Schizophrenia*, published in 1972, in which both Freud and Marx are indirectly denounced for encouraging narrow minded and ill-founded theorizing. All the more irritating for their opponents, Deleuze and Guattari approach the grand masters by elegantly taking apart the attempts to reconstruct the strategies, undertaken with respect to Freud by the lesser master Lacan, and with respect to Marx by the lesser master Althusser. Deleuze and Guattari thus set the intellectual terms of entry into this debate very high indeed.

There are various problems with lining out Adorno and Habermas, the two German Marxian philosophers of modernity and human progress over against Foucault and Deleuze, the two French post-modernist post-Marxian, so-called poststructuralists. This line out obscures what Deleuze and Adorno have in common, and serves to divide the radical from the liberal feminist projects. More trivially, the term 'poststructuralist', like the term 'postmodernist' assumes an understanding of a predecessor, 'structuralism' or 'modernism', neither of which have self-evident meaning or usefulness. Since both 'structuralism' and 'modernism' are primarily terms picking out respectively particular kinds of theoretical enquiry and particular kinds of artistic practice, it is far from self-evident they can be used unproblematically as terms designating temporal epochs, which can then be deemed to have come to an end. The confusion is made greater by the reluctance of most of those labelled by others as 'structuralist' to accept the label, generating the suspicion that the label was invented in the process of packaging them for wider consumption. The situation is complicated in the case of modernity and postmodernity, modernism and postmodernism by the now customary division of history into three epochs, the ancient, the Middle Ages, and the modern, with perhaps the eschatological additions of the Judaeo-Christian time before in Paradise, and time after the coming of Messiah. Postmodernity then appears to lay claim to the quasi-posthistorical status, claimed by Marx for the post-revolutionary phase, in which history as the exercise of human freedom would first become possible. There is then a tension between this Marxian claim about historical process and the postmodernist declaration of a postmodern age.

The question of an epoch, modernity, is addressed in German under the term *die Neuzeit*, whereas the cultural formation identified discursively through the music of Schoenberg and the writing of Joyce is referred to under the term *die Moderne*, with its connections to a conception of ephemeral fashion, *die Mode*. This paper presupposes that Benjamin, in his study *Baudelaire: Lyric Poet of High Capitalism*, has shown how modernism as developed by Baudelaire is a response to and articulation of the condition of modernity. Furthermore, it supposes that Adorno's cultural Marxism is a development of Benjamin's analysis of modern cultural production as the articulation of the modern age, although the precise nature of their agreements and disagreements remains to be clarified. Their work establishes a connection of some kind between the condition of modernity and the cultural formation called 'modernism'. No such connection has been established between a condition called 'postmodern' and a cultural practice called 'postmodernism'. Habermas's paper, mentioned earlier, suffers from its presupposition that both connections have been established, when there is only an established connection between modernity and modernism. The production of the terms 'postmodernity' and 'postmodernism' seem to be responses to the demands of a product hungry market for cultural goods, rather than the result of identifying genuinely new phenomena for analysis. Thus in fact Habermas is right to be impatient with the will to celebrate in postmodernism the advent of a new age. He identifies the phenomena collected together under the term 'postmodernist' as complementary and contemporaneous, not successive and antipathetical to the phenomena collected together under the term 'modernist'. It is however a sign of his preference for the modernist over the postmodernist that he understands the proponents of postmodernism to be suggesting that the postmodern condition is a distinctively new epoch, following on from the epoch of modernity. Such a notion of temporal sequence is not available to postmodernist thinking, for the very notion of a postmodernism, positing an epoch after modernism, contradicts the postmodernist denial of such temporal sequence. Furthermore, Habermas's preference for the modernist over the postmodernist, depends on the availability of certain conceptions of history, of temporal sequence and of progress. These conceptions however only become available, at the cost of silencing women and other members of the human community, who have assigned to them silenced and subordinate roles in the structures invoked under the term 'history', 'progress' and 'temporal sequence'.[4]

Structuralism is a name used to pick out the supposedly shared, and new, features of the enquiries produced by a number of Parisian intellectuals, including Lévi-Strauss, Barthes, Lacan, Foucault and really anyone else who appeared at the time to be doing something interesting and novel. For structuralists, meaning is to be understood on the model of Saussurean linguistics, not as independently constituted systems, mapping on to a real world, which can thus be represented to an already constituted subject, but as a system through which meanings, the world and the possibility of subjectivity itself, are produced. One of the primary qualifications for being labelled a structuralist was a supposed opposition to Sartre and to phenomenology. This opposition may however have been more apparent than real, since most theorists called structuralist, with the possible exception of Lacan, had undoubtedly spent time studying both phenomenological and Sartrean themes. Said points out a theme common to both Barthes and Sartre, which is particularly important for those traditionally excluded from high culture: the female and the non-European. Both Barthes and Sartre seek to counteract the appropriation of high culture by an academic elite and seek to return its products to a non expert audience. Comparing the 'structuralist' Barthes to the American 'new critics', Said writes:

> For about four decades then in both France and the United States
> the school of 'new' critics were committed to prying literature and
> writing loose from confining institutions. However much it was to
> depend upon carefully learned technical skills, reading was in
> very large measure to become an act of public depossession. Texts
> were to be unlocked or decoded, then handed on to anyone who
> was interested. The resources of symbolic language were placed at
> the disposal of readers who it was assumed suffered the
> debilitations of either irrelevant 'professional' information or the
> accumulated habits of lazy inattention.

Thus French and American New Criticism were, I believe, competitors for authority with mass culture, not other worldy alternatives to it. Because of what became of them, we have tended to forget the original missionary aims the two schools set for themselves. They belong to precisely the same moment that produced Jean Paul Sartre's ideas about an engaged literature and a committed writer. (p. 139)[5]

There is a second important parallel between structuralism and phenomenology. Saussurean linguistics sacrifices the philological emphasis of historical etymology in favour of emphasizing meaning as constituted through systems of sound and meaning inter-dependency, which invoke non-historical conceptions of synchrony, simultaneity, and diachrony, sequence. Neither Husserlian nor Heideggerian phenomenology nor Sartre's version of Marxism how-ever were particularly strong in the analysis of historical process and of historical specificity. Thus one of the characteristic features of structuralist theory, its lack of an historical dimension, was in fact shared by its supposed arch opponent. In *The Order of Things*, Foucault questions this supposed opposition and instead asserts that structuralism and phenomenology are parallel and interdependent theoretical structures.[6]

Fredric Jameson identifies this absence of historical dimension, which is transmitted from structuralism to poststructuralism, as distinctive of postmodernist theorizing. He introduces two marks of postmodernism, the tendency to pastiche and to schizophrenia thus:

I want here to sketch a few of the ways in which the new postmodernism expresses the inner truth of that newly emergent social order of late capitalism, but will have to limit the description to only two of its significant features, which I will call pastiche and schizophrenia: they will give us a chance to sense the specificity of the postmodernist experience of space and time respectively. (p. 113)[7]

The use of the term 'expression' and the postulation of an 'inner truth' indicate that Jameson is still firmly theorizing within the parameters of a project of modernity. He then identifies one of these characteristic features of postmodernism in terms which indicate that for him the poststructuralism of Derrida, at least, is a paradigm case of postmodernism: 'I want now to turn to what I see as the second basic feature of postmodernism, namely its peculiar way with time- which one could call "textuality" and "écriture" but which I have found it useful to discuss in terms of current theories of schizophrenia' (p. 118). Jameson locates this 'current theory of schizophrenia' in the work of Lacan, and joined to the use of Derrida's term 'écriture', in the description of postmodernism, this suggests but does not argue a close association between poststructuralism and the postmodernism under discussion. This is a suspect sleight of hand.

Jameson connects up the theme of schizophrenia to that of a fragmentation of a sense of temporality and to the disruption of a sense of historical process. These fragmentations disrupt the use of notions of temporal sequence and of history. Jameson describes the schizophrenic condition thus: 'as temporal continuities break down the experience of the present becomes powerfully, overwhelmingly vivid and material: the world comes before the schizophrenic with heightened intensity, bearing a mysterious and oppressive charge of affect, glowing with hallucinatory energy' (p. 120). The oddity about this description is that it seems to fit the atmosphere evoked by Kafka, one of the supposedly modernist canon. Thus the will to impose distinctions, for the purposes of political analysis, on top of terms of literary classification produces distortions in those literary classifications. Jameson's description of a schizophrenic condition is not intended as a description of clinically definable states of individuals, but of cultural products. This allies Jameson's theme of schizophrenia more closely with the schizophrenia discussed by Deleuze and Guattari in *Anti-Oedipus* than with that discussed by Lacan, which still has some tenuous footing in the analysis of individuals. Deleuze and Guattari criticize the crudeness of reducing all psychological states and conditions to the status of effects of one single structure: Daddy, Mommy, Me, derived from Freud's reading of the epic of Oedipus. Similarly in their oblique critique of Marx and Marxism, Deleuze and Guattari have no patience with treating as demonstrable truth the emancipatory fables surrounding the analysis of surplus value in *Capital*. In *Anti-Oedipus* Deleuze and Guattari propose a substitute for psychoanalysis: schizanalysis, by arguing the greater significance and less reactionary nature of the schizophrenic over the paranoiac pole of psychological states. They are eager to emphasize that their concern is to describe processes, not to classify individuals:

We have only spoken of a schizoid pole in the libidinal investment of the social field, so as to avoid if possible the confusion of the schizophrenic process with the production of schizophrenia. The schizophrenic process (the schizoid pole) is revolutionary in the very sense that the paranoiac method is reactionary and fascist: and it is not these psychiatric categories freed of all familialism that will allow us to understand the politico-economic determination, but exactly the opposite. (p. 380)[8]

Thus Deleuze and Guattari claim that the direction of their determination of concepts is from the politico-economic to the psychiatric, in traditional Marxist terms, from the economic base to the ideological superstructure of psychiatric theory and practice. The resonance with feminism at this point is the questioning of the central and indispensable role which the concept of the family plays in almost all versions of Freudian theory, and the opening up of the possibility of questioning the effects, especially for women, of thus taking the family structure to be a pregiven of the psychoanalytical scene. The invocation of 'schizanalysis' resonates with Kristeva's 'semanalysis', introduced in her book *Semiotike*, published in 1969, but neither Deleuze and Guattari, nor the summaries offered by Lecercle and Frank comment on this.[9]

Deleuze and Guattari replace the traditional Marxian analysis of conflicting interests as the motor of political process, with its presuppositions about class position and identity, with their conception of desire:

If we put forward desire as a revolutionary agency, it is because we believe that capitalist society can endure many manifestations of interest but not one manifestation of desire, which would be enough to make its fundamental structures explode, even at the kindergarten level.[10]

Interests, in their view, can always be bought off; desire has no interest at all, and therefore can have no interest in conserving a given social order in the name of avoiding greater social evils. In effect, Deleuze and Guattari are suggesting that Marxian ways of conceiving of politics and of political agency are complicit in the self-interested evils of capitalist organization and exploitation, and that radically new forms of conceptualization are needed to make sense of radically new forms of activity. Deleuze and Guattari theorize the productive potential of fragmenting the conception of personal identity which underpins the theory of possessive individualism of capitalist accumulation and also underpins the Marxist analysis of the conflict of interests between the possessing and the dispossessed. This conception of personal identity is interdependent with a conception of temporal sequence and of historical process, which also fragment under the pressure of the critique. Deleuze and Guattari draw the consequence of fragmenting conceptions of identity, of temporal sequence and of historical process by refusing any theorizing of connections between belief, action and event, and by refusing a connection between such analysis and the construction of a global account of reason, history, progress.

Similarly, Adorno's negative dialectic does not offer an account of reason and history, nor does he take for granted a conception of self and of family. Indeed, the text called *Negative Dialectic* (1966) picks up from where Adorno and Horkheimer's *Dialectic of Enlightenment* (1944) left off. In *Dialectic of Enlightenment* there is an account of the constitution of identity as founded in an arbitrary separation between self and context, between knowledge and morality, and as motivated by a will to develop a technical mastery of nature. This is understood as leading to the destruction of nature, and all its products, including human beings. The image of enlightenment, for Horkheimer and Adorno, is not of Oedipus, acquiring wisdom through suffering, but of Ulysses, acquiring knowledge through passivity. Adorno analyses these divisions, between self and context, and between knowledge and morality, as constitutive of modern sensibility, and he sees no point in wishing it otherwise. Instead, in analysing this condition, he affirms it, seeking to show what may yet be achieved, even in this condition of self-division. Occasionally nostalgia for a lost unity and contentment does burst through Adorno's writing, and the theme of the possibility of reconciliation is undoubtedly posed, but in this negative form of that which cannot be posited by dialectics in the age of fragmentation. He is by no means a theorist of the necessary coming of the proletarian uprising.

Neither Adorno, nor indeed Habermas are obviously developing a Marxian analysis of the necessary triumph of communism. Neither analyses the economic processes of production and consumption, which should bring about the crisis of capitalism, leading to revolution and communism. Neither shows much interest in the proletariat:

Habermas is always theorizing the conjunction of the theories of yet another pair of German and American sociologists and systems theorists; Adorno's entire analysis of culture is predicated on the failure of the proletariat to identify its own interests as opposed to those of the owners of the means of production. Where Lukács maintained an interest in the dispossessed, Adorno looked to the abstractions of high modernism to provide a challenge to commodity capitalism, precisely through its detachment from particular social context. He would thus seem to be on the side of the modernists over against the postmodernists, with respect to the postmodernist tendency to oppose abstraction and detachment, and to celebrate consumption and consumability. Adorno's views on *Gebrauchsmusik*, background music, and on popular culture are definitely negative. However, Adorno is inclined to push his own enquiries and concepts to the point at which distinctions between different kinds of enquiry, between metaphysics and ethics, between epistemology and aesthetics begin to break down, and this break down is a sign rather of a postmodern mode of philosophizing than of the modern, which seeks to maintain a detached control over such distinctions and conceptual boundaries. In their radical critiques of philosophy, returning to Plato in the attempt to grasp what the point of the philosophical project might be, and in their critiques of the classical texts constitutive of the history of philosophy, Adorno and Deleuze are in profound sympathy.

THE CHARACTERISTIC FEATURES OF POSTMODERN PHILOSOPHIZING

Hegel invokes the centrality of self-consciousness as a defining feature of philosophizing in the modern age. This modern age Hegel supposes to have begun around the time of Descartes, Bacon and Hobbes, the theorists of self-certainty, of scientific experimentation, and of the pragmatist state. Hegel privileges Descartes' declaration *Cogito ergo sum*, I think therefore I am. This declaration of a supposed self-evident truth is the mode of enquiry which underpins the American Declaration of Independence: 'We hold these truths to be self-evident . . .' It also underpins the mode of enquiry used by Wollstonecraft in her *Vindication of the Rights of Women*, in which she writes: 'in the present state of society it seems necessary to go back to first principles in search of the most simple truths and to dispute with some prevailing prejudice over every inch of ground'.[11] This appeal to self-evident principles links liberal feminism to Cartesian philosophy and also links Cartesian philosophy back to Aristotle's *Metaphysics*, in which the philosophical project of deriving truths from self-evident first principles is first announced in the history of western philosophy. Implicit already in the Cartesian mode is a conception of human beings as autonomous rational and self-determining, and this is the central theme of the political theorizing of the next 300 years, through Locke, Rousseau, Kant, Hegel, Marx. Hegel's project is an attempt to reconstruct the spatial domain of experience, as theorized by Descartes, in terms of a temporal horizon of expectation, in which human potentialities may be elaborated and fulfilled. This horizon of expectation is transformed by Benjamin into the future in which the unfulfilled expectations of the dispossessed of past epochs may be remembered. It is Hegel then who challenges the elision of temporal dimension in the modern philosophical project. His reconstrual of the project requires a construal of subjectivity as developing in time and in history, thus positing history and time as the stance from which the altering structures of subjectivity may be theorized.

Heidegger subverts Hegel's reconstrual of the project of modernity by first accepting the determination of subjectivity in temporal process, and by then suggesting that history and time can be grasped only through their contingent effects as experienced by human beings, and cannot be deduced as Hegel sought to do as given necessary structures with given necessary effects. This radically disrupts the traditional status of philosophy, as the study of the unchanging framework of human existence. First Hegel construes subjectivity as alterable, within a single temporal process, up until some final apocalyptic culmination. Then Heidegger denies the availability of a conception of that encompassing constant, the temporal process, thus abolishing the unchanging object of philosophical reflection. It is for this reason that the study of both Heidegger and Hegel is resisted by those who insist on the immutability of their object of study. Heidegger proposes a critique of the concepts of representation and of expression as a supplement to Hegel's account of subjectivity as the distinguishing feature of modernity. He questions the status of both the process of representing states of affairs in the world, and the status of that to which those representations are presented, the self-present foundation of knowledge for the modern project, the subject.

Parallel to this conception of the representation of an object to a subject is the positing of inner states of the subject, which then are expressed in the subject's actions and utterances. Heidegger thus criticizes both parts of this complementary pair of structures, composed of the entity itself, the subject or the object, and its emanation, the representation or expression. It is this model of a subject, expressing a meaning, through which the world is presented to that subject, which is put in question by Saussurean linguistics. The theme of representation introduces a moment of transgression into philosophy, already signalled by Plato in the *Republic*: the distortion of truth in the acceptance of a mere representation in its place. This theorist of the pure philosophical state bans such simulacra and bans the construction of utopian fictions, at the very moment when he is himself constructing a utopian fiction, about the ideal republic. This is the founding paradox of philosophy, which, in proposing a quest for truth, must either presuppose itself to be in error, or proposes a quest for truth while already being in possession of it. Heidegger's theme of representation disrupts the self-evident certainties of self-presence, since the evidences the self has available to it are merely evidences, and not the states of affairs themselves, of which they are evidence. This is a theme which spans the history of philosophy not just from the moment of Cartesian doubt to the present, but from Plato on. It is this theme which motivates Plato's expulsion of the artists from the *Republic*.[12]

A third theme, supplementing and subverting both Hegel's principle of subjectivity and Heidegger's theme of representation, is the concept of experience. Anglo-American philosophy, in line with the humanist ideals of the Cartesian 'cogito', posits an unselfconscious subject of Promethean capacity, who, by daring to think, can bring about a just and free society. There is a feminist objection to be made to this conception of experience, and to the conception of the subject, on which it rests, for women are not permitted to be unselfconscious, nor are we encouraged to identify with the infinite powers of the subject, embodied in Prometheus' endeavours. We are rather encouraged to identify with the sister-in-law, Pandora, who, in a gesture curiously reminiscent of the received version of Eve in Paradise, is supposed to have let loose all the evils of human existence on an unsuspecting world. These three themes, the principles of subjectivity, in its various forms, the theme of representation, and the concept of experience, underpinned by conceptions of sexually undifferentiated human being, reason and progress, are put in question by a postmodernist philosophizing, which is to be found in the work of Nietzsche, Heidegger, Adorno, Deleuze, Kristeva and Irigaray. The central theme is the questioning of the continuity and givenness of subjectivity and the parallel questioning of the continuity and givenness of historical process.

Habermas, in the opening essay of his book *The Philosophical Discourse of Modernity*, identifies four key features of modern thinking: the neutralization of tradition, the generalization of norms and values, the broadening of the base for the exchange of opinion, and the emphasis in socialization on the development of the individual. Just how clearly these four distinguish modernism from the ideals of Plato's *Republic* is however not at all clear. In Habermas's defence it might be said that this is the point of modernism: the revival of classical ideals in a form which is compatible with contemporary conditions. Then Habermas must show how those classical ideals are to be separated from the economic preconditions in which they functioned: the extraction of surplus value from a domestic economy managed by women, and from a labour power provided by slaves, and the exclusion of both groups from the political community. A further feature of the modern period, in Germany at least, is the emergence of a conception of history, as a collective singular, a single process composed of a multiplicity of discrete events. Again, it is not clear that the histories of Thucydides and Herodotus were not at least tendentially invoking such a conception of history. More significant still, this relationship between the one and the many, this time conceived as history, is a rewriting of Parmenides' discussion of the relation between the one and the many, as repeated in Plato's eponymous dialogue at the beginning of western philosophy.

The shift away from understanding history as a single heroic process, as posited by Hegel and by Marx, to the sedimentations proposed by Braudel and by Foucault, is paralleled by the fragmentation of narrative in the novel, and the fragmentation of character. Indeed the rise and fall of the conception of writing total history parallels the move away from the fragmentations of picaresque and epistolary novel form, towards the narrative unities of Scott and Trollope, and back to the fragmentations of Joyce and of Calvino. While Benjamin cites Nietzsche approvingly, concerning the antipathy between destiny and character, for 'if man has a character, he has an experience which continually recurs',[13] nevertheless history has been conceived, by Hegel indeed, as the composite of the intended and unintended effects of just these recurrences. The dissolution of history into histories, the dissolution of the distinction between story telling and telling it how it was, and the dissolution of the self-determining autonomous human subject, underpinning this conception of character, into a series of encounters, into the subject in process, is welcomed by those written out of the histories, as putting pressure on the unacknowledged maleness and whiteness of that humanist subject, and on the maleness and whiteness of the interests in the light of which that history has been told. This humanist subject turns schizophrenic only too rapidly, in to the unreconcilable elements of a masculine struggle for self-mastery and a feminine agony of self-sacrifice; and through the application of a little unreconstructed biological essentialism, women become martyrs, and men end up bound to the mast of a ship, imprisoned in Plato's cave.

Instead of these depressing stereotypes, it becomes possible with a postmodern mode of philosophizing to conceive of gender difference as an optional participation in socially variable processes of becoming a mother or becoming a father. The attribution of authority to fathers is a social attribution, and the self-sacrifice associated with being a mother is a social construct, which are then demonically turned into fixed invariable attributes of male authority and female self-sacrifice. It is not then accidental, but as a result of this kind of consideration that Kristeva and Irigaray have questioned the connections between the symbolic meanings of sacrifice and motherhood. The problem is to resist the pressure to generalize and to naturalize. Any set of images which seeks to challenge the domination of institutionalized images of women's weakness and suitability for sacrifice will tend to make appeal to some figurative point of origin, easily misconstrued as a naturalization, in order to hold off the pressure to surrender once more to the dominant mode. Thus Kristeva and Irigaray are pressurized into idealizing and reifying the figures of motherhood and lesbianism respectively, in order to provide themselves with sufficient leverage over against established images of the passivity and incompetence of women in order to affirm female spontaneity and self-determination.

POSTSTRUCTURALISM, POSTFEMINISM, FEMINISM: IRIGARAY AND KRISTEVA

The three themes to be identified in the workd of Kristeva and Irigaray are then the questioning of systems of representation, the questioning of the givenness and self-evidency of the conception of the subject and the questioning of the givenness and self-evidency of a conception of historical process. Women do not fit into the mould of subjectivity constructed in the philosophy of modernity, because women are not encouraged to assert autonomy and to assert a capacity for self determination. Thus questioning the adequacy of this conception of subjectivity assists the feminist cause, the cause of women, by bringing into question one of the mechanisms of differentiation whereby the oppression of women is reproduced. Women have been excluded from historical process, not in the trivially and obviously false sense that women have not taken part in historical events, but in the sense that theorizings of history have assigned no place to women, either as theorists, or as an interest group within history with specific concerns. Both in the piecemeal Rankean what happened in history mode and in the Marxian globalizing history as the liberation of humanity, there is a failure to consider the implications of subsuming the interests of women under the interests of the men, who also happen to do most of the theorizing. Thus questioning this inclusive conception of continuous history, through which the elision of women's interests has been accomplished, also advances the feminist cause.

There is of course a problem here. Many self-professed feminist activists in France such as Christine Delphy, in the group Nouveau Questions Feministes, reject the work of Irigaray and Kristeva, as a conservative, antifeminist theorizing of a neofemininity, which affirms a difference between women and men, by naturalizing and reifying it. Irigaray and Kristeva are accused of discussing sexual difference as just one in a series of shifting metaphysical differences, instead of theorizing the centrality to social process of a socially produced, and therefore socially alterable, oppression of women by men. Such critics can find confirmation of antifeminism in Kristeva's explicit denunciations of feminism as a humanist error, and anticipation of postfeminism.[14] This declaration for postfeminism is bluntly subverted by the neglect of the women poststructuralists in three recent surveys of poststructuralism undertaken from very different angles: the survey of Manfred Frank, the German theorist of hermeneutics; the survey by Jean-Jacques Lecercle, presenting the Parisian 'philosophy of desire' to an eager Anglo-Saxon market; and the survey offered by Peter Dews, in the cause of affirming Marxian hegemony over high theory. While Kristeva may declare herself postfeminist, she needs feminist friends and sympathizers to remark the way in which yet again the women are being written out of the history of theory.

A close connection between feminism and postmodernism is of course suggested in Craig Owen's paper in the Hal Foster collection. There he identifies the feature, common to feminism and postmodernism, of blurring the boundaries of various activities taken by modernism to be distinct:

> Many modernist artists of course produced texts about their own production, but writing was almost always considered supplementary to their primary work as painters, sculptors, photographers etc., whereas the kind of simultaneous activity on multiple fronts that characterises many feminist practices is a postmodern phenomenon. And one of the things it challenges is modernism's rigid opposition of artistic practice and theory. (Foster, p. 63)

Owens invokes the image of a Leonardo *uomo universale*, capable of transforming itself like Tiresias from man into woman. Here, undoubtedly, there is a revival of a classical ideal at work. Clearly, the questioning of boundaries between practices and disciplines is common to feminism and to postmodernism. However the male practices of such questioning, for example that of Lacan, Derrida, Deleuze, Foucault tend to be developed from the security of fully tenured positions within the academy. Feminists, conversely, often make themselves unemployable by questioning and undermining the specialist boundaries in advance of becoming certified practitioners. The kind of questioning which poses a challenge to the discipline when developed by the professor, simply excludes the less well-placed questioner from the practice in question.

Owens also suggests that the ironizing of the relation between artist and work is a feature of women avant garde artists, this irony also being for him a characteristic of postmodernism. However he rapidly runs into difficulties as a result of a failure to consider the different trajectories with which female and male artists arrive at that ironic stance. He proposes the following centre for discussion: 'Here we arrive at an apparent overcrossing of the feminist critique of patriarchy and the postmodernist critique of representation: this essay is a provisional attempt to explore the implications of that intersection.' (p. 59). 'We' on closer inspection turns out to be Owens and his men friends, Derrida, Lyotard, and Heath, whose work he uses to establish the parameters of his discussion. Owens does quote Cixous, at second hand, and cites Irigaray, Kristeva and Michele Montrelay, but in his immediately preceding discussion of Montrelay he gives the game away: 'Montrelay, in fact, identifies women as the "ruin of representation": not only have they nothing to lose; their exteriority to Western representation exposes its limits.' (p. 59). What interests me in Owens' paragraph is the naming of women as 'they', in contraposition to the inclusive 'we' of the following paragraph. He had no option, grammatically, but, with a gesture of mock humility in the direction of Nietzsche, we have not got rid of sexism until we have got rid of grammar, or certain features of grammar at any rate.

Women have entered into systems of representation only as the representation of something else, as justice, liberty, philosophy, or indeed some less abstract more human objectification of men's desire. The difference between the nudity of Michelangelo's David and of Botticelli's Venus should indicate the kind of difference intended. One is self-regarding, self-defining, self-assertive, admittedly representing the autonomy of the Florentine state; the other is only too acutely aware of the spectator, half draped, in order to appear modest, and to suggest an infinite sensuality. Here, then, women are not so much exterior to the system of representation, as subordinated to a system controlled from elsewhere. The issue becomes all the more pressing, if representation, Kant's *Vorstellung*, is understood as a central feature of modernity, such that a problematic relation to representation generates a problematic relation to modernity. The grammatical constraint on Owens' discussion, noted above, indicates that this problematic status of women is not an issue only for modernism, but is carried over, at least as a residue of modernism, into postmodernism. However postfeminist we may all be inclined to feel, then, there is still an outsider/insider disjunction at work here, which, running true to a the time-honoured Aristotelian essentialism, places men inside and women out. To point out the functioning of such an essentialism is not to endorse either the effects of such a system, nor the system itself. Such essentialism is certainly not in the interests of those who are placed beyond the sphere in which values are produced, although not beyond the sphere of their application. Irigaray would advise us to ask: in whose interests then is it? The following Nietzschean remark from Irigaray's *Speculum of the Other Woman* points the question:

> Either let truth carry the day against deceitful appearance, or else, claiming once more to reverse the optics, let us give exclusive privilege to the fake, the mask, the fantasy, because at least at times they mark the nostalgia we feel for something more true. We will continue to waver indecisively before this dilemma unless we interpret the interest and interests involved here. Who or what profits by the credits invested in the effectiveness of such a system of metaphor? (pp. 269–70)

Irigaray is suggesting, of course, that it is not women but men who profit. Irigaray thus gestures towards the systems of power relations, within which metaphors of desire and the textuality of philosophy unfold.

Irigaray and Kristeva, in their reappropriations of Plato's *chora* and of Plato's cave, suggest that women are not just the empty signifier, which can be used to represent any object of desire; they suggest that women form the ground, or condition of possibility, of representation. Irigaray in *Speculum* identifies Plato's cave of self-delusion as the womb, from which imprisoned men are led up to the sun of enlightenment by the philosophy tutor. By metonymy, then, women are the condition of possibility for men discovering truth:

> The project or process whereby the hystera, or cave, is displaced, transposed, transferred, metaphorised, always already holds them (the prisoners) captive. The transposition of anterior to posterior of the origin to the end, the horizon, the telos, envelops and encircles them; it is never susceptible of representation, but produces, facilitates, permits all representations since all are always already marked, or re-marked, in the incessant repetition of this same work of projection. Which yet is impossible, or cannot be completed at least. The hystera, faceless, unseen, will never be presented, represented as such. But the representational scheme and sketch for the hystera- which can never be fulfilled- sub-tends,

englobes, encircles, connotes, overdetermines every sight, every sighting, face, feature, figure, form, presentification, presence. Blindly.

Certain men, then – sex undetermined (?) – are chained up in/ by this transposition of the hystera. In no position to turn their heads, or anything else. (*Speculum*, p. 245)

This schizophrenic separation of representation from its frame, of assertion from its ground, of activity from the metanarrative, which justifies and awards points for accuracy and truthfulness becomes menacing when, as Susan Griffin analyses in her book *Pornography and Silence*, another series of oppositions are put in play. Sensuality, passion, mortality and bodiliness, in short sexuality, are denied in order to generate the heroic confrontations of Ulysses, and permit the freer expression of their opposites, intellect, immortal fame, action, self-discipline. There is here, in short, a repression of context in order to make visible that which appears. When that sensuality, sexuality, mortality, bodiliness are attributed to women, who are then punished for possessing the fallibilities from which men have disassociated themselves, the question of whether that punishment is sadistic or masochistic becomes secondary to the problem of a double pressure from the initial constraint imposed on women, and the retribution extracted for it. The schizophrenia with respect to temporal structure, identified in postmodernism, is thus paralleled by a schizophrenia with respect to a system of meaning and values, dating back not just to Kant, nor to Descartes, but to Plato. It is of course Nietzsche's challenge to this system which renders him an ally of feminism, for all the surface abuse. The writing of women out of history also generates a schizophrenia for women with respect to history, for women are at one and the same time in history and not in history. This triple schizophrenia is picked up by Irigaray and Kristeva in their questioning of the givenness of conceptions of a unified subject and of continuous temporal process, and it underpins the resonance between the postmodernist theoretical constructs, and the theoretical constructs motivated by the question to the maleness of the subject at the centre of philosophical enquiry.

Kristeva questions conceptions of a unified subject. She demonstrates the way in which the Freudian and Lacanian accounts of the constitution of individuals as subjects posits the feminine as outside that process of self-constitution. For Kristeva, Lacan and Freud, the female body constitutes a ground of possibility for the construction of identity, but in so far as identity is attainable, it is in the image of the father, with whom the production of meaning and identity is inextricably connected via the affirmation of the Oedipus complex. The materialist critique of Christine Delphy then asks why Kristeva refuses to address the way in which social relations and expectations bring it about that it is overwhelmingly women who take up these self-renouncing feminine positions outside the practices of the production of meaning and identity, leaving the masculine positions of assertion and innovation to men. The position appears all the more antifeminist in that the creative aspect of the feminine, the capacity to resist the ordering and pragmatism of the construction of a masculine identity, subordinated to an economy of need, instead taking part in an economy of desire, is realized not as might be expected by women, but by the great avant garde poets and novelists, celebrated by Kristeva: Mallarmé, Joyce, Artaud.

Irigaray, in her book *Speculum*, challenges the adequacy of the Freudian scenario of the Oedipus complex by generating a whole series of paradoxes and self-refutations in Freudian theory, simply by reading Freudian texts and refusing to forget that such a reading for women is blocked and excluded by Freud's manner of presentation and by his theory of sexuality. Freud's account of sexuality constructs feminine sexuality as the structure required by an autonomously generated masculine sexuality. Women are the sex which isn't one, leaving open the two possibilities: of there being no feminine sexuality, except as men imagine it, as Freud imagines and supposes; or the possibility which Irigaray takes up in *The Sex Which Isn't One*, that feminine sexuality is dual, indeed schizophrenic: that it is both the one subordinate to the needs and desires of men; and autonomous, explorable only within a separatist women's movement, since the very presence of men means that women are always already appropriated into the model set up to satisfy the needs and desires of the dominant group. As a result of the publication of this book in 1974, two years after the publication of *Anti-Oedipus*, with which it has the critique of Freud in common, Irigaray was expelled from the Lacanian psychoanalytical school.

Kristeva questions the conception of unified continuous temporality in her paper 'Woman's Time'. She takes up an opposition from Nietzsche's essay 'On the uses and drawbacks of history for living', between the time of linear, cursive history, and a cyclical, monumental time of symbolic social systems, like nations. Curiously she leaves out Nietzsche's third notion of time: critical history. He writes: 'History is necessary to the living man in three ways: in relation to his action and struggle; his conservatism and reverence; his suffering and his desire for deliverance.'[15] The activities proposed by a liberal feminism require a notion of linear, cursive time in which the achievements of one generation can be passed on to the next. The analysis of patriarchy requires a monumental notion of time, in which all human history is understood as a repetition of the oppression and exploitation of women by men. This cyclical, monumental time is identified by Kristeva with the time of matri-archal myths, which are excluded from the histories written by a male centred tradition. She identifies this notion of time with the powers of the feminine, which she understands as being excluded from the symbolic order constructed by the powers of the masculine. This symbolic order is the time of European history. Kristeva writes: 'There are in any case three attitudes on the part of the European feminist movements towards this conception of linear temporality, which is readily labelled masculine and which is at once civilisational and obsessional.'[16] The liberal feminist takes up an affirmative stance towards this mode of linear history, and engages in campaigns to end oppression and inequalities around the themes of rights.

Kristeva correctly identifies the monumentalism of radical separatism as rejecting traditional political activity, with its emphasis on representational process, and as rejecting as delusions the modernist project of self-assertion within linear temporal process. Radical feminism proposes a monumental account of history as a single monolithic process in which the oppression of women is repeated and reproduced. Of the third attitude she writes:

> Finally it is the mixture of these two attitudes – insertion into history and the radical refusal of the subjective limitations imposed by this history's time as an experiment carried out in the name of the irreducible difference – that seems to have broken out in the past few years in the European feminist movements particularly in France and in Italy.[17]

The vagueness of the characterization of this third attitude is a result of the impossibility of making a general statement with regard to Nietzsche's third source for a need for history: human suffering and a desire for deliverance. It is also the result of Kristeva's lack of sympathy for the claim that women might be suffering, and might therefore be in need of deliverance, as the following remark from the same essay indicates:

> It could be said, with only slight exaggeration, that the demands of the suffragists and existential feminists have, to a great extent, been met in these countries, since three of the main egalitarian demands of early feminism have been or are now being implemented despite vagaries and blunders: economic, political and professional equality.[18]

In Kristeva's defence it should perhaps be pointed out that she wrote this in 1979, when perhaps such complacency was more excusable. She continues:

> In this third attitude, which I strongly advocate – which I imagine? – the very dichotomy man/woman as an opposition between two rival entities may be understood as belonging to metaphysics. What can "identity" even "sexual identity" mean in a new theoretical and scientific space, where the very notion of identity is challenged?[19]

Thus Kristeva consigns the distinction between woman and man to the age of metaphysics which she supposes to have been surpassed. With the transcending of identity, the constraints of sexual identity have also supposedly been transcended. However she herself admits that this transcending of the opposition is imagined, and not necessarily accomplished. Thus in her positing of a postfeminist space there is this ambiguity between the transcendence of the constraints of expectations concerning what women can do, necessary for any spontaneous action by women at all, and the indefensible claim that all distinctions between women and men have in fact been abolished and transcended. This will to transcend the tiresome limitations of historical, indeed of gender specificity is directly reminiscent of Plato's rejection of the transient constraints of particular human existence in favour of the eternal perfection of unchanging ideas.

In *Speculum*, Irigaray constructs a spectacular history of philosophy, in reverse, which begins by confronting the Janus-faced double act of Freud and Lacan, and concludes with a confrontation with that other famous double act, Plato and Socrates. Irigaray proposed a reading of Freud's undelivered lecture on femininity, from the *New Lectures on Psychoanalysis*, composed under threat of Nazism in 1932. Freud writes:

> Throughout history, people have knocked their heads against the riddle of femininity. . . . Nor will you have escaped worrying over this problem – those of you who are men; to those of you who are women, this will not apply: you yourselves are the problem.
> (p. 146)

Lacan challenges Freud's emphasis on the development of actual individuals, and on the analysis of dreams and descriptions as belonging to a single identifiable person. Lacan shifts and focus to the structures through which meaning and subject positions are produced, but by retaining the Freudian framework, Lacan produces the result that all subject positions are masculine, and thus easier for men than for women to attain. Irigaray therefore suggests that for women the choice between Freud and Lacan is no choice at all. Similarly the choice between Plato and Socrates, for women, is no choice at all. Men may choose between the speaking master and the writing disciple, but for women Socrates offers only the gesture of appropriation and dismissal. He identifies himself as the midwife of the thoughts to which young men give birth, and he sends the women away from the *Symposium*, before the philosophical discussion can begin, and away from the prison in the *Phaedo*, when he is about to commit suicide. Plato in the *Republic* offers women the status of second rate men, always inferior and falling short of the standards set by men.

Furthermore, Irigaray suggests that the choice between psycho-analysis and philosophy for women is no choice at all: that both would prefer to exclude women, and failing that, seek to appropriate and subordinate the specificities of women's existence as subsidiary to the much more interesting task of thinking about men. As far as Irigaray is concerned, for women it makes no difference whether you talk about Freud or Lacan, Socrates or Plato; if you start in the twentieth century and tell history backwards, or start in the fifth century before the common era, and talk about Socrates; it makes no difference if you talk about Freud and Socrates, and their emphasis on speech and talking, or if you write about Plato and Lacan and their written appropriations of the speech of psychoanalysis and of philosophical diagnosis. For Irigaray in *Speculum*, for women, there is no temporal direction, underpinned by a conception of progress, in which the project of modernity takes up the ideals of antiquity, and seeks to develop them, since those ideals are misogynist, and since the project of modernity has not been constructed to include women. History for women is a process from which women have been elided; it is not a process in which women, too, have been permitted to take up and develop the achievements of past generations. Thus with a gesture characteristic of philosophy, of radical feminism and of postmodernism, as diagnosed by Jameson, Irigaray denies the significance of temporal and historical difference.

In conclusion then, constructing an opposition between the French poststructuralists, in the form of Deleuze and *Anti-Oedipus*, and the German dialecticians, in the form of Adorno and *Negative Dialectics*, serves to obscure the commonality between them, and to obscure the collective interests of women, as the repressed of culture and of philosophical history. The opposition serves to support a misleading division between liberal feminist strategies, within a project of modernity, and radical feminist eschatologies, in which the oppression of women is theorized as one unchanging social system, which is nevertheless produced within society, and therefore changeable within society. The supposed opposition between Adorno and Deleuze furthermore serves to obscure their common neglect of the challenge to cultural analysis which feminism and the claims of women pose, and it has served to excuse a general failure to engage with, indeed to read, Irigaray and Kristeva.

NOTES

1 'The Discourse of Others: Feminists and Postmodernists' in Hal Foster (ed.) *Postmodern Culture*, Pluto Press, London 1985.
2 Also in Hal Foster (ed.).
3 See Foucault, 'Governmentality' in *Ideology and Consciousness* no. 6 Autumn 1979; 'What is Enlightenment' part one in Paul Rabinow (ed.) *The Foucault Reader*, Penguin, Harmondsworth 1984; and 'What is enlightenment' part two in *Economy and Society* vol. 15, no. 1 February 1986.
4 See Benjamin's critique of the silencing of the losers in the historical conflict, in his 'Theses on the philosophy of history' pp. 255–67 in Walter Benjamin, *Illuminations*, Jonathan Cape, London 1970.
5 Edward Said, 'Opponents, Audiences, Constituencies, and Community' in Hal Foster (ed.).

6 Michel Foucault, *The Order of Things*, Tavistock, London 1974, p. 299.
7 Fredric Jameson 'Postmodsernism and Consumer Society' in Hal Foster (ed.)
8 Gilles Deleuze and Felix Guattari, *Anti-Oedipus: Capitalism and Schizophrenia*, Viking, New York 1982.
9 Jean-Jacques Lecercle, *Philosophy through the Looking-glass: Language, Nonsense and Desire* in the series Problems in European Thought, Hutchinson, London 1985, and Manfred Frank, *Was ist Neostrukturalismus?*, Suhrkamp, Frankfurt 1983.
10 In Gilles Deleuze and Felix Guattari (op. cit.).
11 In Mary Wollstonecraft, *Vindication of the Rights of Women*, ed. Carol H. Poston, Norton, New York 1975, p. 11.
12 Plato, *Republic* book 10.
13 Walter Benjamin 'Fate and Character' p. 126 in *One Way Street*, New Left Books, London 1979.
14 Julia Kristeva: 'Women's Time' in *Signs* Autumn 1981, vol. 7, no. 3, reprinted as chapter 8 in Toril Moi (ed.) *The Kristeva Reader*, Basil Blackwell, Oxford 1986.
15 *Untimely Meditations* 'The Use and Abuse of History', Cambridge University Press, Cambridge 1986.
16 Toril Moi (ed.), p. 193.
17 Toril Moi (ed.), p. 195.
18 Toril Moi (ed.), p. 196.
19 Toril Moi (ed.), p. 209.

Chapter Six

BENJAMIN'S *FLÂNEUR* AND THE PROBLEM OF REALISM

JOHN RIGNALL

The *flâneur*, strolling the streets of nineteenth-century Paris with cool but curious eye, is for Benjamin a threatened species whom history is about to overtake. Still standing on the margins both of the great city and of the bourgeois class, he is yet to be overwhelmed by either. Balanced as he is on the brink of the alienating system of commodity exchange into which he will eventually be absorbed, he stands as the representative figure of a phase of nineteenth-century culture. The characteristic literary expression of that period is the body of realist fiction which, in his work of Baudelaire and Paris, Benjamin draws upon in passing but does not centrally explore, and which can be seen, like the *flâneur*, in terms of a precariously achieved equilibrium soon to be disturbed. The aim of this paper is to show how Benjamin's account of the *flâneur* can be related to, and can throw light on, the practice and epistemological premises of nineteenth-century realism, and how, at the same time, it points towards that crisis of representation that is to be the mainspring of modernist innovation and the continuing preoccupation of postmodernist experiment. In writing primarily about the first modern poet Benjamin indirectly uncovers the roots of modern fiction by throwing into relief the problematic nature of realism.

The figure of the *flâneur* first appears in Benjamin's writing in 1929 in a review of Hessel's *Spazieren in Berlin* entitled 'Die Wiederkehr des Flaneurs' ('The Return of the *Flâneur*').[1] That title suggests that the *flâneur* is properly a creature of the past, and it is, of course, in Benjamin's later work on nineteenth-century Paris that the figure is examined in its true habitat, playing a central part in the 1935 sketch for the Arcades Project 'Paris – the Capital of the Nineteenth Century'[2] and the two studies of Baudelaire, 'The Paris of the

Second Empire in Baudelaire' written in 1938 and the revised and much altered vision 'Some Motifs in Baudelaire', published in the *Zeitschrift für Sozialforschung* in 1939.[3] Although Benjamin refers in his letters to his theory of the *flâneur* (GS vol. 1, pt. 3, p. 1105), it is difficult to discern anything like a coherent single theory in the various ideas that cluster around that composite and overdetermined figure. Constituted intertextually from Baudelaire's essays and poetry, from Poe's fiction and Balzac's, from Dickens' letters about his own creative practice, from Marx's theory of commodity fetishism, and from documentary and historical writings about Paris, the *flâneur* is at once an observed historical phenomenon, a type among the inhabitants of nineteenth-century Paris, the representation of a way of experiencing metropolitan life, a literary motif, and an image of the commodity in its relation to the crowd. The aspect on which I intend to concentrate here and which is central both to Baudelaire's own use of the term and Poe's story 'The Man of the Crowd', to which Baudelaire refers and which Benjamin analyses, is the aspect of vision.

The intertextual layering of the material in the chapter entitled 'The *Flâneur*' in 'The Paris of the Second Empire in Baudelaire' points to the crucial issue of seeing. In 'The Painter of Modern Life' Baudelaire uses the term *flâneur* in an attempt to define the quality of observation that he admires in the painter of Parisian life, Constantin Guys.[4] This observer of metropolitan life is himself observed and defined with the aid of a literary text about observation, Poe's 'The Man of the Crowd'. Benjamin then observes the observer Baudelaire observing Guys. He reads Baudelaire reading Poe and defining a painter of Parisian life, and uses Baudelaire's own term *flâneur* as a lens through which to see his poetry and Baudelaire's poetry as a lens through which to see Parisian life. Paris, the object of Guys' painting, is brought again before the eyes of Benjamin's reader through a complex series of mediations. We are alerted to the way things are seen by the very disposition of the textual material, and as Benjamin proceeds to develop his notion of the *flâneur* he outlines a distinctive mode of vision. Starting from George Simmel's premise that 'interpersonal relationships in big cities are distinguished by a marked preponderance of the activity of the eye over the activity of the ear' (GS vol. 1, pt. 2, p. 540; CB, p. 38) Benjamin presents the *flâneur* as a characteristic product of urban life in that in him 'the joy of watching is triumphant' (GS vol. 1, pt. 2, p. 572; CB, p. 69). His particular kind of seeing is defined in terms of dialectically related opposites: he sees the city as 'now landscape, now a room' (GS vol. 5, pt. 1, p. 54; CB, p. 170). This latter transformation of the street into a kind of interior is one of the ways in which he makes the alien urban world bearably familiar – 'the street becomes a dwelling for the *flâneur*; he is as much at home among the façades of the houses as a citizen is in his four walls' (GS vol. 1, pt. 2, p. 539; CB, p. 37) – yet that familiarity is at the same time juxtaposed to visionary strangeness in that 'the appearance of the street as an *intérieur*' is one 'in which the phantasmagoria of the *flâneur* is concentrated' (GS vol. 1, pt. 2, p. 552; CB, p. 50). Seeing the city now as open, now as enclosing, now familiar, now phantasmagoric, the *flâneur* also combines the casual eye of the stroller with the purposeful gaze of the detective. His vision is thus both widely ranging and deeply penetrating at the same time.

It is not hard to perceive the affinities between this complex form of seeing in the city and the practice of nineteenth-century realism, in particular the practice of those novelists of metropolitan life like Balzac and Dickens on whom Bejamin himself draws. The city as landscape, lying either desolately or seductively open before the fictional characters, and the city as a room enclosing them either protectively or oppressively; the city as familiar, knowable and known, and the city as mysteriously alien and fantastic; these are the well-established poles of Balzac's and Dickens' urban fiction. And, as Michael Hollington has shown,[5] there is a correlation between Dickens' own nocturnal ramblings through London and his narrative techniques. The impersonal narrator of, for instance, *Bleak House* can be seen as a kind of *flâneur* whose freely ranging yet penetrating gaze can make sense of the urban labyrinth that baffles and repels the innocent eye of Esther Summerson. However, clarification is not the sole function of such a narrator for he performs a dialectically double action of revelation and mystification. He renders the London world familiar and meaningful, and yet at the same time mysterious. If he illumines, then, like the moon that serves as the vehicle for his freely ranging movement in chapter 48 and shines down on the murder of Tulkinghorn, he illumines darkly. With Balzac elucidation rather than mystification is the main thrust of the narrative, and when, in a well-known passage at the beginning of *Facino Cane*, he makes one of his narrators define the nature of his vision, it is the power of visual penetration that is stressed:

I walked the streets to observe the manners and ways of the faubourg, to study its inhabitants and learn their characters. Ill-dressed as the workmen themselves, and quite as indifferent to the proprieties, there was nothing about me to put them on their guard. I mingled in their groups, watched their bargains, heard their disputes, at the hour when their day's work ended. The faculty of observation had become intuitive with me; I could enter the souls of others, while still conscious of their bodies, – or rather, I grasped external details so thoroughly that my mind instantly passed beyond them; I possessed, in short, the faculty of living the life of the individual on whom I exercised my observation, and of substituting myself for him, like the dervish in the Arabian Nights who assumed the body and soul of those over whom he pronounced certain words.[6]

This is the *flâneur* as detective, whilst the act of imaginative substitution with which the description closes precisely parallels a further characteristic of Benjamin's figure, the power of empathy to which, in one of the laconically more obscure passages of the first Baudelaire essay, he is said to abandon himself in the crowd and, in so doing, to share the situation of the commodity (GS vol. 1, pt. 2, p. 557; CB, p. 55). Empathy, the aim and achievement of the realist novelist in his representation of the inner life in relation to the outer, is a facet of the *flâneur*'s vision.

The equation of the *flâneur* with the commodity signals for Benjamin the end of the former's brief existence. The middle chapter of 'The Paris of the Second Empire in Baudelaire presents the freedom of the *flâneur* giving way to the fixity of the purchasable commodity, just as Baudelaire himself is unable to maintain his strolling detachment and ends up harried by creditors and jostled by the crowd. Such a process has numerous analogues in nineteenth-century fiction – the fate of Isabel Archer in *The Portrait of a Lady* is a classic example – but it is not the dramatic potential of the theme that is important in this context but the precarious nature of the *flâneur*'s stance which it reveals. The complex dialectical mode of seeing figured in the *flâneur* and enacted in the narrative practice of realism is inherently unstable, and the epistemological assumptions of that practice are open to question. The privileged role ascribed to the detached individual vision of the novelist as narrator rests on the premise that seeing is equivalent to knowing. As in the case of the narrator of *Facino Cane* to see is to know, to observe acutely is to penetrate to the truth. This equation is a recurrent motif in Balzac's fiction. Those characters, such as the ubiquitous Vautrin, who are in the know, who understand the workings of the social world, are commonly described in terms of their lynx eyes, their penetrating gaze. Knowledge is regularly conveyed by metaphors of vision. And in the metonymical practice of realist description the same premise is implied. The descriptive energy expended on appearances, clothes, buildings, interiors is predicated on the assumption that to see, to observe closely the visible exterior is to gain access to the life of truth within. Seeing is knowing; description yields meaning; representation involves faithfully mirroring what is seen.

The equation of seeing with knowing and the mirror theory of art and knowledge that it implies are not directly addressed by Benjamin, and the precariousness of the *flâneur*'s stance is defined solely in socio-historical terms. The crisis that engulfs him is economic not aesthetic. Nevertheless, Benjamin does indirectly reveal the problematic nature of the aesthetic and epistemological premises of realism in his reading of Poe's story 'The Man of the Crowd'. Approaching Poe's text in both the Baudelaire essays with a different emphasis on each occasion he does not explicitly set out its implications for an understanding of realism, but in his reading and in one respect curious misreading, of Poe in the light of Baudelaire he provides the means by which these implications may be uncovered.

The misreading lies in his interpretation of Baudelaire's reading of Poe and turns on the question of who in Poe's story is to be properly designated a *flâneur*, the narrator looking at the world through the window of a London coffee-house, or the 'man of the crowd' whom he catches sight of on the street outside and eventually follows. The latter, 'this unknown man', is for Benjamin 'the *flâneur*. That is how Baudelaire interpreted him when, in his essay on Guys, he called the *flâneur* "l'homme des foules"' (GS vol. 1, pt. 2, p. 550; CB, p. 48). The text of 'The Painter of Modern Life', however, reveals nothing of the sort. Baudelaire refers to the story to define more precisely the quality of observation he admires in Guys. Describing Poe's narrator as 'a convalescent pleasurably absorbed in gazing at the crowd, and mingling, through the medium of thought, in the turmoil of thought that surrounds him', he proceeds to draw the comparison with Guys: 'Imagine an artist who was always, spiritually, in the condition of that convalescent, and you will have the key to the nature of Monsieur G'.[7] A few paragraphs later he emphatically identifies the *flâneur* with Guys as a passionate observer of the crowd: 'For the perfect *flâneur*, for the passionate spectator, it is an immense joy to set up house in the heart of the multitude, amid the ebb and flow of movement, in the midst of the fugitive and the infinite.'[8] Baudelaire clearly associates the *flâneur* with the act of seeing not with the person seen.

In his second essay on Baudelaire Benjamin partially corrects his own error when he points out that the man of the crowd is not the *flâneur*:

> Baudelaire saw fit to equate the man of the crowd, whom Poe's narrator follows throughout the length and breadth of nocturnal London, with the *flâneur*. It is hard to accept this view. The man of the crowd is no *flâneur*. In him composure has given way to manic behaviour. (GS vol. 1, pt. 2, p. 627; CB, p. 128)

But he still believes that he is exposing Baudelaire's misreading rather than his own. He remains trapped within his own error and never makes the step from maintaining that the man of the crowd is not the *flâneur* to stating that the narrator is.

This misreading may be understood as an example of that tendency which Adorno saw and criticized in 'The Paris of the Second Empire in Baudelaire', a tendency to relate the pragmatic contents of Baudelaire's work directly to adjacent features in the social history of his time (GS vol. 1, pt. 3, p. 1095). The *flâneur* is seen here as a social phenomenon, the object of the materialist historian's gaze rather than the exponent of a certain kind of vision, the seeing subject himself. And when Benjamin partially corrects himself he is still using the figure to illustrate social and economic change: 'he exemplifies what had to become of the *flâneur* once he was deprived of the milieu to which he belonged' (GS vol. 1, pt. 2, p. 627; CB, pp. 128–9). The precariousness of the *flâneur*'s situation is defined solely by the changing circumstances to which he is exposed. What is lacking here is, as Adorno maintains, mediation, the very mediation that the concept of the *flâneur* as representing a way of seeing itself provides. However, Benjamin's blindness may be our insight, indicating by omission the terms that can help make sense of Poe's story and allow it to be related to the precariousness of the *flâneur*'s stance in a more subtly mediated way which takes into account not

117

only what is represented but also the very mode of its representation. Benjamin himself quite properly distinguishes between Poe's text and realism: 'Poe's manner of presentation cannot be called realism. It shows a purposely distorting imagination at work, one that removes the text far from what is commonly advocated as the model of social realism' (GS vol. 1, pt. 2, p. 627; CB, p. 128). But, leaving aside the Romantic trappings of the story, if the gaze of the narrator and the limits of his vision are made the central issue, then it emerges as 'something like the X-ray picture' (GS vol. 1, pt. 2, p. 550; CB, p. 48), not only of a detective story as Benjamin suggests, but also of a realist text and its epistemological assumptions. In the light of Benjamin's other pronouncements on the *flâneur* 'The Man of the Crowd' can be read not only as a mirror of changing historical circumstances but also as revealing the problematic basis of a mirror theory of literary representation.

At the opening of the story the narrator, convalescing from an illness, is in a state of heightened but calm awareness. Although he is seated in a coffee-house rather than strolling the streets his calm and inquisitive interest in all about him corresponds to that of the *flâneur*, and like the latter he becomes absorbed in the spectacle of the crowd. Regarding 'with minute interest the innumerable varieties of figure, dress, air, gait, visage, and expression of countenance' (MC, p. 180), he begins to categorize the passers-by according to their dress and occupation. The signs are unmistakable and he reads the street scene without doubt or hesitation:

> The tribe of clerks was an obvious one. . . . The division of the upper clerks of staunch firms, or of the 'steady old fellows', it was not possible to mistake. . . . The gamblers, of whom I descried not a few, were still more easily recognizable. (MC, pp. 180–1).

Thus, playing the part of the typical narrator of realist fiction, Poe's convalescent makes sense of the world for his reader, even claiming for himself, as night thickens and the fitful glare of the gaslamps takes over, the same kind of omniscience and power of empathy as Balzac's narrator in *Facino Cane*:

> And although the rapidity with which the world of light flitted before the window, prevented me from casting more than a glance upon each visage, still it seemed that, in my peculiar mental state, I could frequently read, even in that brief interval of a glance, the history of long years. (MC, p. 183)

At this juncture he is struck by the sight of a decrepit old man whose face wears an expression of such absolute idiosyncracy as to be not immediately readable. He 'struggles to form some analysis of the meaning conveyed' but can only produce a mere catalogue of disparate and often contradictory qualities, 'the ideas of vast mental power, of caution, of penuriousness, of avarice, of coolness, of malice, of blood-thirstiness, of triumph, of merriment, of excessive terror, of intense – of extreme despair' (MC, pp. 183–4). Instead of analysis he can offer only rhetorical declamation.

Seized by a craving to 'keep the man in view – to know more of him' (MC, p. 184), on the assumption that to see more is to know more, he sets off after him. 'The *flâneur* is thus turned into an unwilling detective' (GS vol. 1, pt. 2, p. 543; CB, p. 40) as Benjamin puts it in another context. After following the man for a whole day he finally stops 'wearied unto death', and gazes 'at him steadfastly in the face' (MC, p. 187). But the gaze cannot penetrate the surface and dispel the mystery. To see the man steadily and to see him whole is to approach no nearer to knowledge, so that all the narrator can offer is another rhetorical declamation, a grandiose but empty label: '"This old man," I said at length, "is the type and the genius of deep crime. He refuses to be alone. *He is the man of the crowd*"' (MC, p. 188). Beyond that the narrator can do no more than acknowledge the limit of his own understanding:

> It will be in vain to follow; for I shall learn no more of him, nor of his deeds. The worst heart of the world is a grosser book than the 'Hortulus Animae', and perhaps it is but one of the great mercies of God that *es lässt sich nicht lesen*. (MC, p. 188)

From reading the signs of the street and making sense of the world easily and confidently the narrator has come finally to admit that the heart of the world cannot be known. *Es lässt sich nicht lesen*; the world cannot be read, and made readable, in the manner demonstrated at the beginning of the story.

In the guise of a Romantic mystery tale, then, Poe's text reflects on the problematic nature of realist narration and its premises, both showing the *flâneur*'s vision at work and prescribing its limits. The narrator, in his vain attempts to attach meanings to the unfathomable face of the man of the crowd, ends up resembling the allegorist whom Benjamin scathingly describes in one of his notes for the Arcades Project: 'the allegorist plucks an item at random from his chaotic fund of knowledge and holds it up next to another to see whether they match: that meaning to this image, or this image to that meaning.'[9] Poe's story, too, reveals the relationship between meaning and image, between world and word, to be arbitrary and mysterious, and by implication, the mirror theory of representation to be without secure foundation. If Benjamin does not draw these conclusions himself in his reading of Poe and Baudelaire, he never-theless points the way towards them. His concept of the *flâneur* becomes an instrument for the deconstruction of realism.

The *flâneur* can thus be seen as a forerunner of the modern and Poe's story as both a diagram of realism and an anticipation of its end. The doubleness which Benjamin explicitly identifies in 'The Man of the Crowd' is a socio-historical one, but it has implications for literary history of a related kind. In seeing the story as prefiguring the end of the *flâneur* in the development of the department store he points to a change that has its literary equivalent in the transition from realism to naturalism, that is to a mode of fiction that is at once the product and the critique of developed consumer society. Where the street was once an interior for the *flâneur*, now in the department store the interior has become a street:

> And he roamed through the labyrinth of merchandise as he had once roamed through the labyrinth of the city. It is a magnificent touch in Poe's story that it includes along with the earliest description of the *flâneur* the figuration of his end. (GS vol. 1, pt. 2, p. 557; CB, p. 54)

This image of the individual as a consumer in thrall to the power of the commodity no longer suggests affinities with the stance and practice of contemporary novelists, and the kind of vision required to penetrate this society and its values is altogether more deliberate than that of the stroller. The naturalist novelist, combining the roles of observer and experimentalist, performs an act of deliberate looking *into* the social which is more systematic and theoretically self-aware than the explorations of his realist predecessors.[10] He takes over and intensifies the purposeful, detective quality of the *flâneur*'s vision, but what is lost is the casualness which nicely epitomizes the com-paratively unreflective, untheoretical, and epistemologically naive nature of earlier realist practice. The transient figure of Benjamin's *flâneur* captures precisely the precariousness of that literary mode and, at the same time, indicates the complex process of its supersession by the different but related experimentalisms of naturalism and modernism.

Abbreviations

CB   Walter Benjamin, *Charles Baudelaire: A Lyric Poet in the Era of High Capitalism*, trans. Harry Zohn, Verso Editions, London 1983.

GS   Walter Benjamin, *Gesammelte Schriften*, ed. Rolf Tiedemann and Hermann Schweppenhäuser, Suhrkamp, Frankfurt am Main 1974–85.

MC   Edgar Allan Poe, 'The Man of the Crowd', in *Selected Writings*, ed. David Galloway, Penguin Books, Harmondsworth 1967.

NOTES

1 GS vol. 3, pp. 194–9.
2 GS vol. 5, pt. 1, pp. 45–59; CB, pp. 155–76.
3 GS vol. 1, pt. 2, pp. 511–653; CB, pp. 9–154.
4 Charles Baudelaire, *Oeuvres Complètes*, ed. Claude Pichois, Gallimard, Paris 1976, vol. 2, pp. 683–724; *The Painter of Modern Life and Other Essays*, trans. and ed. Jonathan Mayne, Phaidon Press, London 1964, pp. 1–40.
5 Michael Hollington, 'Dickens the Flâneur', *The Dickensian*, vol. 77, 1981, pp. 71–87. Hollington gives a good account of the affinities between realist practice and the *flâneur's* vision, stressing the dialectical nature of the latter.
6 Honoré de Balzac, *La Comédie Humaine*, ed. Pierre-Georges Castex, Gallimard, Paris 1977, vol. 6, p. 1019; *La Comédie Humaine of Honoré de Balzac*, trans. Katharine Prescott Wormeley, Athenaeum Press, London n.d., pp. 154–5.
7 *Oeuvres Complètes* vol. 2, p. 690; *The Painter of Modern Life*, p. 7.
8 *Oeuvres Complètes* vol. 2, p. 691; *The Painter of Modern Life*, p. 9.
9 Cited in Walter Benjamin, *Charles Baudelaire: Ein Lyriker im Zeitalter des Hochkapitalismus*, ed. Rolf Tiedemann, Suhrkamp, Frankfurt am Main 1974, p. 204. My translation.
10 See Rachel Bowlby, *Just Looking: Consumer Culture in Dreiser, Gissing and Zola*, Methuen, New York and London 1985, p. 15.

Chapter 7

TRADITION AND EXPERIENCE: WALTER BENJAMIN'S *SOME MOTIFS IN BAUDELAIRE*

ANDREW BENJAMIN

Benjamin starts his discussion of Baudelaire by repeating, to some extent, Baudelaire's own beginning of *Les Fleurs de mal*, Baudelaire questions the possibility of comprehension. Benjamin is at the same time more dramatic and more reasonable. He is concerned to explain Baudelaire's own predicament. It is of course an explanation not simply of the predicament of Baudelaire, but the one in which Baudelaire finds himself. It is to that extent therefore Benjamin's own predicament, the secular. Benjamin's initial stated concern is to establish and explain the reason why the conditions no longer pertain for a 'positive reception of lyric poetry'. The reason Benjamin adduces is that it 'may be due to a change in the structure of experience (*Erfahrung*)'.[1] In order to construct a frame within which to trace the interplay of experience and tradition in Benjamin's *Ober einige Motive bei Baudelaire*[2] I want to look, albeit briefly, at the way in which experience figures in his short study of the Russian writer Nikolai Leskov, *Der Erzähler*.[3] Central to this particular study is the problem of experience, since Benjamin will explain the disappearance of the storyteller as contemporaneous with the 'atrophy' of experience.

In any analysis of texts as complex as Benjamin's there is always the risk that the issues at play in them and which emerge from them can get displaced by the task of exposition. Consequently it is worth noting in advance the central issues at stake in experience and tradition and which are under study here. It should be pointed out of course that fundamental components of any investigation of tradition and experience are the concepts of identity and difference in terms of which they are articulated. The central problems in this instance are the subject of experience and the temporality of experience; clearly of course they are related. It shall be argued in the latter stages of this paper that a critique of Benjamin's work provides the possibility of thinking anew the interplay of subjectivity, agency and time.

THE COMMUNITY OF LISTENERS DISAPPEARS

The Storyteller opens with an important and intriguing reference to time. It is located in the claim that despite the familiarity of the storyteller's name, in terms of his 'living effectivity' (*lebendingen Wirksamkeit*) he is no longer present. The storyteller, in other words, is no longer at hand and therefore no longer part of the present. The time of the storyteller is past. The ending of the time of storytelling is described by Benjamin in terms of there no longer being 'the ability to exchange experiences' (*Erfahrungen auszutauschen*). The storyteller draws on experience and in narrating turns that experience into the experience of the listener. Narrating is lodged within and therefore comes to articulate 'the community of listeners'.

In the opening sections of the paper Benjamin contrasts information and the story. Even though the manner in which he distinguishes between the temporality of each (the temporality of the instant as opposed to the temporality of survival) is of great significance, the important point here is the link established between the story and memory. Developing an understanding of tradition necessitates unpicking Benjamin's different conceptions of memory, since it is memory as *Errinnerung* which he argues 'creates the chain of tradition'. The first important link between memory and experience occurs in section VIII. Here it is argued that a story is easily committed to memory (*Gedächtnis*) if it does not necessitate psychological analysis. If in other words its comprehension involves immediate integration into the experience of the listener. Benjamin argues that to the extent that this occurs the listener is liable to repeat the story. Having made this move Benjamin's argument takes a remarkable turn. He next suggests that the taking over of the story, its assimiliation and hence possible repetition, demands 'relaxation'. What is intended by the reference to 'relaxation' and the one to 'boredom' can be seen later in the section when he invokes the 'rhythm of work'. 'Relaxation' and 'boredom' are not negative characteristics. It is rather that they denote a state of mind in which the activity of work demands less and less conscious attention and therefore the worker is open both to the hearing of stories and their repetition. The repetition of work

involves a forgetting which allows the possibility of listening. Forgetting yields listening. This is why Benjamin can argue that then
'the gift for listening is lost . . . the community of listeners disappears.
For storytelling is always the art of repeating stories and this art is
lost when stories are no longer retained (*behalten*)'.[4] Memory
(*Gedächtnis*) plays a fundamental role in the coherence of the
'community of listeners'. However, because listening and relaxation
involve, as has been indicated, the 'self-forgetful (*selbstvergessener*)
listener', it is essential to differentiate this type of forgetting from the
forgetting that would stem from the unravelling of the community of
listeners. It is in section XIII of *The Storyteller* that these points are to
some extent clarified.

The section begins with the position already established: namely,
that fundamental to the listener is the possibility of reproducing
what has been said. A remembering, in other words, that will
occasion repetition. It is the importance of both retaining and
repeating that is signalled in the connection established by Benjamin
between memory and epic.

> Memory (*Gedächtnis*) is the epic faculty par excellena. Only by
> virtue of a comprehensive memory can epic writing absorb the
> course of events on the one hand and, with the passing of these,
> make its peace with the power of death on the other.[5]

Memory as *Gedächtnis* retains by absorbing 'the course of events' and
in repeating and hence in the continual possibility of repetition it
'makes its peace with the power of death'. It should of course be
added that this is an easy peace for it cheats death of its own power;
the power to end, to preclude therefore the possibility of repetition.
The epic is for Benjamin to be understood in relation to its muse,
Mnemosyne. The relation introduces a distinction between memory
(*Gedächtnis*) and remembrance (*Erinnerung*) because Mnemosyne, the
muse of epic is also the rememberer. The epic in its origin contains
both the story and the novel. However remembrance (*Erinnerung*)
has a different form in each. The rest of section XIII is concerned
with outlining this difference.

It is precisely at this point that Benjamin makes the important
claim already cited above, that it is 'remembering' (*Erinnerung*) that
'creates the chain of tradition'. The form taken by storytelling within
the epic involves taking over, retaining and repeating. The repeating
is not simply the repetition of the same. It is not therefore simply a

repetition on the level of narrative content. It is rather a repetition of the narrative form. Benjamin indicates this when he cites Scheherazade 'who thinks of a fresh story (*eine neue Geschichte*) whenever her tale come to a stop'.[6] The interplay of retention and repeating is described by Benjamin as 'epic remembrance' (*episches Gedächtnis*). It endures as the 'Muse-inspired element of the narrative'. Now the capacity to retain as well as repeat means that on one level the time of the story does not admit of death. Though on another level the story can end if it can no longer be passed on. The end of the story is the end of community. It remains a question however the extent to which it is possible to hold these levels as separate.

The origin of the novel is linked to memory (*Erinnerung*) in a different way. It involves that element in epic that necessitates and shows what Benjamin calls 'perpetuating remembrance' (*verewigende Gedächtnis*). A conception of memory that Benjamin contrasts with the 'short lived reminiscences of the storyteller'. There is on the surface something odd about this distinction. Not only does the time scale proper to memory seem wrong – the novel as 'perpetuating' and the story as 'short lived' – the difficulties are compounded by his relating the novel to unity (it 'is dedicated to one hero, one odyssey, one battle') and the story to diversity ('to many diffuse occurences'). It goes without saying that the conceptions of unity and diversity at work here do not lend themselves to any automatic or easy summation.

Each individual story – each telling – is a unique event within a general repetition. Repetition is of course tradition and that is why memory as *Errinerung* is essential to the unfolding of tradition. The novel however is unique. It is not lodged within the process of taking over, retaining and repeating. This is why Benjamin approves of Lukacs's description of it as 'the form of transcendental homelessness'. There is a very real sense in which, for Benjamin, the novel neither articulates nor continues the tradition. It clearly takes a place within it. However its place does not function to continue tradition. The story and the novel both demand memory and it is the different conceptions of each that are identified by Benjamin in his description of their initial unity in epic.

It is . . . remembrance (*Eingedenken*) which as the muse derived element of the novel, is added to reminiscence (*Gedächtnis*), the corresponding element of the story the unity of their origin in memory (*Errinerung*) having disappeared with the decline of the epic.[7]

Memory (*Errinerung*) contains therefore both remembrance and reminiscence. They are combined in the epic though with its decline they separate, giving rise on the one hand to the novel and on the other to the story. The novel opens an enclosed world closed off from the world of repetition. The world it opens is self-enclosing and within it the novel is preoccupied with a unique happening. The novel finishes at the border of its own enclosure. The impossibility of repetition is therefore inscribed within the actual identity of the novel itself. The intricacy and complexity of its singularity demands what Benjamin has called 'perpetuating remembrance'. It is of course a remembrance that perpetuates within the self-enclosed world of the novel. The story on the other hand is brief. It passes with the moment and yet potentially its end is infinitely deferred. The story both in terms of form and content can be repeated *ad infinitum*, if of course the conditions for its reception also endure. Benjamin establishes this interplay of time and memory in both the novel and the story in the following way.

> There is no story for which the question of how it continued would not be legitimate. The novelist, on the other hand, cannot hope to take the smallest step beyond that limit at which he invites the reader to a divinatory realisation of the meaning of life by writing "Finis".[8]

As this passage makes clear the temporality of the novel differs profoundly from that of the story. It is of course commensurate with this difference that the concepts of memory also differ. The task at hand is to link these different conceptions to the initial problem raised by Benjamin; namely the growing impossibility of exchanging experiences. Towards the end of *The Storyteller* Benjamin makes a general claim about the nature of storytelling. It is a claim that is worth pursuing because not only does it forge an important distinction between the experience of the individual and what he calls 'collective experience' (*Kollectiverfahrung*) but it also introduces the concept of 'shock' (*Chock*) which, as we shall see, plays a vital role in his study of Baudelaire:

> All great storytellers have in common the freedom with which they move up and down the rungs of their experience as on a ladder. A ladder extending downward to the interior of the earth and disappearing in the clouds is the image for a collective

experience (*das Bild einer Kollectiverfahrung*) to which the deepest
shock of every individual experience, death, constitutes no
impediment or barrier.[9]

What is at stake here is a distinction between two different realms; a
difference of kind. The ladder, the experiences of the storyteller,
mark a type of totality. It is not the simple accretion of all the
storyteller's experiences. A number of those experiences are no more
than the result of having listened and therefore of having retained
and repeated. The totality is tradition. Its past does not exist as a
series of discrete events in themselves. Rather it endures as ritual.
While Benjamin does not argue it as such, there is a distinction
between the past proper to history and the past proper to ritual. It
will be in relation to ritual that a conception of experience that
involves allegory will emerge. Events are particularized and cannot
be repeated. The continuity of ritual is the repetition of the storyteller.
The ladder along which the storyteller moves could be seen as the
repetition and living out of tradition.

The experience of the individual must be understood as not simply
the opposite of collective experience but more importantly as the
unique experience that takes place outside community. However
even this formulation is not completely accurate. For in taking place
outside of community it undermines the possibility of both the
continuity of tradition and the community of listeners. The link
between memory and experience that pertains to the individual
differs fundamentally from the link within tradition, community and
collectivity. Tradition and repetition do not unfold into an empty
space. Nor are they merely taken over by passive subjects. (There is
an enormous difference between boredom and passivity.) Tradition
in Benjamin's sense demands and creates unity. Not only must the
community of listeners be unified, the story and the storyteller must
also refuse the possibility of fragmentation. The agent of repetition
must repeat and be repeated. Community and collectivity can be
seen as metaphors for a present that is fragmenting. It is one where
it is no longer possible to understand the present as a unified site in
which the unity of tradition is taken over and repeated. Fragmentation
leads to a present that is not an envisaged end for tradition. The
question – the philosophical question – to which this gives rise is
how is the present to be understood without the singularity tradition?
In other words, in the absence of the unity of tradition; not of course

in the absence of the plurality of tradition. Having traced some of the themes that emerge in *The Storyteller* it is now possible to return to the initial puzzling formulation of the present as that in which, 'experience has fallen in value'. It is now clear that what is at play in this claim is the possibility of community itself. What has to be determined therefore is how this description of the growing impossibility of community is to be understood.[10]

Perhaps the most direct encapsulation of the problem of community is the claim of Benjamin's that has already been noted, namely, that with the loss of the 'gift for listening . . . the community of listeners disappears'. The community therefore is structured by storytelling. But it is also the case that the community constructs the storyteller as storyteller. There is an identity-giving reciprocity between story-teller and community. The link between them, however, is not simply in terms of identity for it is also the case that they are both sites of repetition, and hence indispensable for the continuity of tradition. (The question that emerges here is how is repetition to be understood?) It could be the case for example that repetition continually returns and repeats the same. Or there could be a Nietzschean conception within which repetition involves the always *different*; a repetition where the eternal return of the same was always both same and different. At this stage the problematic nature of repetition can only be noted rather than resolved.

If emphasis is placed on tradition then continuity means that the repetition of tradition is to be understood in terms of repetition giving to tradition its mode of being as being present; as the always at hand. The fragmentation of community and hence the absence of the site of tradition gives rise to a number of specific problems. The first is the absence of the place of repetition. The second is the construction of the present as a site of loss. It is this construction which structures the nature of the task that Benjamin identifies as flowing from the present. There is therefore an important reciprocity between the way the present is construed and the task that is presented as at hand. The third is a cleavage in experience. In regard to the latter it is not simply that there is a growing impossibility to exchange experiences, it is also that experience has become divided between the relatively unproblematic experience of that which is at hand and the problem of the possibility of experiencing that which has been lost. Fragmentation divides experience. There are therefore two distinct objects of experience and therefore the need for two different experiences. It is precisely these problems which may be traced in *Some Motifs in Baudelaire*. Not only must their unfolding be noticed, their viability must also be questioned.

THE CLEAVAGE IN EXPERIENCE

It is tempting to begin any examination of Benjamin's writings on Baudelaire by commenting on their plurality and by noting developments as well as lacunae and lapsus throughout texts as diverse as those gathered together to form the English language collection, *Charles Baudelaire: A Lyric Poet in the Era of High Capitalism* as well as the enigmatic *Zentralpark*[11] and of course the relevant section of *Das Passangen-Werk*.[12] The sheer diversity of these texts invites such an approach. Resisting it and thereby focusing almost exclusively on one text, seems to demand some type of justification. What needs to be identified here is therefore the specificity of *Some Motifs in Baudelaire*. It is to be found in the links that exist between the task already identified and established in *The Storyteller* and those at play in this particular text on Baudelaire. The links can be seen to take place in terms of a systematic reworking and development of the relationship between experience and tradition. The way this relationship unfolds in the earlier paper has already been noted. Furthermore what has also emerged is a number of questions. Taking them up opens the point of connection between these two texts. On a thematic level this connection is established by Benjamin himself in the opening section of *Some Motifs in Baudelaire*: 'Experience (*Erfarhgung*) is indeed a matter of tradition (*eine Sache der Tradition*) in collective existence (*Kollektiven*) as well as private life.'[13] The immediate question that arises here concerns the meaning of 'matter' (*Sache*). It will be in clarifying this 'matter' that the parameters for an understanding of the relationship between tradition and experience will begin to emerge.

For Benjamin the poetry of Baudelaire is attentive to a specific problem. It is apparent throughout Baudelaire's work though most strikingly and with most dramatic force in poems such as 'Une Passante', 'Correspondances' and 'Le Soleil' amongst others. In them Benjamin notes Baudelaire's attempt to return to and to dwell on that which is no longer at hand. The 'correspondances' established by Baudelaire are Benjamin's continual point of reference. What these 'correspondances' actually are remains the difficult question.

That they are the focus of Benjamin's interest is exemplified thus: 'the correspondances record a concept of experience which includes ritual elements. Only by approaching these elements was Baudelaire able to fathom the full meaning of the breakdown which he, a modern man, was witnessing'.[14] The difficulty here is that the concept of experience in this text needs to be explained. The cleavage in experience is marked by the use of the words *Erfahrung* and *Erlebnis*. It must be added of course that merely explaining the difference will not capture what is at stake in it. It is vital, in this instance, to recognize that each brings with it a different temporality of experience.

Our task must be to trace the relationship between *Erfahrung* and *Erlebnis* in order then to go on and examine the important consequences that stem from the nature of their difference. Perhaps one of the most important moments in Benjamin's text that allows for an understanding of *Erfahrung* concerns the following description of the unskilled worker: 'The unskilled worker is the one most deeply degraded by the drill of the machines. His work has been sealed off from experience. (*Seine Arbeit ist gege Erfahrung abgedichtet*).'[15] Benjamin is alert to a possible response to this description, namely that the continuity of work – the rhythm of work itself – should construct the continuity of action that establishes itself as experience; as *Erfarhung*. His reply is the following: 'The manipulation of the worker at the machine has no connection with the preceding operation for the very reason that it is its *exact repetition*.' (my emphasis)[16] At play here is a completely different conception of repetition than the one that was observed at work in *The Storyteller*. In that instance the importance of repetition was that it involved a repeating that took over and handed on. Repetition became that through which the tradition was continued. The same was never the same because it was supplemented by its own repetition. However the storytelling – the narrative practice – as the image of Scheherazade suggests, contains within it its own supplementarity. There is a sense in which the continuity of storytelling can only end, as has already been noted, if the site – the community – of storytelling becomes fragmented. The site is the unity constructed by and hence enabling the exchange of experience (*Erfarhung*).

The worker at the machine does not repeat by taking over. The repetition breaks the continuity because the act of repeating – the 'retelling' – is in each instance the same and therefore new. The logic of repetition within which the worker is locked means that he is, in Benjamin's words, 'sealed off' from *Erfarhung*. What is the force of being sealed off? How is this particular cleavage to be understood? A way of answering these questions is suggested by an intriguing passage that contains, in an abbreviated form, Benjamin's critical stance in relation to symbolism.

In his analysis of Baudelaire's sonnet 'La Vie antérieure' and prior to his quoting the lines which he believes exemplifies the point he is trying to make, Benjamin states the following:

> The images of caves and vegetation, of clouds and waves which are evoked at the beginning of this second sonnet rise from the warm vapour of tears, tears of homesickness. . . . There are no simultaneous correspondences, such as were cultivated by the symbolists later. The murmur of the past may be heard in the correspondences, and the canonical experience of them has its place in a previous life.[17]

The 'previous life' is captured by Baudelaire's own use of the past tense, 'C'est là que j'ai vécu', 'Le printemps adorable a perdu son odeur'. What must be pursued is the connection between the critique of symbolism and the past tense, in order to develop an understanding of what is at play in the description of the worker as 'sealed off'. These interconnections will display the 'matter' of tradition.

The 'simultaneous correspondences' involve a conception of symbolism in which the symbol provides automatic access to the symbolized. The experience of one was the experience of the other. The at hand gave the not at hand. The cleavage was no sooner opened than it was sealed. The symbolized is therefore present within simultaneity. Symbolism does not raise the problem of memory. It is thus that they are not sealed off from the experiencing subject. Correspondence on the other hand marks the cleavage in experience. It involves the experience in the present which is the experience of that which can no longer be experienced. It is experienced as loss. The past tense marking that which is no longer present. There can be no return within present experience. What has been lost is no longer an object within memory. This accounts in part for Benjamin's interest in Proust. His conception of involuntary memory provides the possibility of access to the past – the past of the past tense, the 'that' from which the worker has been sealed off – that does not occur via an intentional act of memory.

At play here is the fundamental distinction between *Erfahrung* and *Erlebnis*. Benjamin connects the passer-by of Baudelaire's sonnet 'Une Passante' to the worker at the machine in the following way: 'The shock-experience (*Chockerlebnis*) the passer-by has in the crowd, corresponds to what the worker experiences (*Erlebnis*) at his machine'.[18] The worker at the machine does not experience *Erfahrung*. Each moment is new. A repetition of the same, of newness (novelty). The experience (*Erlebnis*) at the machine is not even noticed as it enters consciousness. It is located within memory without having been the object of conscious recognition. Modernity causes the forgetting of experience. Benjamin's reference to Freud is precisely in these terms. He uses psychoanalysis to argue for the possibility of an event entering into psychic life without the subject being aware of the event. What is at stake here is not the viability of Benjamin's reading of Freud but the conception of the subject proper to forgetting. It will be essential to return to this point.

The time of *Erlebnis* differs fundamentally from the time of *Erfahrung*. The first involves the temporality of the unique and fragmented moment while the second involes the sequential continuity within tradition. What is emerging here, of course, is a conception of alienation and hence of modernity as loss. It is moreover a loss which cannot be overcome, in other words that which has been lost, or that which has been fragmented cannot attain again its original status. It is none the less the case that access is provided; occurring either in terms of Proustian involuntary memory or Baudelaire's correspondances. Benjamin makes a significant reference to Baudelaire's rare use of what could be called temporal markers, e.g. 'one evening';

> They are days of recollection (*Eingedenken*), not marked by any experience (*Erlebnis*). They are not concerned with other days but stand out from time. As for their substance Baudelaire has defined it in the notion of the correspondences, a concept that in Baudelaire stands side by side and unconnected with the notion of modern beauty.[19]

There is an important connection here with the distinction drawn in *The Storyteller* between the novel as 'perpetuating' and the story as 'short lived'. The novel is unique, a solitary and single event. It does not form part of the tradition. It is neither repeated nor handed down. It is the place of 'transcendental homelessness'. The days of recollection which stand out from chronological time are themselves situated within continuity and tradition. This is why 'correspondences record a concept of experience which includes ritual elements'. Correspondances overcome the results of fragmentation but without overcoming the fragmentation of the present. They do not return what has been lost but allow for an experience that is not jeopardized by the shocks of *Erlebnis*. That is why they are connected to a more original form of beauty, namely a conception that, 'one would define as the object of experience in the state of resemblance'. The reference to Plato is clear. However the important point here is that beauty pertains to *Erfahrung* – to that which is infused by ritual – but which cannot be experienced as such; hence correspondances and therefore resemblance. The importance of Baudelaire's poetry is that it has allowed *Erlebnis* to be enframed by *Erfarhung*. For Benjamin, Baudelaire's battling the crowd 'is the nature of something lived through (*Erlebnis*) to which Baudelaire has given the weight of experience (*Erfahrung*).'[20] Baudelaire turned *Erlebnis* into *Erfahrung*. Perhaps this is Benjamin's final conclusion. It is of course a conclusion, the possibility of which, has already been gestured at in *The Storyteller*. There Benjamin attributes an aesthetic dimension to the death of the art of storytelling. He described this death, not as modern but as secular, and therefore as part of the historical process of secularization. He then goes on to add that this death

> is . . . only a comcomitant symptom of the secular productive
> forces of history, a concomitant that has quite gradually removed
> narrative from the realm of living speech and at the same time is
> making it possible to see a new beauty in its vanishing.[21]

Here is an aesthetic, not of decay, nor even of the modern, but one yielded by the growing incompleteness and fragmentation of the present. The new beauty is made possible by the cleavage in experience.

It is in Baudelaire's poetry however that the point of contact between these two forms of experience – the two sides of the cleavage – takes place. One is given the significance of the other. It is a relationship between them that differs fundamentally from the connection that Benjamin attributes to Bergson. Quoting Horkheimer to the effect that Bergson has 'suppressed death', Benjamin goes on to add that

> The durée from which death has been eliminated has the miserable endlessness of a scroll. Tradition is excluded from it. It is the quintessence of the passing moment [*Erlebnis*] that struts around in the borrowed garb of experience. The spleen on the other hand is exposing the passing moment in all its nakedness.[22]

In this passage and within the distinction between *Erlebnis* and *Erfahrung*, Benjamin has situated, albeit in a negative form the 'matter' of tradition. Baudelaire's poetry – the spleen – reveals the reality of *Erlebnis*. Why is it that tradition is excluded from the endlessness of the scroll? The response is based on the fact that for Benjamin what Bergson has done is construct the lived – the passing moment – in terms of an unending continuity. It is of course continuity that is proper to tradition and therefore to *Erfarhung*. Hence the description of *Erlebnis* strutting 'around in the borrowed garb of experience'. The absence of death is the exclusion of history (and prehistory, the time of ritual). The scroll can be read as standing for the mechanical work that seals the worker off from tradition. It is therefore the continual repetition of the same. At play here is what must be seen as a fundamental aspect of Benjamin's understanding of tradition. It involves a particular form of repetition; one within which action plays a central role. Repetition is a handing on. Tradition is thus linked to a specific conception of action. A conception that is exemplified by the figure of the storyteller; who by telling a story (i.e. by acting) takes over and hands on. The storyteller emerges therefore as the figure within tradition. Action causes the tradition to endure and hence facilitates its continuity. It should always be remembered however that this action is only possible if the community in which it takes place is unified. Modernity renders this impossible because of the fracturing of the site of community.

Despite its initial attraction it should be remembered that Benjamin's conception of modernity is articulated within the distinction between *Erlebnis* and *Erfahrung*. It is only in terms of this distinction that it is possible to, say, characterize the worker as 'sealed off' from the possibility of a place within the continuity that is tradition, because he is 'sealed off' from *Erfarhung*. The consequence of this distinction is, as has been suggested, that it yields a conception of the present as a place of loss. Clearly, of course, what is important here is the way in which loss is to be understood. Within any understanding of such a construction of the present it is vital to take account of the conception of subjectivity implicit both within the cleavage in experience and therefore which inhabits the present as the locus of loss.

In his discussion of beauty Benjamin quotes Goethe and then goes on to make the important additional point concerning correspondances and their role in understanding beauty: 'Beauty in its relationship to nature can be defined as that which remains true to its essential nature only when veiled. The correspondances tell us what is meant by the veil.'[23] The correspondances have allowed Baudelaire to give to the passing moment the 'weight' of an experience. Benjamin's conception of modernity does not sanction the possibility of a return or a recovery of what is no longer at hand. The aesthetic, here finding its most intense expression in beauty, is constrained to adopt resemblance. Benjamin uses Goethe's point that the aesthetic representation of nature must aim at resemblance and not an exact copy. It is to this extent that nature is unrepresentable. Once again the shadow of Plato can be seen haunting both Goethe and Benjamin. The additional point made by Benjamin is that it is Baudelaire's correspondances which allow for an understanding of the resemblance; an understanding that includes both its necessity and its function. It is at exactly this point that Benjamin and Goethe differ. Goethe is making a claim about representation within aesthetics, and hence the veil is simply an aesthetic category. Benjamin on the other hand gives to the veil an historical specificity. The veil emerges within – and hence also, in part, constructs – modernity. To redeploy the imagery of *The Storyteller*, the veil marks the absence of 'the community of listeners'. The veil therefore smothers the 'matter' of tradition. It is the historical specificity introduced by Benjamin that further reinforces the argument that his position is both dependent upon as well as advancing a conception of the present as a place of loss.

The experiencing subject is no longer (and it is the 'longer' that must be emphasized) articulated within the continuity of tradition. The possibility of the 'no longer' – of what was identified before as Baudelaire's 'past tense' – necessitates the cleavage in experience. It is clear that at work here there is what could be called, a 'discursive reciprocity'. The 'no longer' and the cleavage in experience are mutually interdependent. The conception of alienation inherent in Benjamin's description of the worker at the machine is neither economic nor even overtly political. It is rather that modernity is the place of an alienation from the continuity of tradition. It is essential not to employ the language of causality. It is not as though, either implicitly or explicitly, alienation has its source in the development of technology. Implicitly, however, alienation is dependent upon the subject proper to the cleavage in experience. In other words a subject articulated within – and hence which articulates – the distinction between *Erfahrung* and *Erlebnis*.

The consequence of this interarticulation is that because it demands a conception of the present as a locus of loss it advances a related understanding of action that is itself based on the overcoming of loss. Such a conception of the present and therefore the particular orientation of the active is not unique to Benjamin. A similar conception is found in the work of Heidegger and Marx. The unique contribution made by Benjamin, however, is that instead of directing action in terms of a recovery or retrieval of that which has been lost (and where therefore the experience of that through which the lost can itself become the object of an experience emerges as central) Benjamin's position gestures towards the future. It is precisely this gesturing 'toward' that marks the Messianic in his work. It is a conception of the Messianic that can be politicized, as is found in some of his later writings. It is also however equally present as the conception of totality as the end of history that is found in *The Origin of German Tragic Drama*. This latter point emerges in Benjamin's argument that 'There takes place in every original phenomenon a determination of the form in which an idea will constantly confront the historical world, until it is revealed fulfilled, in the totality of its history.'[24] The revealed fulfilment of the idea is itself based on the impossibility of the idea to be actually present. Benjamin's argument is based on Plato and yet his conception of the future is Messianic. It is not that Benjamin reworks this precise formulation in his text on Baudelaire. It is rather that inherent in each is a futural dimension that necessarily depends upon a conception of the present either as incomplete or as the locus of loss.

In order to take these deliberations a step further it is necessary to return to what is in fact the central philosophical problem here, namely, the relationship between experience and the subject of experience. Consistent with both the cleavage in experience, and the present as loss and the resolution or overcoming of loss as futural, is a conception of the subject of experience as that which while modern (secular) – since it is located in the site of the fractured community –

can at the same time see itself as a divided unity, and hence will be able to see itself as no longer alienated and therefore as reunited. The cleavage in experience demands the experience of the overcoming of that division. The important point here is that while the subject of experience may be divided, the nature of what may be antagonistic and perhaps even conflictual it none the less gestures towards its own unity, in the same way as the idea is revealed as fulfilled 'in the totality of its history'.

When it is argued that alienation can be overcome, this must be understood as arguing that the present as the locus of loss can be overcome. Within the present it is the aesthetic which is privileged by Walter Benjamin as providing access to the nature of the present as well as the possibility of redemption. However, what must be remembered is that the aesthetic takes place within – if not as – experience. Developing a critique of Benjamin should not involve taking the aesthetic as its object but rather as the subject and place of aesthetic experience. Fundamental to such a task is the inherent unity that marks both the subject in the present and in the future. While it is true that the subject in the present is divided by the cleavage in experience, this division is the consequence of the process of loss. There is an interesting parallel here with tradition. When it is argued that modernity means that tradition is no longer a possible object of experience, it is presupposed that prior to this state of affairs there was a necessary communication between the subject of experience and tradition. A communication that is no longer present within modernity. The consequence of this is that the conception of the present and the conception of the subject of the present both derive their mode of existence – which could be described as a mode of self-irreconcilability – from their having been an original state of unity (perhaps this could also be called an original state of reconciliation). The cleavage in experience means that the subject is not reconciled with itself. The absence of community is a state of social irreconcilability where it is the image of the past which opens up the possibility of the future.[25]

What is emerging here is the negative characterization of the present that seems to dominate the philosophical orientation of modernity. A characterization, the overcoming of which is conditional upon accepting change as the overcoming of negativity, where negativity is the collapse of an initial unity. For Benjamin fragmentation, in subjectivity and within the social, must be sublated

only because it is the mark of collapse. It is at this precise point that
the limits of Benjamin's work can be traced. The problem is that if
the present is understood either as incomplete or as a site of loss –
where the designation of the incomplete or loss comes from the past
and therefore demands a futural projection for either completion or
the overcoming of loss – then this precludes any conception of the
present as agonistic. If alienation, for example, is explained in terms
of the relationship between the past and the present (it should of
course be added that it is a past constructed by the present) such
that it is also possible to argue that the difference between the past
and the present is explicable in terms of alienation, then the agonistic
moment is precisely the divide between the past and the present. In
relation to the fragmentation of the community of listeners the agon
becomes the moment of fragmentation. It is not located in the
community as fragmented but in the distinction between the
community as unity and its fragmentation; between the past and the
present. The agon is not part of the present but merely the construction, and hence perhaps also the definition, of history.

Within Benjamin's work it is the relationship between the past
and the present which gives rise to the possibility of conflict, the
resolution of which is necessarily futural. Indeed the possibility of
the future is the possibility of resolution. It is of course resolution as
totality. Not necessarily a return to the totality that was, but rather
to a future totality, the consequence of this, of course, is that it both
demands, as well as gives rise to, a conception of the future as a
synthesized totality, where identity must always precede and ground
difference. It is clear from this description the extent to which
Benjamin's position is Messianic. However that is not the most
significant problem. It is rather the impossibility within the
temporality of the scheme he presents of thinking the present as
agon. It is only if the present can be thought as an agonistic plenitude
that it is possible both to develop as well as situate critique. Furthermore, even if it is accepted that fragmentation is descriptive of both
the subject and the social – and in sum therefore descriptive of the
postenlightenment, i.e. the epochal present beyond synthetic unity –
fragmentation in this sense demands neither an initial unity nor the
need to define the present in terms of loss.

The philosophical challenge at the present – indeed of the present –
is to map the interarticulation of the desire for unity with the
necessity of differential plurality. The limiting element in Benjamin's

conception of the interplay between tradition and experience is that it is unable to meet this challenge. The location of this limit is at the hinge separating the modern and the postmodern.[26]

NOTES

1 SMB, 110, GS. 1, 608.
2 All references to Benjamin's text 'Some Motifs in Baudelaire' will be to the translation by Harry Zohn that appears in *Charles Baudelaire: A Lyric Poet in the Era of High Capitalism*, Verso Editions, London 1983. They will take the form OB plus page number. I have also provided the page and volume number of the *Gesammelte Schriften*, edited by R. Tiedmann and Herman Schweppenhauser, Surkhamp, Frankfurt am Main 1908.
3 References to this text will be to Harry Zohn's translation in *Illuminations*, Fontana, London 1973. They will take the form ST plus page number. Once again there will be the accompanying reference to the *Gesammelte Schriften*.
4 ST, 91, GS, 2, 446.
5 ST, 97, FS, 2, 453.
6 While it cannot be pursued here it is worth drawing attention to the link between *Geschichte* as story and *Geschene* as the 'happening' – though equally historicizing – that is passed from one generation to another in the 'chain of tradition' created by memory (*Errinerung*).
7 ST, 98, GS, 2, 454.
8 ST, 100, GS, 2, 455.
9 ST, 102, GS, 2, 457.
10 The problem of community is emerging as a central philosophical issue. The reason for this is in part due to the emergence of what I have called in this paper the 'postenlightenment'. By this term I mean the relationship between on the one hand the desire for unity (indeed at times the need for unity) that is a direct result of the Enlightenment, and on the other the existence of a differential plurality that marks amongst other things contemporary multiracial societies.
11 GS, I, 655–691.
12 For an important discussion of the issues that emerge from this text see H. Wisman (ed.) *Walter Benjamin et Paris*, LeCerf, Paris 1986.
13 OB, 110, GS, 1, 608.
14 OB, 139, GS, 1, 638.
15 OB, 133, GS, 1, 632.
16 OB, 133, GS, 1, 632.
17 OB, 141, GS, 1, 639–40.
18 OB, 134, GS, 1, 632.
19 OB, 139, GS, 1, 637.
20 OB, 154, GS, 1, 652–3.
21 ST, 87, GS, 2, 442.
22 OB, 145, GS, 1, 643.
23 OB, 140, GS, 1, 639.
24 Walter Benjamin, *The Origin of German Tragic Drama*, trans. John Osborne, New Left Books, London 1977, pp. 45–6; GS, 1, 227.
25 Richard Wolin in *Walter Benjamin. An Aesthetic of Redemption*. Columbia University Press, New York 1982, also uses the expression reconciliation. While recognizing

the importance of Wolin's position I have however tried to deploy the term in a different way.

26 I wish to thank Peter Osborne for the many valuable comments he made on an earlier draft of this paper.

Chapter 8

THE INVISIBLE *FLÂNEUSE*: WOMEN AND THE LITERATURE OF MODERNITY

JANET WOLFF

THE EXPERIENCE OF MODERNITY

The literature of modernity describes the experience of men. It is essentially a literature about transformations in the public world and in its associated consciousness. The actual date of the advent of 'the modern' varies in different accounts, and so do the characteristics of 'modernity' identified by different writers. But what nearly all the accounts have in common is their concern with the public world of work, politics and city life. And these are areas from which women were excluded, or in which they were practically invisible. For example, if the chief characteristic of modernity is the Weberian idea of increasing rationalization, then the major institutions affected by this process were the factory, the office, the government department. There have, of course, always been women working in factories; the growth of bureaucracies was also to some extent dependent on the development of a new female work force of clerks and secretaries. Nevertheless, it is appropriate to talk of this world as a 'male' world, for two reasons. First, the institutions were run by men, for men (owners, industrialists, managers, financiers), and they were dominated by men in their operation and hierarchical structure. Second, the development of the factory and, later, the bureaucracy coincides with that process, by now well documented, of the 'separation of spheres', and the increasing restriction of women to the 'private' sphere of the home and the suburb.[1] Although lower middle-class and working-class women continued to go out to work throughout the nineteenth century, the ideology of women's place in the domestic realm permeated the whole of society, at least in England, as evidenced by the working-class demand for a 'family wage' for men.[2] The public sphere, then, despite the presence of some women in certain contained areas of it, was a masculine domain. And in so far as the experience of 'the modern' occurred mainly in the public sphere, it was primarily men's experience.

In this essay, however, I shall not pursue the more orthodox sociological analyses of modernity, which discuss the phenomenon in terms of the rationalization process (or perhaps the 'civilizing process' – this, of course, places the event at a much earlier date). I want to consider the more impressionistic and essayistic contributions of those writers who locate the specially 'modern' in city life: in the fleeting, ephemeral, impersonal nature of encounters in the urban environment, and in the particular world-view which the city-dweller develops. This focus is not foreign to sociology; the essays of George Simmel immediately come to mind as studies in the social psychology of city life,[3] and the more recent sociology of Richard Sennett has revived interest in the diagnosis of the modern urban personality.[4] But a particular concern for the experience of modernity has also run through literary criticism; here its early prophet was Charles Baudelaire, the poet of mid-nineteenth-century Paris.[5] Walter Benjamin's essays on Baudelaire, written in the 1930s, provide a fascinating (though typically cryptic and fragmentary) series of reflections of Baudelaire's views on 'the modern'.[6] As a starting-point for the investigation of this particular literature of modernity, I take Baudelaire's statement, in the essay written in 1859–60, *The Painter of Modern Life*: 'By "modernity" I mean the ephemeral, the fugitive, the contingent, the half of art whose other half is the eternal and the immutable'.[7] This is echoed in Marshall Berman's recent book on the experience of modernity, which describes the 'paradoxical unity' of modernity:

> A unity of disunity: it pours us all into a maelstrom of perpetual disintegration and renewal, of struggle and contradiction, of ambiguity and anguish. To be modern is to be part of a universe in which, as Marx said, 'all that is solid melts into air'.[8]

It also recalls Simmel's account of the metropolitan personality: 'The psychological basis of the metropolitan type of individuality consists in the *intensification of nervous stimulation* which results from the swift and uninterrupted change of outer and inner stimuli,'[9] (italics in original).

For Simmel, this is closely related to the money economy, dominant by the late nineteenth century. It is worth stressing that, although cities were not new in the nineteenth century, the critics (and defenders) of modernity believed that urban existence took on an entirely different character around the middle of the nineteenth century. Though any such dating is, to some extent, arbitrary (and will vary, anyway, from Paris to London to Berlin),[10] I think it is useful to take this period of accelerated urbanization, coupled with the transformations in work, housing and social relations brought about by the rise of industrial capitalism, as the crucial years of the birth of 'modernity'. Berman gives modernity a prehistory, in those elements of the modern which began to appear in the period before the French Revolution and which found their expression in Goethe's *Faust*.[11] Bradbury and McFarlane, who focus on the later period of 1890 to 1930, credit Baudelaire as an 'initiator' of modernism.[12] But they are writing about the rather different phenomenon of *modernism* in the arts; although 'modernism' and 'modernity' are often conflated, I do not think anyone has claimed that Baudelaire was a modernist poet, in the sense of revolutionizing poetic language and form.[13] There is no contradiction in locating the early experience of 'modernity' in the mid-nineteenth century, and its later expression in the arts at the end of the century.

The peculiar characteristics of modernity, then, consist in the transient and 'fugitive' nature of encounters and impressions made in the city. A sociology of modernity must, ultimately, be able to identify the origins of these new patterns of behaviour and experience, in the social and material aspects of the contemporary society. Simmel, as I have said, relates the metropolitan personality and what he calls the 'blasé attitude' to the money economy. Marshall Berman, beginning from Marx's account of the 'melting vision',[14] seems to take over at the same time Marx's analysis of the basis of this vision in the radical changes wrought in society by the bourgeoisie and the capitalist mode of production. Baudelaire, on the other hand, considers the phenomenon itself, and not its causes. It is not my task here to provide a sociology of modernity, and so I shall not assess competing accounts of the social or economic base of the modern experience, nor even examine very closely the adequacy of the conceptions of 'modernity' I discuss. What I do want to do is to take those accounts which do describe, more or less sociologically, the modern urban experience, and consider them from the point of view of gender divisions in nineteenth-century society. To that extent, it does not really matter whether a particular account is adequately grounded in a social-historical understanding of the period, or even whether an account is internally consistent. (As Berman shows, Baudelaire employs several different conceptions of 'modernity', as well as changing evaluations of the phenomenon.)[15]

Baudelaire's comments on modernity are most explicit in his writings on art criticism, though the same themes can be found in his poetry and in his prose poems. An early reference appears at the end of his review of *The Salon of 1845*, appended almost as an afterthought in the final paragraph. Here he commends contemporary painting, but laments its lack of interest in the present.

> No one is cocking his ear to tomorrow's wind; and yet the heroism of *modern life* surrounds and presses upon us. We are quite sufficiently choked by our true feelings for us to be able to recognize them. There is no lack of subjects, nor of colours, to make epics. The painter, the true painter for whom we are looking, will be he who can snatch its epic quality from the life of today and can make us see and understand, with brush or with pencil, how great and poetic we are in our cravats and our patent-leather boots. Next year let us hope that the true seekers may grant us the extraordinary delight of celebrating the advent of the *new*.[16]

But the following year was no better, and again Baudelaire bemoans the absence of any really contemporary art, concerned with modern themes and characters in the way that Balzac's novels are. This time he devotes several pages – the final section of the review of *The Salon of 1846* – to the theme of 'the heroism of modern life'. Modern life here begins to acquire some identifiable features: the uniform drabness of the colours of people's dress, the modern phenomenon of the 'dandy' who reacts against this, the 'private subjects' which Baudelaire extols as far more 'heroic' than the public and official subjects of painting:

> The pageant of fashionable life and the thousands of floating existences – criminals and kept women – which drift about in the underworld of a great city; the *Gazette des Tribunaux* and the *Moniteur* all prove to us that we have only to open our eyes to recognize our heroism. . . . The life of our city is rich in poetic and marvellous subjects.[17]

These subjects are itemized in more detail in 'The Painter of Modern Life' of 1859–60. By this time, Baudelaire has found a painter he considers equal to the task of depicting the modern: Constantin Guys, the subject of the essay. Guys' watercolours and drawings are generally considered to be talented but superficial works, of little importance in the history of art – though judgments like these do, of course, beg all sorts of questions about critical assessment. Berman dismisses Guys's 'slick renderings of the "beautiful people" and their world', and wonders that Baudelaire should think so highly of an art which 'resembles nothing so much as Bonwit's or Bloomingdale's ads'.[18] Nevertheless, the essay is interesting for its expansion of the notion of 'modernity'. Guys, the 'painter of modern life', goes out into the crowd and records the myriad impressions of day and night.

> He goes and watches the river of life flow past him in all its splendour and majesty. . . . He gazes upon the landscapes of the great city – landscapes of stone, caressed by the mist or buffeted by the sun. He delights in fine carriages and proud horses, the dazzling smartness of the grooms, the expertness of the footmen, the sinuous gait of the women, the beauty of the children. . . . If a fashion or the cut of a garment has been slightly modified, if bows and curls have been supplanted by cockades, if *bavolets* have been enlarged and *chignons* have dropped a fraction towards the nape of the neck, if waists have been raised and skirts have become fuller, be very sure that his eagle eye will already have spotted it from however great a distance.[19]

This is the passage Berman dismisses as 'advertising copy'. But if it is an inventory of the superficial and the merely fashionable, then that is the point – the modern consciousness consists in the parade of impressions, the particular beauty appropriate to the modern age. And, more importantly, it is in this essay that Baudelaire suggests the formal features of the modern mind, which grasps 'the ephemeral, the fugitive, the contingent'. The dandy appears again, to be compared and also contrasted with Guys, similar in their concern for appearance and for personal originality, divided by the blasé and insensitive attitude of the former which Guys (according to Baudelaire)[20] abhors. Guys is the *flâneur*, in his element in the crowd – at the centre of the world and at the same time hidden from the world.[21]

The *flâneur* – the stroller – is a central figure in Benjamin's essays on Baudelaire and nineteenth-century Paris. The streets and arcades of the city are the home of the *flâneur*, who, in Benjamin's phrase, 'goes botanizing on the asphalt'.[22] The anonymity of the crowd provides an asylum for the person on the margins of society; here Benjamin includes both Baudelaire himself as a *flâneur*, and the victims and murderers of Poe's detective stories (which Baudelaire translated into French).[23] For Benjamin, however, the city of the *flâneur* is historically more limited than for Baudelaire. Neither London nor Berlin offers precisely the conditions of involvement/non-involvement in which the Parisian *flâneur* flourishes; nor does the Paris of a slightly later period, when a 'network of controls' has made escape into anonymity impossible.[24] (Baudelaire, and Berman, on the contrary, argue that the Paris increasingly opened up by Haussmann's boulevards, which broke down the social and geographical divisions between the classes, is even more the site of the modern gaze, the ambit of the *flâneur*.)[25]

The *flâneur* is the modern hero; his experience, like that of Guys, is that of a freedom to move about in the city, observing and being observed, but never interacting with others. A related figure in the literature of modernity is the stranger. One of Baudelaire's prose poems is entitled *L'Étranger*.[26] It is a short dialogue, in which an 'enigmatic man' is asked what or whom he loves – his father, mother, sister, brother? his friends, his country, beauty, gold? To all of these he answers in the negative, affirming that he simply loves the passing clouds. For Simmel, the stranger is not a man without attachments and involvements, however. He is characterized by a particular kind of 'inorganic' membership of the group, not having been a member from its beginning, but having settled down in a new place. He is 'the person who comes today and stays tomorrow';[27] in this he differs from both the *flâneur* and Baudelaire's *étranger*, neither of whom will settle down or even make contact with those around him. But Simmel's stranger is always a 'potential wanderer': 'Although he has not moved on, he has not quite overcome the freedom of coming and going'.[28] These heroes of modernity thus share the possibility and the prospect of lone travel, of voluntary up-rooting, of anonymous arrival at a new place. They are, of course, all men.

WOMEN AND PUBLIC LIFE

It is no accident, and no fault of a careless patriarchal use of language, that Richard Sennett's book on modernity is called *The Fall of Public Man*. The 'public' person of the eighteenth century and earlier, whose demise is charted, and who passed the time in coffee-houses, paraded in the streets and at the theatre, and addressed strangers freely in public places, was clearly male. (Although Sennett says that it was quite proper to address strange women in the parks or the street, as long as men did not thereby assume that a reply meant they might call on the woman at home, there is no suggestion that *women* might address strangers.)[29] In the nineteenth-century city, no longer the arena of that public life, the *flâneur* makes his appearance – to be watched, but not addressed.[30] Men and women may have shared the privatization of personality, the careful anonymity and withdrawal in public life; but the line drawn increasingly sharply between the public and private was also one which confined women to the private, while men retained the freedom to move in the crowd or to frequent cafés and pubs. The men's clubs replaced the coffee-houses of earlier years.

None of the authors I have discussed is unaware of the different experience of women in the modern city. Sennett, for example, recognizes that the 'right to escape to public privacy was unequally enjoyed by the sexes', since even by the late nineteenth century women could not go alone to a café in Paris or a restaurant in London.[31] As he says, '"The lonely crowd" was a realm of privatized freedom, and the male, whether simply out of domination or greater need, was more likely to escape in it.' He notes, too, that in the earlier period of 'public life' women had to take a good deal more care about the 'signs' of their dress, which would be scrutinized for an indication of their social rank; in the nineteenth century, the scrutiny would be in order to differentiate 'respectable' from 'loose' women.[32] Simmel, whose essayistic sociology I have used very selectively, also paid much attention elsewhere to the condition of women. He wrote essays on the position of women, the psychology of women, female culture, and the women's movement and social democracy.[33] He was one of the first to permit women in his private seminars, long before they were admitted as full students at the University of Berlin.[34] Berman, too, considers women, acknowledging somewhat belatedly (on page 322 of his book) that they have a totally different experience of the city from that of men. He suggests that Jane Jacobs' *The Death and Life of Great American Cities* gives a 'fully articulated woman's view of the city'.[35] Published in 1961, Jacobs' book describes her own daily life in the city – a life of neighbours, shopkeepers, and young children, as well as work. The importance of the book, says Berman, is that it reveals that 'women had something to tell us about the city and the life we shared, and that we had impoverished our own lives as well as theirs by not listening to them till now'.[36]

The problem is, though, that it is also the literature of modernity which has been impoverished by ignoring the lives of women. The dandy, the *flâneur*, the hero, the stranger – all figures invoked to epitomize the experience of modern life – are invariably male figures. In 1831, when George Sand wanted to experience Paris life and to learn about the ideas and arts of her time, she dressed as a boy, to give herself the freedom she knew women could not share.

> So I had made for myself a *redingote-guérite* in heavy gray cloth, pants and vest to match. With a gray hat and large woollen cravat, I was a perfect first-year student. I can't express the pleasure my boots gave me: I would gladly have slept with them, as my brother did in his young age when he got his first pair. With those little iron-shod heels, I was solid on the pavement. I flew from one end of Paris to the other. It seemed to me that I could go round the world. And then, my clothes feared nothing. I ran out in every kind of weather, I came home at every sort of hour, I sat in the pit at the theatre. No one paid attention to me, and no one guessed at my disguise. . . . No one knew me, no one looked at me, no one found fault with me; I was an atom lost in that immense crowd.[37]

The disguise made the life of the *flâneur* available to her; as she knew very well, she could not adopt the non-existent role of a *flâneuse.* Women could not stroll alone in the city.

In Baudelaire's essays and poems, women appear very often. Modernity breeds, or makes visible, a number of categories of female city-dwellers. Among those most prominent in these texts are: the prostitute, the widow, the old lady, the lesbian, the murder victim, and the passing unknown woman. Indeed, according to Benjamin, the lesbian was for Baudelaire the heroine of modernism; certainly it is known that he originally intended to give the title *Les Lesbiennes* to the poems which became *Les Fleurs du mal*.[38] (Yet, as Benjamin also points out, in the major poem about lesbians of the series, 'Delphine et Hippolyte', Baudelaire concludes by condemning the women as 'lamentable victims', bound for hell.)[39] The prostitute, the subject of the poem 'Crépuscule du soir' and also discussed in a section of 'The Painter of Modern Life'[40] elicits a similarly ambivalent attitude of admiration and disgust (the poem comparing prostitution to an anthill, and to a worm stealing a man's food). More unequivocal is Baudelaire's sympathy for those other marginal women, the old woman and the widow; the former he 'watches tenderly from afar' like a father, the latter he observes with a sensitivity to her pride, pain and poverty.[41] But none of these women meet the poet as his equal. They are subjects of his gaze, objects of his 'botanizing'. The nearest he comes to a direct encounter, with a woman who is not either marginal or debased, is in the poem, 'A une passante'.[42] (Even here, it is worth noting that the woman in question is in mourning – *en grand deuil*.) The tall, majestic woman passes him in the busy street; their eyes meet for a moment before she continues her journey, and the poet remains to ask whether they will only meet again in eternity. Her return of his gaze is confirmed in the last line: 'Ô toi que j'eusse aimée, ô toi qui le savais.' Benjamin's interpretation of this poem is that it is the very elusiveness of the passing encounter which fascinates Baudelaire: 'The delight of the city-dweller is not so much love at first sight as love at last sight.'[43] The meeting is characterized by the peculiarly modern feature of 'shock'.[44] (But if this is the rare exception of a woman sharing the urban experience, we may also ask whether a 'respectable' woman, in the 1850s, would have met the gaze of a strange man.)

There is, in any case, an apparently common assumption that women who do participate in 'the public' on anything like the same terms as men somehow manifest masculine traits. One of the widows observed by Baudelaire is described as having mannerisms of a masculine character.[45] His mixed admiration for the lesbian has much to do with her (supposed) 'mannishness', according to Benjamin.[46] Benjamin himself explains that, as women in the nineteenth century had to go out to work in factories, 'in the course of time masculine traits were bound to manifest themselves in these women'.[47] Even Richard Sennett (without much evidence, and despite the benefit of contemporary perspectives on the construction of gender) claims that women at the end of the nineteenth century who were 'ideologically committed to emancipation' dressed like men and developed bodily gestures which were 'mannish'.[48] But perhaps this perception of the 'masculine' in women who were visible in a man's world is only the displaced recognition of women's overall exclusion from that world. Baudelaire's general views on women, in his letters and his prose, are illuminating as a context for his poetic expressions of fascination with 'women of the city'. This is his own admission, in a letter to one of the women he idolized and idealized: 'I have hateful prejudices about women. In fact, *I have no faith*; you have a final soul, but, when all is said, it is the soul of a woman'.[49] Woman as a non-person is extolled in 'The Painter of Modern Life':

> Woman, in a word, for the artist in general, and Monsieur G. in particular, is far more than just the female of Man. Rather she is a divinity, a star, which presides at all the conceptions of the brain of man; a glittering conglomeration of all the graces of Nature, condensed into a single being; the object of the keenest admiration and curiosity that the picture of life can offer its contemplator. She is a kind of idol, stupid perhaps, but dazzling and bewitching, who holds wills and destinies suspended on her glance. . . . Everything that adorns woman, everything that serves to show off her beauty, is part of herself; and those artists who have made a particular study of this enigmatic being dote no less on all the details of the *mundus muliebris* than on Woman herself. . . . What poet, in sitting down to paint the pleasure caused by the sight of a beautiful woman, would venture to separate her from her costume?[50]

The classic misogynist duality, of woman as idealized-but-vapid/real-and-sensual-but-detested, which Baudelaire displays (and to which his biographers attest) is clearly related to the particular parade of women we observe in this literature of modernity.

But the other authors I have discussed were not misogynists; they were or are, on the contrary, sympathetic to women's condition and to the case of women's emancipation and equality with men. We need to look deeper than particular prejudices to explain the invisibility of women in the literature of modernity. The explanation is threefold, and lies in 1) the nature of sociological investigation, 2) the consequently partial conception of 'modernity', and 3) the reality of women's place in society. Much of this has been discussed in the recent work of feminist sociologists and historians, but it is worth rehearsing here in the specific context of the problem of modernity.

THE INVISIBILITY OF WOMEN IN THE LITERATURE OF MODERNITY

The rise and development of sociology in the nineteenth century was closely related to the growth and increasing separation of 'public' and 'private' spheres of activity in western industrial societies. The condition for this was the separation of work from home, with the development of factories and offices. By the mid-nineteenth century, this had made possible the move to the suburbs in some major cities (for example, the industrial cities of England, such as Manchester and Birmingham).[51] Although women had never been engaged on equal terms (financial, legal or otherwise) with men, this physical separation put an end to their close and important involvement in what had often been a family concern – whether in trade, production, or even professional work. Their gradual confinement to the domestic world of the home and the suburb was strongly reinforced by an ideology of separate spheres.[52] At the same time, a new public world was in process of formation, of business organizations, political and financial establishments, and social and cultural institutions. These were almost invariably male institutions, though women might occasionally be granted some sort of honorary membership or allowed minimal participation as guests on particular occasions. In the second half of the century, the rise of the professions excluded women from the other expanding areas of activity, some of which they had traditionally been engaged in (like medicine), some of which had already excluded them (like the law and academic occupations), and some of which were new (the education of artists, for example). The two major implications for sociology as a new discipline were, first, that it was dominated by men, and second, that it was primarily concerned with the 'public' spheres of work, politics and the market place.[53] Indeed, women appear in the classic texts of sociology only in so far as they relate to men, in the family, or in minor roles in the public sphere. As David Morgan has said about Weber's *The Protestant Ethic and the Spirit of Capitalism*:

> It cannot have escaped many people's attention, at least in recent years, that women are very much hidden from this particular

history; the lead parts – Franklin, Luther, Calvin, Baxter and Wesley – are all played by men and women only appear on the stage fleetingly in the guise of German factory workers with rather traditional orientations to work.[54]

And, to the extent that 'the separation of spheres' was a very incomplete process, many women still having to go to work to earn a living (though a very high proportion of these did so in domestic service), even these women, in their factories, mills, schools and offices, have been invisible in traditional sociological texts. The public institutions in which they did participate were rarely those accorded most importance by analysts of contemporary society.

This also meant that the particular experience of 'modernity' was, for the most part, equated with experience *in* the public arena. The accelerated growth of the city, the shock of the proximity of the very rich and the destitute poor (documented by Engels – and in some cities avoided and alleviated by the creation of suburbs), and the novelty of the fleeting and impersonal contacts in public life, provided the concern and the fascination for the authors of 'the modern', sociologists and other social commentators who documented their observations in academic essays, literary prose or poetry. To some extent, of course, these transformations of social life affected everyone, regardless of sex and class, though they did so differently for different groups. But the literature of modernity ignores the private sphere and to that extent is silent on the subject of women's primary domain. This silence is not only detrimental to any understanding of the lives of the female sex; it obscures a crucial part of the lives of men, too, by abstracting one part of their experience and failing to explore the interrelation of public and private spheres. For men inhabited both of these. Moreover, the public could only be constituted as a particular set of institutions and practices on the basis of the removal of other areas of social life to the invisible arena of the private.[55] The literature of modernity, like most sociology of its period, suffers from what has recently been called 'the oversocialisation of the public sphere'.[56] The skewed vision of its authors explains why women only appear in this literature through their relationships with men in the public sphere, and via their illegitimate or eccentric routes into this male arena – that is, in the role of whore, widow or murder victim.[57]

The real situation of women in the second half of the nineteenth

century was more complex than one of straightforward confinement
to the home. It varied from one social class to another, and even
from one geographical region to another, depending on the local
industry, the degree of industrialization, and numerous other factors.
And, although the solitary and independent life of the *flâneur* was not
open to women, women clearly were active and visible in other ways
in the public arena. Sennett, as I have already mentioned, refers to
the importance of careful attention to dress which women must
maintain, a point made much earlier by Thorstein Veblen:

> It has in the course of economic development become the office of
> the woman to consume vicariously for the head of the household;
> and her apparel is contrived with this object in view. It has come
> about that obviously productive labor is in a peculiar degree
> derogatory to respectable women, and therefore special pains
> should be taken in the construction of women's dress, to impress
> upon the beholder the fact (often indeed a fiction) that the wearer
> does not and cannot habitually engage in useful work.[58]

Here, the particular visibility of women is that of sign of their
husbands' position. Their important role in consumption is stressed:

> At the stage of economic development at which the women were
> still in the full sense the property of the men, the performance of
> conspicuous leisure and consumption came to be part of the
> services required of them. The women being not their own
> masters, obvious expenditure and leisure on their part would
> redound to the credit of their master rather than to their own
> credit; and therefore the more expensive and the more obviously
> unproductive the women of the household are, the more
> creditable and more effective for the purpose of reputability of the
> household or its head will their life be.[59]

The establishment of the department store in the 1850s and 1860s
provided an important new arena for the legitimate public appearance
of middle-class women.[60] However, although consumerism is a
central aspect of modernity, and moreover mediated the public/
private division, the peculiar characteristics of 'the modern' which I
have been considering – the fleeting, anonymous encounter and the
purposeless strolling – do not apply to shopping, or to women's
activities either as public signs of their husband's wealth or as
consumers.

We are beginning to find out more about the lives of women who were limited to the domestic existence of the suburbs;[61] about women who went into domestic service in large numbers;[62] and about the lives of working-class women.[63] The advent of the modern era affected all these women, transforming their experience of home and work. The recovery of women's experience is part of the project of retrieving what has been hidden, and attempting to fill the gaps in the classic accounts. The feminist revision of sociology and social history means the gradual opening up of areas of social life and experience which to date have been obscured by the partial perspective and particular bias of mainstream sociology.

It is not at all clear what a feminist sociology of modernity would look like. There is no question of inventing the *flâneuse*: the essential point is that such a character was rendered impossible by the sexual divisions of the nineteenth century. Nor is it appropriate to reject totally the existing literature on modernity, for the experiences it describes certainly defined a good deal of the lives of men, and were also (but far less centrally) a part of the experience of women. What is missing in this literature is any account of life outside the public realm, of the experience of 'the modern' in its private manifestations, and also of the very different nature of the experience of those women who *did* appear in the public arena; a poem written by 'la femme passante' about her encounter with Baudelaire, perhaps?

NOTES

1 Catherine Hall, 'Gender Divisions and Class Formation in the Birmingham Middle Class, 1780–1850', in *People's History and Socialist Theory*, ed. Raphael Samuel, Routledge & Kegan Paul, London 1981; Leonore Davidoff and Catherine Hall, 'The Architecture of Public and Private Life: English Middle-class Society in a Provincial Town 1780–1850', in *The Pursuit of Urban History*, ed. D. Fraser and A. Sutcliffe, Edward Arnold, London 1983.
2 Hilary Land, 'The Family Wage', *Feminist Review* 6, 1980; Michèle Barrett and Mary McIntosh, 'The "Family Wage": Some Problems for Socialists and Feminists', Capital & Class 11, 1980. The ideology of separate spheres, and even of the equation of male/public/rational, has persisted to the present day, its recent sociological expression being found in Parsonian theories of the family. Talcott Parsons, 'Family Structure and the Socialization of the Child', in *Family, Socialization and Interaction Process*, Talcott Parsons and Robert F. Bales, Routledge & Kegan Paul, London 1956.
3 George Simmel, 'The Stranger' and 'The Metropolis and Mental Life', in *The Sociology of George Simmel*, ed. Kurt H. Wolff, The Free Press, New York 1950.

4 Richard Sennett, *The Fall of Public Man*, Cambridge University Press, Cambridge 1974.

5 Charles Baudelaire, 'The Painter of Modern Life', in *The Painter of Modern Life and Other Essays*, trans. and ed. Jonathan Mayne, Phaidon Press, Oxford 1964 (first published 1863). For Baudelaire's other writings on modernity, see below.

6 Walter Benjamin, *Charles Baudelaire: A Lyric Poet in the Era of High Capitalism*, New Left Books, London 1973.

7 Baudelaire, op. cit., p. 13.

8 Marshall Berman, *All That is Solid Melts into Air*, Verso, London 1983, p. 15.

9 Simmel, op. cit., pp. 409–10.

10 Benjamin, for example, argues that conditions in the three cities were significantly different. Benjamin, op. cit., pp. 128–31.

11 Berman, op. cit., pp. 16–17 and chapter 1.

12 Malcolm Bradbury and James McFarlane, 'The Name and Nature of Modernism', in their (ed.) *Modernism 1890–1930*, Penguin, Harmondsworth 1976, p. 36.

13 For example, Joanna Richardson, translator of Baudelaire's poems, says in her introduction to *Baudelaire: Selected Poems* (Penguin, Harmondsworth 1975, p. 20): '*Les fleurs du mal*, may not be technically original. The only poem in which Baudelaire really seems to have invented his rhythm is 'L'invitation au voyage'. His one revolutionary innovation is in the versification, it is the complete suppression of the auditive caesura in a certain number of lines.'

14 The title of his book, *All That is Solid Melts into Air*, is a quotation from the *Communist Manifesto*.

15 Berman, op. cit., pp. 133–42.

16 Charles Baudelaire, 'The Salon of 1845', in *Art in Paris 1845–1862*, Phaidon Press, Oxford 1965, pp. 31–2. Italics in original.

17 Charles Baudelaire, 'The Salon of 1846', op. cit., pp. 118–19.

18 Berman, op. cit., p. 136.

19 Baudelaire, 1964, op. cit., p. 11.

20 Baudelaire, 1964, op. cit., pp. 26–9.

21 Baudelaire, 1964, op. cit., p. 9.

22 Benjamin, op. cit., p. 36.

23 Benjamin, op. cit., pp. 40 and 170. However, elsewhere Benjamin argues that Baudelaire is *not* the archetypical *flâneur*. Benjamin, op. cit., p. 69.

24 Benjamin, op. cit., pp. 49, 128, 47.

25 Berman, op. cit., pp. 150–5.

26 Charles Baudelaire, *Petits Poèmes en Prose (Le Spleen de Paris)*, Garnier-Flammarion, Paris 1967, p. 33.

27 Simmel, op. cit., p. 402.

28 Simmel, op. cit., p. 402.

29 Sennett, op. cit., p. 86.

30 Sennett, op. cit., pp. 125, 213.

31 Sennett, op. cit., p. 217. However, there were exceptions to this. See Robert Thorne, 'Places of Refreshment in the Nineteenth-Century City', in *Buildings and Society*, ed. Anthony D. King, Routledge & Kegan Paul, London 1980.

32 Sennett, op. cit., pp. 68 and 166. In these references to Sennett's book, I am again considering fairly uncritically (from any other point of view) a text on modernity. For a critical review of his use of evidence, his historical method, and his sociological explanation for the changes in manners, see Sheldon Wolin, 'The Rise of Private Man', *New York Review of Books*, 14 April 1977.

33 David Frisby, *Sociological Impressionism. A Reassessment of George Simmel's Social Theory*, Heinemann, London 1981, pp. 15, 17, 27, 139.

34 Frisby, op. cit., p. 28.
35 Berman, op. cit., p. 322.
36 Berman, op. cit., p. 323.
37 Quoted in Ellen Moers, *Literary Women*, Anchor Press, New York 1977, p. 12.
38 Benjamin, op. cit., p. 90; Richardson, op. cit., p. 12.
39 Benjamin, op. cit., pp. 92–3; Charles Baudelaire, *Selected Poems*, Penguin, Harmondsworth 1975, p. 224.
40 Baudelaire, 1967, op. cit., p. 185; 1964, op. cit., pp. 34–40.
41 Baudelaire, 1975, op. cit., p. 166; 1967, op. cit., pp. 63–5.
42 Baudelaire, 1975, op. cit., p. 170.
43 Benjamin, op. cit., p. 45.
44 Benjamin, op. cit., p. 125; also pp. 118 and 134.
45 Baudelaire, 1967, op. cit., p. 64.
46 Benjamin, op. cit., p. 90.
47 Benjamin, op. cit., p. 93.
48 Sennett, op. cit., p. 190.
49 Letter to Apollonie Sabatier, quoted in Richardson, op. cit., p. 14. Italics in original.
50 Baudelaire, 1964, op. cit., pp. 30–1.
51 Maurice Spiers, *Victoria Park Manchester*, Manchester University Press, Manchester 1976; Davidoff and Hall, op. cit.
52 Catherine Hall, 'The Early Formation of Victorian Domestic Ideology', in *Fit Work for Women*, ed. Sandra Burman, Croom Helm, London 1979.
53 Margaret Stacey, 'The Division of Labour Revisited or Overcoming the Two Adams', in *Practice and Progress: British Sociology 1950–1980*, ed. Philip Abrams et al., Allen & Unwin, London 1981; Sara Delamont, *The Sociology of Women*, Allen & Unwin, London 1980, chapter 1.
54 David Morgan, 'Men, Masculinity and the Process of Sociological Enquiry', in *Doing Feminist Research*, ed. Helen Roberts, Routledge & Kegan Paul, London 1981, p. 93.
55 Sennett does discuss, in passing, some changes in the home – for example, the development of a 'private' form of dress – but his central focus is on the public sphere, and he does not present a systematic account of the private or of the relationship between the two spheres. Sennett, op. cit., pp. 66–7.
56 Eva Gamarnikow and June Purvis, Introduction to *The Public and the Private*, ed. Eva Gamarnikow et al., Heinemann, London 1983, p. 2.
57 References to the murder victim, whom I have not discussed, originate in Poe's detective stories, which greatly influenced Baudelaire. Benjamin, op. cit., pp. 42–4.
58 Thorstein Veblen, *The Theory of the Leisure Class*, Unwin Books, London 1970, p. 126. First published in 1899.
59 Veblen, op. cit., pp. 126–7.
60 Thorne, op. cit., p. 236.
61 Davidoff and Hall, op. cit.; Catherine Hall, 'The Butcher, the Baker, the Candlestick-Maker: The Shop and the Family in the Industrial Revolution', in *The Changing Experience of Women*, ed. Elizabeth Whitelegg et al., Martin Robertson, Oxford 1982.
62 Leonore Davidoff, 'Mastered for Life: Servant and Wife in Victorian and Edwardian England', *Journal of Social History*, vol. 7, no. 4, 1974.
63 Ivy Pinchbeck, *Women Workers and the Industrial Revolution 1750–1850*, Frank Cass, London 1977. First published in 1930. Sally Alexander, 'Women's Work in Nineteenth-Century London. A Study of the Years 1820–1850', in *The Rights and Wrongs of Women*, ed. Juliet Mitchell and Ann Oakley, Penguin, Harmondsworth 1976: also in Whitelegg et al. (eds.) op. cit.

Chapter Nine

ON SOME JEWISH MOTIFS IN BENJAMIN

IRVING WOHLFARTH

A MARXIST'S GENESIS

In the beginning was the word.

The Fall, according to Benjamin, is first and foremost the fall of language. It is a fall from the god-inspired language of names and, concomitantly, from the 'birth of the *human* word' (GS, 11, 153; O, 119).[1] As it falls from its original state of being into having, language becomes synonymous with 'abstraction', 'judgment' and 'meaning'. It ceases to be a 'medium', and degenerates into a 'means' of intersubjective 'communication'. 'The word', writes Benjamin, 'must communicate *something* (outside of itself). That is the Fall of the spirit of language' (GS, 1, 153; O, 119). The Fall is thus the origin of reification, the birth of the 'thing' (*Sache*) *qua* 'something', and, by the same token, the genesis of the subject and the law. Man had named the world; the subject reifies it. In the process, Creation is reduced to mere quantitative matter, an object governed by a subject, an accusative subjected to the egocentric dictates of a nominative which, far from naming things once and for all, will never cease to belabour them. If the Paradise of names had been a self-enclosed inside without an outside, the fall now opens up, indeed invents, the abyss of exteriority. It marks the exteriority of mere 'knowledge' (*Wissen*) to real 'knowing' (*Erkenntnis*), of 'signs' to 'names'; and, within the sign, that of the signifier to the signified, as opposed to the 'immanent magic' (GS, 11, 153; O, 119) of unfallen language. Upon eating of the tree of knowledge,[2] man abandons the magic circle, the plenitude, of pure speech. The crime calls forth its punishment: to exile oneself from pure language is already to be expelled from Paradise.

The Fall is the degeneration of the *proper* name into the *arbitrary* sign. Not that *all* signs are arbitrary. Already in the Garden of Eden, Benjamin recounts,

> God gives each beast in turn a sign, whereupon they each appear before man to be given their names. In an almost sublime fashion, the community of God's language with a speechless creation is thus rendered in the image of the sign. (GS, 11, 152; O, 118)

If man's signs betray the name, God's signs inspire it. Having 'breathed his breath' (GS, 11, 147; O, 114) into man, the Lord summons a general assembly at which the whole of Creation may bear witness, in His presence, to His greater glory. Seeing that it is good, He rests content, on the seventh day, with the role of prompter. Having motioned to the animals to appear before man, He calls on man to give them names.[3] Man is, as it were, named God's lieutenant: appointed, without being named, to speak in the name of a mute Creation. By naming it, he re-presents it; by representing it he does it justice – a justice prior to the judgment of good and evil to be subsequently derived from the tree of knowledge. Each name man bestows on Creation is its sole, its true name: *le mot juste*. For it corresponds to/with the divine Logos from which both name and thing jointly spring. It is consubstantial with the ubiquitous breath of the Word. Endowed with an 'immanent magic' which enables it to partake, in person, of the presence of what it represents, namely God in and through His Creation, the name roughly approximates to what modern linguistics would term an icon or a symbol. In his poem 'Correspondances' Baudelaire evokes the 'profound and mysterious unity' of such a 'forest of symbols'.[4]

Fallen signs, on the other hand, are the language of the arbitrary despot portrayed in Baudelaire's third and fourth *Spleen* poems. With the fall comes 'the triumph of subjectivity and the arbitrary rule over things' (GS, 1, 407; OGTD, 233). The arbitrary sign merely *refers* to things in an indifferent, unilateral fashion. The latter no longer have any say in the matter, if indeed they ever did. But before the Fall they did not communicate 'something': they communicated *themselves*. To name things, therefore, prelapsarian man had merely to listen to them. Communicating themselves to themselves, they communicated themselves to him. This self-reflexive circuit of communication partook of the general circulation of a self-addressing Word. According to the analogous epistemology of the early German Romantics expounded by Benjamin in his dissertation, there are no objects, only subjects, all partaking of a common 'medium of reflexion'. Through such self-reflexion they radiate self-knowledge; and, knowing themselves, make themselves known to us (GS, 1, 53–61). German Romanticism converges here with Jewish theology.

'The name which man gives to the thing', Benjamin writes in his early theological essay on language,

> depends on how the latter is communicated to him. Within the name the Word of God is no longer creative, for it becomes in some part receptive, though receptive to language (*empfangend, wenn auch sprachempfangend*). This receptivity is turned towards the language of things themselves, from which, in turn, the word of God silently radiates forth in the speechless magic of nature. (GS, 11, 150; O, 117)

Naming is thus active spontaneity and passive receptivity. Adamic language does not yet subject woman-nature to an arbitrary despotism. Impregnating itself with her language, it has yet to lose its original bipolarity. But the sole origin of Adam's bisexual language is God's creative Word, which engenders the world entirely on its own. It is therefore (like libido for Freud) an entirely male affair, a monologue addressed by a monotheistic God to no one but Himself.[5] 'Let there be' (cit. GS, 11, 148; O, 115): this inaugural speech act gives parthogenetic birth to Creation 'in an absolutely unlimited and infinite manner' (GS, 11, 149; O, 116). The question inevitably arises whether such an unprecedented, performative act of 'spontaneous creation', which cannot by definition contain any 'part' of receptivity, does not thereby already contain its share of arbitrariness. Much the same question applies to name-giving, that masterful activity of human language which is most closely modelled on the absolute spontaneity of the divine Word. Is it, then, possible to name nature without already doing her a certain *in*justice? Even as God's word 'silently radiates forth in the speechless magic of nature', the first intimations of her inarticulate lament are perhaps already beginning to make themselves heard.

Names, in semiological terms, are partly 'motivated' and partly 'unmotivated'. Man freely 'bestows' their names upon the beasts. He is, admittedly, 'summoned' to do so by a God whose word itself already 'names' creation (GS, 11, 148; O, 115), but God does not dictate the actual terms. And yet man merely translates the silent 'password' (GS, 11, 157; O, 123) of Creation into speech, thereby relaying[6] it back to its founding Father. We have, in this translation or correspondence, a theological model of what Benjamin will, more than twenty years later, term 'aura'. 'To experience the aura of a phenomenon,' he will write, 'means to lend it the capacity to raise (*aufschlagen*) its gaze' (GS, 1,647; IU, 188). (Man no longer 'bestows' (*verleihen*) but 'lends' (*belehnen*), and he does so not by naming but by way of poetic reverie.) The pristine theological aura of a thing would thus originally have been the radiance of its name. In which case, the 'loss of aura' that Benjamin will later associate with the advent of mechanical reproduction would date back as far as the Fall.

> In stepping outside the pure language of the name, man makes language into a means (that is, a form of knowledge inappropriate to him), and thereby, at least in part, into a *mere* sign; and this led later to the plurality of tongues. (GS, 11, 153; O, 120)

Was it, then, the Fall – a fall 'into the abyss of the mediateness of all communication (*den Abgrund der Mittelbarkeit aller Mitteilung*)' (GS, 11, 154; O, 120) – that inaugurated the 'age of mechanical reproduction'?! Was the sign *qua* means the technological beginning of the end? And the proliferation of signs and languages which furnish only 'external knowledge' and an 'uncreative imitation of the creative Word' (GS, 11, 153; O, 119), the writing on the wall, the sign of things to come?

The fall of language is immediately identified with the curse of labour. With the expulsion from Paradise, man is condemned to till the fields (*Acker*) by the sweat of his brow. Nature is now an object of technical manipulation, something to belabour, no longer the object of auratic contemplation, a silent language to be listened to. Proper names therewith degenerate into the inappropriate babble of Babel. This latter consequence of the Fall, Benjamin notes, comes about only 'later'. In his reading of Genesis, however, such consequences seem almost contemporaneous, if not indeed synonymous, with the Fall. It is therefore difficult to distinguish cause from effect. Benjamin's version of Genesis is, in this sense, less of a 'genetic' narrative than it first appears. The story it recounts is, in fact, the very genesis of history as such: the 'original history of meaning (*Urgeschichte des Bedeutens*)' (GS, 1,342; OGTD, 166) seen as a fall into the abyss of subjectivity. This primal scene is as real as it is chimerical. At once

160

utter 'evil' and utter 'nothingness' (GS, 1,406; OGTD, 233), it marks the loss of all foundations, all metaphysical realism. It thus prefigures all the distracting 'phantasmagorias' (GS, 1,406 and V, 45 ff; OGTD, 232 and R, 159) to come. Lacking any *fundamentum in re*, the abyss is, in all senses, groundless. In such a perspective, redemption will alternately appear close at hand or out of reach. The merest of gestures would perhaps suffice to dissipate the encircling unreality; but this would also seem to constitute an almost impossible feat.

To erect oneself as subject is already to fall. Benjamin's early theological writings equate the fall not only, like Baudelaire, with the essence of laughter, but more generally with the 'theological essence of the subjective'. 'Evil as such reveals itself to be a subjective phenomenon' (GS, 1,406–7; OGTD, 233). And since evil also stands revealed as empty 'nothingness', subjectivity turns out to be, for all its arbitrary despotism, the epitome of powerlessness. It is sheer vanity: the idle babble, the monumental narcissism, of an abortive project, called Babel. What others term the 'emancipation of the individual' or the 'rise of the bourgeoisie', Benjamin, for his part, calmly puts down to the Fall.

The Fall of man is thus synonymous with the genesis of the subject. It is also the origin of all improper knowledge (*Wissen*), all alienation, all epistemological dualisms. An abyss now yawns between man and nature, the subject and object of human labour. A general subjection ensues. To subject Creation to one's arbitrary rule is not merely to reduce nature to an object. It is also to subject oneself, like the sorcerer's apprentice, to the enslavement of one's own mastery, to the machinations of means without end. But this incipient master/slave dialectic disappears as quickly as it has loomed into view. The enslavement of the master is not accompanied by a liberation of the slave. Man seems rather to drag Creation down with him in his wake.

Thus, the Fall is already, in some sense, the infernal machine of modernity; and modernity, the free fall of history. The Fall may indeed be described, in quasi-historical terms, as the brutal transition from a self-sufficient, 'feudal' economy to a restless dynamic that seems recognizably 'bourgeois'. In terms of the history of philosophy, the shift from names to signs would roughly correspond to the passage from realism to nominalism: from ideas that have a *fundamentum in re* to concepts that are mere *flatus vocis*.[7] But the Fall is less a historical catastrophe than a lapse *into* history. This would imply, on the one hand, that it is not itself describable in historical terms; and, on the other hand, that obliviousness to the Fall may prove to be one of its most baleful historical consequences. As Baudelaire put it, one of the devil's most insidious ruses is to persuade us that he does not exist. The Fall does not, in effect, figure among the objective facts that the modern historian steadily amasses. These facts nevertheless add up to a story he does not know he tells. They amount to the true, though blind, reflection of a 'mounting pile of debris' (GS, 1,698; IU, 258): the junk-heap of history. Benjamin's verdict on 'historicism' as a methodical exercise in oblivion, condemned to perpetuate the Fall it innocently ignores in no way contradicts Nietzsche's diagnosis of it as a hypertrophe of memory. 'A storm', he writes, 'is blowing from Paradise.' This storm is what 'we call progress'. Where 'we' perceive only a 'chain of events', the angel of history 'sees one single catastrophe' (GS, 1,697–8; IU, 257–8). 'We' are, in effect, wedded to progress, historicists to a man, imprisoned in the phantasmagoria of an 'objective', immanent interpretation of history as an orderly progression of events. Benjamin, for his part, takes literally the empiricist quip about history being 'one damned thing after another'. The fading memory of Paradise would constitute the one point of reference which makes it possible to measure the increasing velocity of the Fall.

The Fall is, in short, a self-perpetuating act of forgetting. It originally takes the form of a 'distraction' (*Abkehr*) from that 'contemplation' whereby 'the language of things enters into man' (GS, 11,154; O, 121). Losing the element of passivity that had grounded it in things, language becomes an empty, confused, inflationary activity. Failing to name things, it 'over-names' them (GS, 11,155; O, 122), and falls from 'nobility' (*Adel*) into 'enslavement' (*Verknechtung*). There is, as it were, a political economy of the sign. The story of the Fall parallels that of the sorcerer's apprentice, to whom Marx in turn likened the bourgeoisie. The primitive accumulation of signs already shows all the signs of anarchic over-production. '*Signs* must become confused', writes Benjamin, 'when things are entangled' (GS, 11,154; O, 121). The Garden of Eden turns into a labyrinth. It is as if the fall into the bourgeoisie also marked a relapse into the world of myth. Kafka and Baudelaire, among others, will furnish 'dialectical images' of this process.

Like historicism, the theory of the arbitrary nature of the sign, which Benjamin dismisses as a 'bourgeois view of language' (GS, 11,144; O, 111), is oblivious to the Fall. It does not suspect *how* arbitrary the sign really is. Instead of comprehending the fall of language into signs, structural linguistics, like the historicism it opposes, would unwittingly serve to ratify the effects of the Fall. The sign would be the transcendental commodity of the bourgeoisie, the *a priori* condition of its traffic. Benjamin's early theology of language is not without analogies here to his later materialism. For modern semiology would, in this perspective, possess much the same status that bourgeois theories of political economy had for Marx, or that modern art – 'the distortion of a distorted world' – was to have for the later Lukács. In all three cases, a double reification would be at work: a mimetic redoubling of the perversion one ought to be engaged in comprehending. Language should not, theologically speaking, be said to *be* arbitrary, but rather to have *become* so. *L'arbitraire du signe*, the axiomatic basis of all Saussurean linguistics, would thus not be an innocent category, an objective, structural fact of language, but a crying shame; it would be synonymous with the arbitrary despotism exercised by a *fallen* language. Oblivious to this fundamental truth, modern semiology would be equivalent to 'ordinary language' philosophy. It would merely reflect the present parlous state of language, thereby exacerbating a malady of which it was not a diagnosis but another symptom. Its pretensions to 'science' (*Wissenschaft*) would merely amount to a fallen, 'inappropriate', 'subjective' type of 'knowledge' (*Wissen*).

For the indefinite reference from one sign to another is not considered by Benjamin, as it is by Saussure and his followers, to be the differential *condition*[8] of all language, but its original *catastrophe*. What Derrida terms *différance* is, in Benjamin's eyes, nothing other than the 'nomadic'[9] wandering of the fallen, errant sign. Means have, by deferring their end, lost their way to the 'goal' of language, which is synonymous with its 'origin' (GS, 1,701; IU, 261). The infinite progress/regress of signs *qua* means coincides with the viscous flow of a 'homogeneous, empty time' (GS, 1,701; IU, 262): the lapsed chronology of a 'progress' that progressively propels itself away from Paradise. But signs never completely erase the original names.[10] It is only within a fallen *theory* of the sign that the original language could have disappeared without trace. Just as 'scientific' historiography methodically eliminates 'every resonance of "lament" from history' (GS, 11,231), so modern linguistics banishes 'cratylist' beliefs in the non-arbitrary nature of the sign to the realm of poetic reverie.

The hegemony of signs is, in Benjamin's narrative, an edifice built over an abyss. If their proliferation unleashes the endless power of technological means, it also exhibits a monumental powerlessness. The tower of Babel, which, instead of reaching to the heavens, survives only as a ruined skyscraper, is its allegorical emblem. 'In this distraction from things, which was enslavement, the plan for the tower emerged, and with it the confusion of tongues' (GS, 11,154; O, 121). Such confusion is built into the original project. Babel is doomed from the outset, and the crime once again brings down its subsequent punishment upon itself. Moreover, the busy work of planning it foreshadows the entrepreneurial chaos of bourgeois capitalism. If Babel, the collective 'folly' of windowless monads, anticipates the insanity of the capitalist market-place, there is no 'invisible hand' to guide its fortunes. It is, on the contrary, destined for divine destruction. The ruins of Babel are the allegorical writing on the wall. Seen through the staring eyes of the 'angel of history', they continue to 'grow skyward' in the form of a 'heap of ruins' piled up by the whirlwind of 'progress' (GS, 1,697; IU, 257–8). Such is the 'true image' (GS, 1,695; IU, 255) of the present, as seen by a 'backwards turned prophet'.[11] The pile of rubble, which recalls Eliot's 'heap of broken images' as well as the Kabbalistic 'breaking of the vessels', is more precisely identifiable as a pile of broken names or disused signs. Not for nothing does Benjamin reject the nominalist reduction of ideas to signs as being the hot air it denounces. Where God's creative breath had once animated all Creation, the parodic *flatus votis* of degraded language has now become a gale-force wind which leaves only wreckage in its wake. The storm may call itself progress, but, as Baudelaire observed in a celebrated prose fragment, it 'contains nothing new'.[12] Read against Benjamin's early theology of language, the noise made by the storm of history is that of a god-forsaken language whistling through the abyss of prattle (GS, 11,154; O, 120), a tale told by an idiot, all its 'signification' finally signifying nothing. The Fall is thus the beginning of the end. The ruins of Babel prefigure Golgotha, the leitmotif of baroque allegory; the 'bleak confusion of the charnel-house' (GS, 1,405; OGTD, 232) is in turn a 'dialectical image' of modernity; and modern progress, as witnessed by the *angelus novus*, is a *Trauerspiel* which began with the Fall and progressively regresses towards it.

But Golgotha is not merely the quintessential emblem of mortality.

It also represents 'the allegory of resurrection': 'Allegory departs empty-handed. Unmitigated evil (111) exists only in allegory, is sheer allegory, means something other than what it is. Namely, the non-existence of what it presents' (GS, 1,406; OGTD, 233). Allegory, like the dream that it is, 'contains its end within itself' (GS, V, 59; R, 162), and gropes towards its awakening. It becomes, as it were, its own allegory, the allegory of allegory, and thereby dissolves into its essential nothingness. Awakening from its phantasmagorias, it performs a somersault which reverses the direction of the Fall. In so doing, it exposes the meaning of meaning, the nothingness of signification, to the full light of day. *De profundis*, amidst the ruins of modernity, at the heart of the 'age of perfect culpability',[13] the epileptic aura of the apocalypse prefigures Paradise regained.

What emerges from this reinterpretation of Genesis is, among other things, the prehistory of one strain of western Marxism. The young Benjamin retells the story (both in his essay *On Language as such and on the Language of Man* and in *The Origin of German 'Trauerspiel'*) by way of a theology of language; the young Lukács tells it (in *The Theory of the Novel*) as a history of genres. The new element that both these complementary variations on a millennial, millennarian theme share in common is their identification of the Fall with the advent of bourgeois society. The origins of the present crisis are implicitly located in the origins of history. Only by recalling these origins is it possible to call history to account. For history originates with the forgetting of its origins. Bourgeois society is, in other words, a hell that does not recognize itself as such. Not only is Paradise lost, so too is the very awareness of its loss. Fallen man has forgotten that he has forgotten; like Spinoza's stone, he does not know that he is falling. To start regaining Paradise, we would have to begin to remember that we had forgotten. The crisis is at bottom a metaphysical one; all other crises are merely its consequences; and the way out of the abyss seems to lie in a certain leap of faith. Such is the theological paradigm of alienation, of alienation from alienation, and of redemption as the memory of an oblivious fall.

If this paradigm provides the underlying structure of Benjamin's subsequent materialism, it will also be profoundly altered by what it anticipates.[14] The difficulty lies in deciding which of the two is the 'substructure' of the other. The devious answer contained in Benjamin's closing statement on the matter seems to be: both and neither. It is imperative, according to the first thesis, that the 'apparatus' of historical materialism retain the services of a *deus in machina*. In the guise of a little hunchback he is, it is true, a mere shadow of his former self. But if God were truly dead and buried, historical materialism might not survive him. In more or less secularized guise, his ghost will, at all events, continue to haunt at least one school of western Marxism. Lukács's 'antinomies of bourgeois consciousness', along with the concomitant quest for a 'subject-object' which would transcend the mirror opposites of subjectivism and objectivism; the critique of 'instrumental reason' (Horkheimer) or 'communication' (Adorno) as a fetishism of means without end; the 'dialectic of Enlightenment' as the relapse of modernity into mythical prehistory, and the notion of ideology as an impenetrable, yet insubstantial, veil, the 'enchantment' (*Bann*) of a disenchanted world; the 'wager' (Goldmann) on 'the' revolution as the (un)dialectical reversal of history, be it as its acceleration or as a 'Messianic cessation of happening' (GS, 1,703; IU, 263) – all this is, despite the vast distance that separates a near-mystical theory of language from the practice of historical materialism, latently contained in a version of Genesis which derives the Fall from a fatal slip of the tongue.

Ex- and anti-Marxists have regularly denounced Marxism as 'the god that failed'. Benjamin, for his part, never recanted. It may be that authentically theological versions of Marxism are that much better equipped to weather its so-called 'crisis'. Partly because crisis is already built into their theological paradigm as its crucial, postlapsarian phase; but chiefly because theology, unlike its surrogates, has no need to worship false idols. It is, indeed, on the basis of a certain theological interpretation of the world that profane reality can be effectively rid of its religious inhibitions and thereby left to its own secular devices. Not in the sense of a 'Protestant ethic' which fosters capitalist book-keeping and baroque melancholy. Rather in terms of a Messianic will to fulfillment which ecstatically affirms the world. While such a self-affirmation of the profane world is based on a profoundly theological conception of the profane, the theology in question will prove capable, within certain limits, of whittling away at itself in the name of its own profane imperatives.[15]

THE LAMENT OF NATURE

Nous célébrons tous quelque enterrement.[16]
Faire parler les silences de l'histoire. (Michelet)

In Paradise, at least, everything seems to be in place. God's in his heaven, and all's right with the world. The great chain of being is ordered according to 'degrees of existence . . . already familiar to scholasticism' (GS, 11,146; O, 113). This hierarchy entails a series of asymmetrical relationships. God confers the gift of language on man, but human speech still lacks the creative omnipotence of the Word. Man names the beasts, but does not grant them the faculty of speech. *Noblesse oblige* – but in conferring nobility the nobleman elevates the ennobled to a rank lower than his own. Thus far, though, things still seem more or less in place. Addressing itself to itself, the Word finally returns home. Benjamin describes this circular trajectory in the closing sentences of his early essay on language, which concludes with the same ringing finality as the Word itself:

> The uninterrupted flow of this communication traverses the whole of nature from the lowest forms of existence to man and from man to God. . . . The language of nature is like a secret password that each sentry relays to the next in his own language, but the content of the password is the sentry's language itself. All higher language is a translation from a lower one, until its ultimate clarity unfolds the Word of God, which is the unity of this movement of language. (GS, 11,157; O, 123)

In passing on the Word, nature's sentinels hymn God's praises. Only two pages earlier, however, Benjamin had paused to dwell not on the happiness but on the sadness of Creation. Thereby he had momentarily suspended the 'uninterrupted flow' of the Logos. Beware, warned Gide, of being carried away by your own *élan* (*cit.* GS, IV, 501). Benjamin develops this maxim into a technique of meditation, from whose scrutiny not even the word of God, the stream of the Logos, will be spared. In the face of nature's mourning, the essay on language observes a moment's silence. It will, however, only be a moment. The mourning period is as circumscribed, as symbolic, as a token strike. The parenthesis is then closed, and the Logos resumes

circulation. Towards the end of the book on baroque *Trauerspiel*
nature's lament will be repeated almost verbatim;[17] and there too it
will give way to a final apotheosis. Nature's silence never has the last
word. But it cannot ever be reduced to a quasi-Hegelian 'moment'
within a dialectical movement. 'Thinking involves not only the
movement of thought,' Benjamin will later observe, 'but its arrest as
well' (GS, 1,702; IU, 278). Such thinking here brings the self-
relaying Word to a 'Messianic standstill'. For nature, as she passes
on the Word, is also passed over by it. There is always a remainder
which no *summa theologica* can ever fully comprehend, perhaps because
it is that very summation which forever reproduces it. The irresistible
Logos, like some seducer, never ceases abandoning nature to her
fate. Her stifled lament is the open wound of a closed system.
Benjamin writes that:

> The life of man in pure language was blissful. Nature, however, is
> mute. True, it can be clearly felt (*es ist zwar . . . deutlich zu fühlen*) in
> the second chapter of Genesis how this muteness, named by man
> itself, became bliss only of a lower degree. . . . After the Fall,
> however, when God's word curses the tilling of the soil, the
> appearance of nature is profoundly altered. Now begins her other
> muteness, which is what we mean by the deep sadness of nature.
> It is a metaphysical truth that all nature would begin to lament
> (*klagen*)if it were endowed with language (*wenn Sprache ihr verliehen
> würde*). (And here 'to endow with language' means much more
> than 'to have her speak' (*machen, dass sie sprechen kann*).) This
> proposition has a double meaning. It means, firstly, that nature
> would lament language itself (*über die Sprache selbst klagen*).
> Speechlessness is the great sorrow of nature (and it is for the sake
> of her redemption that the life and language of *man*, and not only,
> as is commonly supposed, that of the poet, are in nature). The
> proposition means, secondly, that she would lament. Lament is,
> however, the most undifferentiated, the most impotent expression
> of language; it contains scarcely more than a sensuous breath; and
> even when there is only a rustling of plants, there is always a
> lament in the air. It is because she is mute that nature mourns
> (*trauert*). Yet the inversion of this proposition leads still deeper
> into the essence of nature: it is her mourning that makes her mute
> (*macht sie verstummen*). There is in all mourning (*Trauer*) the deepest
> inclination to speechlessness, which is infinitely more than the

inability or reluctance to communicate. That which mourns (*Das Traurige*) feels itself to be known through and through by that which is unknowable. To be named – even when the name-giver is god-like and blessed – perhaps always carries with it an intimation of mourning. But how much sadder it is to be named not out of the one blessed paradisical language of names but out of the hundreds of human languages in which the name already withered, yet which, according to God's pronouncement, have knowledge of things. Things have no proper names (*Eigennamen*) except in God. For God's creative Word called them forth by their proper names. In the languages of men, however, they are overnamed . . . overnaming as the deepest linguistic reason for all sadness (*Traurigkeit*) and (as seen from the thing) all silence (*Verstummen*). (GS, 11,154–5; O, 121–2)

If nature were endowed with language, it/she would lament.[18] This hypothesis is said to have not two meanings but rather a single double one. Nature would, in the first place, lament (about) 'language itself'. Already this first meaning invites various interpretations. It is, moreover, unclear whether, as in Kafka, it prompts endless speculation or whether, more traditionally, it demands to be read 'in conformity with the Talmudic doctrine of the forty-nine levels of meaning to be found in each passage of the Torah' (B, 524). How, in turn, distinguish such a doctrine from an over-reading comparable to the 'over-naming' and the 'tragic' 'over-determinateness' (*über-bestimmtheit*) that is here said to obtain between languages since the Fall? (GS, 11,156; O, 122). How, indeed, distinguish here between the tragic and the comic? If nature were no longer mute, what would she still have to complain about? Would she resemble the Jewish mother who, when her son calls, does not stop complaining that he never calls her?

Nature would complain about language 'itself'. Now that she were finally granted language, would she take the opportunity to turn it against itself? Would she be challenging language as such? The first meaning of Benjamin's proposition rapidly engenders a series of logical paradoxes. The plaintiff who is bereft of language has a case, but lacks the means with which to plead it. Once she acquired the latter, she would thereby forfeit the former. How, after all, could language effectively indict itself? Would it not have to swallow its own words? Does it not, by virtue of its very existence, make a cast-iron, albeit biased, case against all have-nots?

Far from shunning language, nature is inevitably drawn to it. Unable to possess it, she aspires instead to its reflected glory. Here as elsewhere the 'image of happiness' is inseparable from that of 'redemption' (GS, 1,693; IU, 256). And it is 'for the sake of her redemption' that man is endowed with speech.

But does his language really redeem nature by naming her? To name nature is no doubt to make her very happy; but it is also to make her somewhat sad. She could, it is asserted, be truly redeemed if she were granted language. But this possibility is inherently un-realizable. Hence the 'metaphysical' nature of its 'truth'. Nothing therefore guarantees that she can or will be saved. She has, in short, every reason to complain.

It is nevertheless equally impossible that she should contest 'language itself'. For that would constitute an equally illogical hypothesis: equally contrary that is, to the workings of the Logos. On the other hand, she would, if she could, 'lament' language – namely, her lack of it. But is not her deprivation endemic to the very logic of creation? Isn't her inarticulateness produced by the self-articulation of the Word? To lament language would, in that case, amount to nothing less than indicting God. Once nature joined the ranks of the haves, however, it would by definition be too late for blasphemy. The verbal complaint she might then voice thus remains as hypothetical as the one she is at present unable – but entitled – to make. But do not the words that Benjamin here voices on her behalf 'represent' her voiceless complaint in both senses of that word? Conversely, isn't her wordless plea all the more disarming for lacking logic, all the more eloquent for being devoid of all rhetoric? Doesn't nature's 'sensuous breath' momentarily stop man's *flatus vocis* in his throat?

The second meaning of Benjamin's hypothesis is intransitive: 'nature would lament'. But lament is, he immediately adds, the most undifferentiated form of language, audible even in the rustling of plants. Nature, then, is *already* complaining. But even if she were able to translate her monotonous lament into language, she would remain more or less inarticulate. Even the most favourable construction that can be placed on Benjamin's hypothesis would scarcely improve her lot.

Its two meanings thus seem to go either too far or nowhere at all. There is therefore no alternative but to start again. What now ensues can best be described in terms of Benjamin's own subsequent analyses, in his meditation on baroque *Trauerspiel*, of the inter-relationship between melancholy and contemplation. 'Method', he there writes, 'is digression' (GS, 1,208; O, 28). The method in question is clearly not Cartesian. For Cartesian discourse is of a piece with the arbitrary despotism of the sign. Both pursue the 'uninterrupted course' of a subjective 'intention' that is oblivious to its resisting objects. The unilinear progress of the 'victors' (GS, 1,696; IU, 256) opens up the commanding perspectives of an 'imperial panorama' (GS, IV, 239) *à la* Haussmann (GS, V, 56–7; R, 159). To this triumvirate of method, subjectivity and domination Benjamin opposes a circuitous discourse which interrupts itself in mid-course in order to renew contact with its objects:

> Thought tirelessly persists in starting afresh, returning painstakingly to the thing itself (*umständlich geht es auf die Sache selbst zurück*). This constant pausing for breath is of the very essence of all contemplation. For in following the various levels of meaning in one and the same object, it receives both the impetus for constantly beginning anew and the justification for its intermittent rhythm. (GS, 1,208; OGTD, 28)

Such is Benjamin's version of a then current philosophical theme: the 'phenomenological' return to the 'things themselves'. One of its distinctive features is the elective affinity that obtains between philosophical contemplation, as Benjamin here defines it, and its chosen object, baroque melancholy. For the latter, too, is charac-terized by an

> astonishing tenacity of purpose, which is perhaps matched among other feelings only by love – and this in no playful sense. For whereas it is not uncommon in the realm of the emotions for the relation between an intention and its object to alternate between attraction and estrangement, mourning is capable of a special intensification, a continual deepening of its intention. Profundity is characteristic above all of sadness. On the road to the object – or rather on the path within the object itself – this intention progresses as slowly and solemnly as the processions of the rulers. (GS, 1,318; OGTD, 139–40)

Whatever the differences that separate the 'continual deepening' of the one from the 'intermittent rhythm' of the other, philosophical contemplation seems to be born, in Benjamin's book on *Trauerspiel*, from the spirit of baroque melancholy. It is as if melancholy contained its own remedy, its philosophical 'anatomy'. Where Cartesian method is arbitrarily applied to *any* object, Benjamin's mimetically adheres to one particular one. Such loving 'epistemo-critical' melancholy runs counter to conventional wisdom. It implicitly judges so-called scientific detachment to be sadly subjective and idealist. Conversely, true objectivity would reside in *another*, materialist sadness, *another* science, that was drawn, gravitationally, to the gravity of things. If the 'progress' of such melancholy contemplation recalls the baroque 'processions of the rulers', these are not to be confused with the 'triumphal procession which leads the present rulers over those who presently lie prostrate' (GS, 1,696; IU, 256). The rhythm is rather that of a funeral procession. The way no longer leads *over* dead bodies, but doubles back *into* its object.

A decisive difference nevertheless distinguishes melancholic from philosophical contemplation. Melancholy, subjectivity and allegory are all, according to Benjamin's reading of Genesis, synonymous with the Fall. 'Tout pour moi devient allégorie', writes the melancholy poet of *Le Cygne*.[19] Melancholy is the Satanic affect of the wilful allegorist who, in projecting his subjectivity on to the world, represents in extreme form the arbitrary despotism of the fallen subject. Here as elsewhere, however, the extremes meet. 'For amidst its knowing [*wissentlich*] degradation of the object', observes Benjamin, 'the melancholic intention keeps faith with its being as a thing in an incomparable manner' (GS, 1,398; OGTD, 225). 'Melancholy', he elsewhere writes,

> betrays the world for the sake of knowledge (*Wissen*). But its
> enduring immersion absorbs dead things into its contemplation in
> order to save them. . . . The persistence which is embodied in the
> intention of mourning is born of its fidelity to the world of things.
> . . . Fidelity, is the rhythm of the . . . descending levels of intention
> in which the rising ones of neo-Platonic theosophy find their
> significantly transformed reflection. (GS, 1,334; OGTD, 157)

In such melancholy, the Fall contemplates itself, and thereby arrests its downward momentum. The 'audacious turn' whereby Renaissance speculation 'discerned in the features of sorrowful contemplation the glimmer of a distant light shining back from the depths of immersion' opens up the prospect of salvation. Benjamin finds this dialectic of redemption enacted in *Hamlet*:

> Hamlet alone is a spectator by the grace of God; but it is only his own fate, not what they play to him, that can satisfy him. His life is the exemplary object offered to his mourning. Before its extinction, it points to Christian providence, in whose womb his mournful images are transformed into blessed existence. Only in such a life as the prince's does melancholy encounter itself and thereby find redemption (*sich einlösen*). (GS, 1,334–5; OGTD, 158)

The true 'play within the play' would thus be Hamlet's encounter with himself. Fallen melancholy looks itself in the face, and is saved by and for contemplation. A significant parallel suggests itself here between this 'exemplary' image of self-contemplation and the relation that obtains, throughout the *Trauerspiel* book, between its own contemplative method and the chosen object of its contemplation: mourning. Just as Hamlet is portrayed as 'passing through [*Durchgang*] all the stations' of the 'intentional space' of melancholy (GS, 1,334; OGTD, 158), so the *Epistemo-critical Prologue* to the book describes the 'course [*Gang*] of an apprenticeship' – an 'ascetic schooling' of the mind intended to enable it to remain in control of its powers in the face of the vertiginous 'depths of the baroque mood' (GS, 1,237; OGTD, 56).[20] The *Trauerspiel* book would thus be a kind of phenomenology that combined Hegel's 'work of the concept' with Freud's 'work of mourning'. It would retrace the stations of the allegorist's journey from the vantage-point of its destination. 'Dürer's genius of winged melancholy' (GS, 1,335; OGTD, 158) would be its emblem. Philosophy would be sublimated melancholy – melancholy which, without falling back into the abyss, could trace 'descending levels of intention' on the 'path within the object'.

This brief digression on the digressive nature of philosophical contemplation, as Benjamin conceives and practises it, may permit a better understanding of the passage before us. We resume where we left it: at the point where *it* seemed to stop and start again. 'It is because she is mute', it resumes, 'that nature mourns.' But it resumes only to break off once again. Benjamin's discourse thereby interrupts the course of the Word, and 'brushes' it 'against the grain'

(GS, 1,697; IU, 257). It is as though thought, by doubling back on itself, were acting in concert with the silence of nature; as if it were indeed gravitating towards nature's gravity. A mimetic, 'auratic' communication would thus be re-established between man and nature. 'Profundity (*Tiefsinn*) is above all characteristic of sadness (*dem Traurigen*).' Such a deep sense of the Fall would in turn be profoundly attuned to the depth of nature's sadness (*Trauer*). Punctuated by intermittent silences and brooding repetitions, Benjamin's meditation lends voice to nature's silence. It thus bids fair to realizing, between the lines, a hypothesis it knows to be impossible.

When it resumes once again, it seems to be reemerging from a deep silence – one that it has momentarily shared with nature. Turning over the proposition it has just advanced, it finally turns it around. This inversion is said to lead 'still deeper' into nature's fallen state: 'it is her mourning that makes her fall silent.' Thus, first, nature *is* mute (*stumm*), therefore she mourns; second, and more profoundly, her melancholy *makes* her mute (*macht sie verstummen*). This is not to imply that under other circumstances nature would have been able to open her mouth. It is rather that, upon further reflection, she can no longer be said to *be* mute, but rather to have *become* so. Or, more precisely, her original silence has been redoubled. After the Fall, we recall, begins her 'other' muteness, 'which is what we mean by the deep sadness of nature'. If, before the Fall, she still communicated her silent language to man, she is no longer able to do so afterwards. The language of silence is henceforth silenced: it is in this sense that she has, since the Fall, 'fallen' silent. Man, the arbitrary despot, no longer listens. Whence her 'deep sadness'. But already her original muteness was the source of a nascent sadness; and it too already had a double cause. Initially deriving from her humble station within the ontological hierarchy of God's creation, it was, Benjamin tentatively suggests, 'perhaps' accentuated by Adam's entry upon the scene. Even before the Fall, the slight but palpable injustice of human language seems to have compounded the ontological inequity of the world. Even prelapsarian naming contains a barely perceptible, structural fault. Such is nature's double bind. For Adamic language also represents the supreme justice of the Word. If man was 'raised above nature' (GS, 1,148; O, 114), it was 'for the sake of her redemption' that his 'life and language' were placed 'in' nature. He thus still represents her only hope of salvation.

There is in all mourning the deepest inclination to speechlessness, which is infinitely more than the inability or reluctance to communicate. That which mourns feels itself to be known through and through by that which is unknowable. To be named – even when the name-giver is god-like and blessed – perhaps always carries with it an intimation of mourning.

Even in Paradise, then, nature's comparative bliss already prefigures her later melancholy. On the one hand, the name of a thing is, we suggested, synonymous with its 'aura'. In both cases, man endows nature with the capacity to respond to his contemplative gaze. On the other hand, the conferral of a name simultaneously appears to involve a 'decline (*Verfall*) of aura' (GS, 1,646; IU, 187), a fall before the fall. For to feel oneself 'known through and through by that which is unknowable' is surely to have been *deprived* of the power to return a look. Two opposite scenarios thus coexist. Nature communicates herself to man; she answers his contemplative look; and the beasts are said to have joyfully 'leaped away' from Adam upon receiving their names (GS, 11,155; O, 121). At the same time, however, being named diminishes nature's responsiveness, so that we also have to visualize her falling silent and casting down her eyes. Traversed by the Word, she seems to be transfixed by the name. The relationship described in Baudelaire's poem *Correspondances* would thus be reversed. It is now *man* who considers *nature* 'with familiar looks'.[21] He knows her 'through and through'. In the process, however, both identifier and identified seem to have lost their identities. They are no longer themselves. Deprived of her gaze, nature is also bereft of her gender. She seems to have become a suffering, allegorical abstraction, an abstract allegory of mourning: *das Traurige*. No sooner is she named – by an equally abstract agency, *vom Unerkennbaren* – than she becomes almost unnameable. This process, moreover, already starts *before* the Fall.

Where, then, is it to be located in the geography and chronology of Genesis? If everything happens before or after the *Fall*, where situate an *incline*? There is in all sadness, writes Benjamin, 'the deepest inclination (*Hang*)' towards silence. Such is the law of its gravity – a law which, Benjamin appears to be hinting, may indeed be a law of nature. Aura is a relation of 'correspondence'. However unequal the partners may be, each responds to the other. Such reciprocity seems nevertheless to be threatened by the unequal order of things: the asymmetrical relations (e.g. knower and known, namer and named) that constitute the ontological hierarchy of Creation. If an 'auratic' communication between man and nature still survives in Benjamin's own meditation on the subject, it does so only in muted form: they jointly mourn its loss.

As long as all was right with the world, a pre-established harmony allegedly obtained between words and things. The act of naming drew its inspiration from the 'selfsame creative Word' (GS, 11,151; O, 118) which called things into existence. Each name was the one and only proper name, which preceded the fall of language into arbitrary signs. Yet names seem, for all their ostensible univocity, to have already been fraught with ambiguity. Even the *mot juste*, it has emerged, was not without its measure of injustice. Such language may have been supposed to say things once and for all, prior to the proliferation of mere words, yet it turns out to require considerable commentary. As seen from below, from the problematic vantage-point of the disadvantaged, as registered, that is, by those they name, names already contain at least an element of the arbitrary. Even in Paradise, then, they had already begun to show the first signs of decay. 'How much more so', we read, once the Fall got underway. But if the all-important distinction between naming and over-naming can be formulated in terms of quantity, and if the absolute opposition between Paradise and the Fall is also a matter of degree, then over-naming, prattle and impropriety would seem to have been more or less present from the very outset. Does not the biblical story, however, stand or fall by the Fall? Can the Word, then, keep its word?

We argued earlier that Benjamin's meditation on Genesis, which is as free as it is faithful, already contains the elements of a certain Marxism. Does it, in the light of the above commentary, now also prompt a 'deconstructive' reading?[22] The latent 'materialism' of its patently 'idealist' discourse – devoted as it is to the Fall of the 'spirit of language' (*Sprachgeist*) – would reside in its messianic capacity to stop itself in its tracks. An affinity would be observable between its meditative technique and the no less intermittent, discontinuous rhythm of materialist intervention. Its deconstructive element, should it exist, would have to do rather with the difficulties it encountered in sustaining its own narrative continuity. Such difficulties do appear to be in evidence. True (*zwar*), the text concedes, it can 'clearly be felt' that nature's bliss is 'only of a lower degree'. A 'but' is rhetorically anticipated which will enable the narrative to proceed. Theology will, as it were, come to its own rescue: reservations are accommodated in advance. Nature will not, however, stay in the place assigned to her – at least not without a murmur. Within the space of a few lines, her 'lower degree' of bliss turns into an 'intimation of mourning'. Once again, however, the story comes to the breach and patches itself up. The Word continues to reproduce itself by multiplying saving distinctions: between silence *before* and falling silent *after* the Fall, between naming and over-naming, etc. Hegel's master slave dialectic sacrificed the master in the interests of its own self-preservation. The divine Word has, for its part, to step over nature's dead body in order to return to itself. Parenthetically, however, Benjamin has it allow nature's wordless lament to give it pause. A timidly audacious 'perhaps' ('To be named . . . perhaps always carries . . .'), underwritten by a robustly apodictic 'truth' which takes the form of a hypothesis ('It is a metaphysical truth that all nature would begin to lament . . .'), has the fleeting effect of blurring the distinctions which keep the theological narrative going.

In attempting to accommodate or contain such aporias, the passage we have been considering does not conceal them from itself. It seems, if anything, to offer them to full view. How, then, decide whether it is powerful enough to accentuate its contradictions or powerless to avoid them? Whether it does its own deconstruction, or rather prompts it? What is the status of its discontinuities? If the rhythm of all meditation requires a constant 'pausing for breath', does this particular pause cut short the breath of the word or, on the contrary, help prolong its existence? For if the focus of nature's lament puts theology to the test, it nevertheless derives from an entirely theological impulse. 'It is for the sake of her redemption that the life and language of *man* . . . are in nature.' Benjamin's meditation seems calculated to save theology from itself. Therein it is perhaps finally closer to Marxism than to deconstruction. Its upshot, at all events, is a latently materialist melancholy born of the spirit of Jewish theology. Nature is the archetype of all those nameless existences whose silence transforms the 'triumphal procession' of the victors into the funeral cortège of the defeated.

THE JUDGMENT OF GOD

> Et dont l'unique soin était d'approfondir
> Le secret douloureux qui me faisait
> languir.[23]

The fall of names into signs is the origin of 'abstraction', 'meaning' and 'guilt'. 'It is in the Fall of man that the unity of guilt and meaning emerges before the tree of "knowledge" in the form of abstraction' (GS, 1,407; OGTD, 233–4).[24] It is also the origin of all 'judgment', which, true to its etymology (*Ur-teil*), is the sign of an original division. Grammatico-logical judgment, dividing sentences into subject and predicate, and moral judgment, distinguishing good from evil, would be two modalities of the selfsame 'prattle'. 'For in reality there exists a fundamental identity between the word that, according to the serpent's promise, knows good and evil, and the word which serves as external communication' (GS, 11,153; O, 119). What we call grammar and ethics would thus rest on distinctions that date back to the Fall.

But abstraction and judgment, while born of the Fall, nevertheless possess the double structure of a *pharmakos*. They designate both the evil and, if not its remedy, at least its corrective. The Fall is evil by virtue of being the *knowledge* of good and evil. Evil thus turns out to be nothing other than human judgment, which is by definition null and void.

For the tree of knowledge provides only *empty* knowledge of good and evil. In a sentence quoted above Benjamin refers to it, accordingly, as the 'tree of "knowledge"'.

> The knowledge [*Erkenntnis*] of good and evil to which the serpent seduces [Adam and Eve] is nameless. It is empty [*nichtig*] in the deepest sense, and this very knowledge [*Wissen*] is itself the only evil that paradise knows [*kennt*]. Knowledge of good and evil abandons the name; it is knowledge from without, the uncreative imitation of the creative Word. . . . The knowledge of things rests [*beruht*] in the name, whereas that of good and evil is 'prattle'. (GS, 11,152–3; O, 119)

Just as the knowledge (*Wissen*, '*Erkenntnis*') of good and evil itself constitutes the very definition of evil, so the 'perfect' knowledge (*Erkenntnis*) of things is, prior to any opposition between good and evil, the only good. 'But already by the seventh day God had known [*erkannt*] with the words of Creation. And God saw that it was good' (GS, 11,152; O, 119). This last sentence should perhaps not be construed as a judgment, but rather as an unspoken blessing, a closing amen. No critical judgment, no dialectical unrest, disturbs the day of rest. Evil has not yet supervened; knowledge is still one with Creation, which God 'knows' in the act of creating it. 'To know' would thus seem to have originally been an intransitive verb ('God had known with the words of Creation'), inasmuch as God would have known nothing outside himself. Fallen knowledge, on the other hand, is always intentional knowledge (*Wissen*) *of* something (outside), a Babel of signs and things, meanings and judgments. Evil, which amounts to the *external* knowledge of good and evil, is thereupon exposed to divine judgment, which summarily enacts the *immediate* knowledge of good and evil. Therein resides the whole difference between good and bad, divine and human, judgment. The saving grace of God's wrath lies in its merciful immediacy.

Just as the name provides the 'ground' (*Grund*) in which the 'concrete elements' of language are 'rooted', so its 'abstract elements . . . are rooted in the word of judgement, the verdict (*im, richtenden Wort, im Urteil*)', which is called forth by the fall of language into the 'abyss [*Abgrund*] of prattle' (GS, 11,154; O, 120). The fall into human abstraction immediately awakens its divine counterpart. 'The prattling man, the sinner' (GS, 11,153; O, 119) is instantly summoned before God's 'Court' (*Gericht*) of judgment. In giving rise to prattling abstraction, the Fall thus also marks the 'origin of abstraction as a faculty of language (*Vermögen des Sprachgeistes*)' (GS, 11,154; O, 120) which has the power to quell, once and for all, the bad infinity of prattle. Despite its abstractness, God's act of judgment shares the definitive immediacy of Adamic language. But in replacing the lost immediacy of the name with that of judgment, God does not restore Paradise to its original state. The 'magic of judgment', unlike that of the name, 'no longer rests blessedly [*selig*] in itself' (GS, 11,153; O, 120).

As an inside without an outside, a present anterior to any differential temporality, Paradise epitomizes what would today be called a 'metaphysics of presence'. Its self-presence is that of a language resting blissfully in itself. But a certain tension already ruffles the calm of its present tense. Paradise is a 'present anterior' or future perfect, a world which will have always already taken place, rather than a purely self-sufficient, self-defining, timeless state. Its perfection is that of a perfect tense, a perfected, inherently anterior past: *selig* also, significantly, means 'blessed' in the sense of 'late', 'dead', 'resting in peace'. 'Happy [*selig*] are those ages when . . .', wrote Lukács of the good old epic days.[25] But was the epic present really as insulated against the future as theorists of the epic such as Lukács, Auerbach and Bakhtin have assumed? 'Not even the existence of the tree of knowledge', Benjamin claims, 'can conceal the fact that the language of Paradise was perfect knowledge' (GS, 11,153; O, 120). Does the tree, then, not even cast an impending shadow on the blissful repose of Paradise? Its disturbing, tempting presence in a perfect world is surely explicable only by a process of tortuous, if not indeed serpentine, logic. If the knowledge it holds out is 'empty', and if 'this very knowledge is itself the only evil that Paradise knows', then the following syllogism can be said to obtain. Paradise already contains the possibility of evil; but such evil is sheer, empty nothingness; *ergo*, Paradise contains nothing evil. But if the tree of knowledge bears only a 'nameless' knowledge, who called it the tree of knowledge in the first place? Was that misleading appellation a sign or a name? What is a misnamed tree doing in the Paradise of names? What is it, in short, if not the ominous, paradoxical presence of the exterior within a garden without exterior, and of a future which will have always already begun sowing division and disseminating difference within a seemingly simple present and/or past?

Divine judgment, the lightning thunderbolt that those who eat the apples bring down upon their heads, has an equally paradoxical status. Where are we to locate a justice which speaks neither the concrete, immediate language of names nor the abstract, instrumental language of signs? Where situate a speech act which is defined as 'immediacy in the communication of abstraction' (GS, 11,154; O, 120)? It can, surely, be both immediate and abstract[26] only if it simultaneously precedes and succeeds the Fall. God's judgment on fallen language retains the 'immediacy', 'purity' and 'magic' of unfallen language. What distinguishes the two is the vigilance with which the one guards over the other. The 'state' of purity yields to a 'more rigorous purity', namely the act of 'purification'. God can no longer 'rest' content when He no longer sees that everything is good. Divine judgment lacks the 'immanent magic' which characterizes a language capable of 'resting' entirely within itself. But if, 'its magic is different from that of names', it must be even more clearly distinguishable from that of signs. For there *is* such a thing, according to Benjamin, as a magic of signs. Magic survives the Fall, however, only by forfeiting its innocence. Stepping outside 'its own immanent magic', language now becomes 'expressly [*ausdrücklich*], as it were externally, magical' (GS, 11,153; O, 119). The magic of divine judgment must, therefore, be located somewhere between that of names and signs, patrolling in advance the frontier that will separate them. Thus, however positive it may be in comparison with the utter vanity of 'prattle', it cannot match the pure positivity of naming, let alone creating. Whereas the name rests intransitively within itself, the 'word of judgment' [*das richtende Wort*] is transitively directed [*sich richten*] against evil.[27] It is as if, in order to bring errant language to justice, the Word had had in turn to step somewhat outside itself. Not that a dialectical relationship with the outside is thereby established. The divine word does not *mediate*; it does not even *sentence*, that is, speak in sentences; it does not, perhaps, even take the form of a grammatico-logical judgment. Divine judgment is the Logos in action; hence the 'immediacy' of its 'abstraction'. Acting in the name of the name, such destruction aims to efface its own traces.[28] For if it should never have been necessary in the first place, it is, by the same token, destined to become superfluous. The 'word of judgment' ought not, for all its finality, to have the final word, but should rather be reabsorbed, without a trace, into the plenitude of the Logos. If it is indeed necessary, as Benjamin observed to Adorno upon returning his thesis on Husserl, to 'cross the icy desert of abstraction', the aim of the exercise is to reach the promised land, the milk and honey of concreteness.[29]

Divine justice can barely even be said to *punish* human judgment. Before God's gaze, earthly justice shrinks into insignificance.

> And while, in the earthly court [*Gericht*] the wavering subjectivity of judgment is deeply anchored in reality by means of punishments, in the heavenly court the illusoriness of evil stands fully exposed [*kommt der Schein des Bösen ganz zu seinem Recht*]. Here self-confessed subjectivity triumphs over the deceptive objectivity of the law [*Recht*], and is incorporated into divine omnipotence . . . as hell. (GS, 1,407; OGTD, 234)

Thus, by a massive paradox, the only human justice worthy of the name would be summary justice without trial.[30] It alone would be beyond all suspicion of being arbitrary. Conversely, due process, the protracted agony of legal justice, would be the epitome of injustice: Kafka's *Prozess*. Like all other institutions erected on the shaky foundations of the Fall, it would, in the perspective of Benjamin's theology of language, be founded on the arbitrariness of the sign.[31] One might, indeed, speak in this context of *L'arbitrage du signe*. Its arbitrary findings stand revealed, in the light of divine justice, as a series of 'wavering' attempts to deny an underlying indecision. Just as all the facts and figures accumulated by historicism in order to fill the void of 'homogeneous, empty time' (GS, 1,701; IU, 260) cannot exorcise a bottomless spleen, no amount of ritual punishment can disguise the inherent vanity of legal justice. 'Deeply anchored' in the 'reality' of the 'abyss', its judgments are so many groundless signs of ontological duplicity. They are therefore incapable of casting the final verdict; they merely prattle on. Too subjective to acknowledge their own subjectivity, they hide behind a facade of objectivity. Subjectivity thus coincides with reification. What we fondly call 'the law' would, like the 'bourgeois conception of language' (GS, 11,144; O, 110), represent fallen man's attempt to legitimate the arbitrary.

The institution of subjectivity and the subjectivity of its institutions emerge, in the light of Benjamin's apocalyptic eschatology, as inseparable consequences of the Fall. If the 'law' is synonymous with 'subjectivity', the subject, conversely, is definable as one who, unlike nature, insists on his rights. He forfeits his right to exist by the very act of asserting it. By raising the question of good and evil, he already falls from grace. The laws he then devises in order to regulate a fallen world merely perpetuate the Fall. Indefinite 'adjournment' of 'the proceedings' (GS, 11,427; IU, 129) is the inevitable upshot. Divine justice, on the other hand, always constitutes a Last Judgment,[32] which is summarily executed with all the performative force of the creative Word: 'This judging [*richtende*] word expels the first human beings from Paradise' (GS, 11,153; O, 119–20). It is effective immediately because, unlike human judgment, it arises from an immediate knowledge of good and evil. If it admits of no deferral, this is because it brooks no 'difference'.[33] And if men's laws are a travesty of divine justice, this is because their language constitutes a 'parody' of the Logos. '*Signs* must become confused, where things are entangled' (GS, 11,154; O, 121). Where signs indefinitely refer to one another, decisions are indefinitely referred elsewhere, constantly deferred until a later time. Such endless deferral is the very structure of fallen time. The bureaucratic maze of human justice is synonymous with the labyrinthine proliferation of fallen, referential language.

Divine justice 'rises', like a phoenix, from the Fall. It regenerates the 'injured' magic of the name. This 'new immediacy' is not, however, as immediate as it seems. For if divine judgment is prompted by original sin, the latter is provoked by the existence of temptation.

> This judging word expels the first human beings from Paradise; they themselves have provoked [*exzitiert*] it, by virtue of the eternal law according to which this judging word punishes – and expects – its own awakening as the only, the deepest guilt. (GS, 11,153; O, 119–20)

Good abstraction thus precedes bad abstraction as its anticipated punishment. Suspended in advance over the potential sinner, divine judgment 'expects' to be awakened by the transgression of its own dormant, eternally pre-existent law. Such transgression is characterized as the loss of an original immediacy. But is not its long-awaited punishment, for all its restoration of immediacy, more premeditated, and thus more 'mediated', than the crime? The wrath of God, it is true, does dispatch the sinner with lightning speed. But if the Logos, in order to protect its self-presence, anticipates its transgression, does it not thereby also betray what it protects? Was not original sin initiated before the fall? Did man fall all by himself, or was he also tripped by a self-fulfilling prophecy?

For all its blissful repose Paradise seems to have been fraught with suspense, excitement and abstraction. If man effectively expels himself from Paradise, God already 'expects' as much. No sooner does he 'excite' His law than he is cited to appear before it and summarily cast outside. One ex-citation, one ab-straction, prompts another. It is as if a jealous God were lying in wait for signs that his name might be taken in vain; as if, like Argus, his law were both awake and asleep.

Paradise implicitly knows what lies outside it. That it should contain the tree of knowledge already indicates as much:

> The tree of knowledge did not stand in the garden of God for the sake of the information it might have supplied concerning good and evil, but as a sign of judgment hanging over the questioner [*Wahrzeichen des Gerichts über den Fragenden*]. This immense irony is

the hallmark [*Kennzeichen*] of the mythical origin of law [*Recht*]. (GS, 11,154; O, 120)

If the tree of knowledge is to be a true, non-arbitrary sign (*Wahrzeichen*) of divine justice, its justification cannot lie in the arbitrary, plural items of 'information' (*Aufschlüsse*) that man will be tempted to seek from it. For it would, in that case, have amounted to an *open* invitation to original sin. Does it not, however, constitute a *tacit* one, both prompting and forbidding sinful thoughts? If transgression is condemned in advance, this is ostensibly in order that the suspended judgment of the law may not actually have to take effect. What provokes the wrath of God is thus nothing other than the fact of having had to be provoked. It is directed solely against those that disturb its peace. But surely it provokes them as much as they provoke it?

Divine justice is, in principle, clearly distinguishable from human judgment. The Word of God is to human language what the original is to a 'parody' (GS, 11,153; O, 119). But, however rigorously such distinctions are maintained, the judgment suspended over the 'questioner' itself raises questions that threaten to blur them. Is the God who lies in wait distinguishable from an evil genius? Is the serpent merely a scapegoat? And Paradise a nascent penal colony? Doesn't the distinction between prohibition and its transgression also transgress itself? Doesn't the irony which turns the question against the questioner, the accusation against the plaintiff, also return to plague its inventor? Doesn't it hang over the judge as well as the judged? Doesn't its duplicity violate the univocal simplicity of the Logos? If Benjamin elsewhere establishes a diametrical opposition between divine justice and the mythical character of human law, does he not in the above-quoted passage collapse this crucial distinction by tracing the latter to the former?[34]

The father in Kafka's strange families battens on the son, lying on top of him like a giant parasite. He preys not only on his strength, but on his right to exist. The punisher (*Der Strafende*) is also the accuser (*der Ankläger*). The sin of which he accuses the son seems to be a kind of original sin. For whom does Kafka's definition fit better than the son? "Original sin, the old injustice committed by man, consists in his unceasing reproach that he has been done an injustice, that an original sin has been committed against him." But who is accused of original sin [*Erbsüde*] – that of having produced an heir [*Erben*] – if not the father by the son? The sinner would in that case be the son. But one should not conclude from Kafka's definition that the accusation is sinful because it is false. Nowhere does Kafka say that it is made wrongfully. It is a never-ending trial that is pending here. . . . Laws and definite norms remain unwritten in the prehistoric world. A man can unsuspectingly transgress them . . . the transgression is not accidental but fated, a destiny which appears here in all its ambiguity. In a cursory consideration of the ancient notion of fate, Hermann Cohen came to the "inescapable conclusion" that "its very ordinances entail this transgression, this defection [*Abfall*]." The same is true of the legal authorities whose procedures are directed against K. One is taken back to some prehistoric world far earlier than the giving of the Law on twelve tablets, written law having been one of the first victories gained over that world. (GS, 11,411–12; IU, 114–15)[35]

What is remarkable, in this context, about the above discussion is that it can, without much prompting, also be read as a subversive commentary on Benjamin's own earlier reading of Genesis. Man committed original sin, according to Kafka, by insisting that it had been committed against him, presumably by his Maker. It is by perpetually claiming that he is its victim that he keeps perpetrating it. Relations between man and God would thus resemble those described in Kafka's letter to his father, where both are implicated in an infinite regress of charges and counter-charges. To be a father or a son is already to be accused thereof. The father accuses the son of the original sin of accusing him of original sin. Conversely, the original sin (*Erbsünde*) of which the father stands accused is to have engendered an heir (*Erben*), to have fathered a son born into the family drama of Genesis. Original sin, or: who started it? Kafka does not, according to Benjamin, adjudicate between the rival accusations. His redefinition of original sin as the complaint about it would thus be neither pious nor blasphemous, neither pro- nor anti- theological.[36] On the one hand, the son remains guilty of protesting too much; on the other the fact that his reproach is inherently sinful does not, Benjamin notes, necessarily deprive it of validity. The trial between father and son is, clearly, a process – a *Prozess* – that can never end.

All this surely sounds by now uncannily familiar. Does not Genesis, as we have read Benjamin's reading of it, say much the same thing? The original sin that consists, according to Benjamin, in awakening its own condemnation bears a remarkable resemblance to the one that, according to Kafka, boomerangs back on the accuser. Our earlier suspicions that Benjamin's theologically impeccable account of the Fall is nevertheless not quite proper may now seem somewhat less far-fetched. They prompt the question whether, for all the alleged immediacy and finality of divine justice, God's impending judgment on fallen man does not institute a never-ending trial between the divine accuser and the filial plaintiff, 'the one who punishes' and 'the one who questions'. Benjamin's God would here resemble Kafka's fathers, those 'giant parasites' whose prohibitions presuppose their transgression and deprive the nascent subject, the son who insists on his rights, of his very right to exist.

How therefore is original sin (*Erbsünde*) to be distinguished from a mythical family curse (*Erbfluch*)? Is not the divine judgment that is 'suspended over man' (GS, 11,157; O, 123) like some sword of Damocles as menacing as the 'ancient notion of fate'? Does monotheism, then, mark no clear and univocal advance over the 'ambiguity' of myth? Adam's sin is committed knowingly. It differs to that extent from preordained, mythical transgression. But it is in the context of *The Trial* – a pre-patriarchal, indeed pre-mythical 'swamp world' (GS, 11,428; IU, 130) extending back far beyond Moses and monotheism – that Benjamin introduces Kafka's definition of original sin. The implicit effect of this montage is to embed monotheism within the 'prehistoric world' of myth. Yet, for Benjamin as for Cohen, monotheism also marks a decisive victory *over* the mythical order. Indeed, a saving distinction between theology and myth constitutes one of the basic axioms of his thought. Without some such critical opposition, history *qua* progress could not even be envisaged. Like Kafka, Benjamin sometimes questions whether any such progress *has* historically taken place (GS, 11,428; IU, 130), the 'storm' we *call* 'progress' (GS, 1,698; IU, 258) having been one long prehistoric catastrophe. But the fact that the law is said, in the above-quoted passage, to have regressed behind its written stage negatively confirms at least the *idea* of progress. The advantage of the narrative chronology implicit in such an idea is its capacity to hold out prospects, to open up perspectives, to locate evil as a stage or moment, and to look, if not to go, beyond it. But given the difficulty we have just encountered in clearly distinguishing between periods, the question arises whether the will to periodize is not motivated by the need to contain an evil too abysmal to be controlled, even as an 'abyss', by a 'genetic' scheme.

Genesis, as read by Benjamin in 1916, foreshadows Kafka. Kafka in turn refers back to Genesis. And Benjamin's essay on Kafka sheds an oblique light on the reading of Genesis he had undertaken eighteen years before. Kafka's universe, he there writes, is subject to a law of 'displacement'; it will, however, take only a 'slight adjustment' on the Messiah's part for everything to fall back into place (GS, 11,433; IU, 135). But does it not, conversely, take equally little for Genesis to fall *out* of place? Gershom Scholem used to tell his students to approach Jewish mysticism by way of Kafka. What is so 'crazy' about Kafka, Benjamin wrote to Scholem in 1938, is that 'this utterly modern world of experience should have been conveyed to him precisely by the mystical tradition' (B, 762; IU, 142). Not only does Kafka's work, on his reading, describe an 'ellipse' between mystical experience and modernity, but the elliptical relationship between these seemingly remote poles is itself uncannily intimate. The incommensurability of modern experience can be measured only in and through the mystical tradition. 'This, of course', Benjamin adds, 'could not have happened without devastating processes within this tradition.' Was, then, the threat to tradition contained, in a double sense, *within* it? In that case, Benjamin would not even have had to 'brush' Genesis 'against the grain' (GS, 1,697; IU, 259) to intuit Kafka's world within it. On discovering Kafka, he would also rediscover the haunting melancholy of his early theological writings. Already there a grave sense of the limits of salvation quietly threatened to exceed the theology that contained it. But only an overarching theology had the resources to limit its mourning to a period and to accommodate its irony as a 'mastered moment' (Kierkegaard).

Man's original sin was to take justice into his own hands, to insist on lodging a complaint. Throughout the ensuing, never-ending trial between father and son, another stifled complaint can be faintly heard. Where is the woman in this male duel? Extrapolating from Benjamin's essay on language, we may identify her with nature. There nature is, unlike man, momentarily entitled to complain – namely, of the original sin committed against her by the father and compounded by the son. Her complaint is, in its way, as persistent as the son's. It is, however, innocent of all legality. But even the highest court is implicated by her testimony.

De profundis, from the depths of the Logos, nature silently laments her immemorial crucifixion. But what if, by some extraordinary turn of events, she were granted her day in court?

> In the mirror which the prehistoric world held before him in the form of guilt [Kafka] merely saw the future emerging in the form of judgment. Kafka did not, however, say what it was like. Was it not the Last Judgment? Does it not turn the judge into the defendant? Is the trial not the punishment? Kafka gave no answer.

'The judgment', we read in *The Trial*, 'does not come all at once; the proceedings gradually turn into the judgment.'

THE TRIAL OF NATURE

> How long such trials last, especially of late.
>
> (Kafka, *The Trial*)
>
> This is perhaps the blasphemous point of the trial: God himself, who punishes man's forgetfulness by the life He assigns him, thereby prevents him from remembering. (GS, 11,1258)

> Kafka does not tire of listening to animals for what has been forgotten. They are not, certainly, the goal, but one cannot do without them. (GS, 11,430; IU, 132)

> Oh, plenty of hope, an infinite amount of hope – but not for us. (Kafka, cit. GS, 11,414; IU, 116)

Idea for a Mystery Play

Represent history as a trial in which man, as the counsel (*Sachwalter*) of speechless nature, lodges a complaint against Creation and the non-appearance of the promised Messiah. But the Court decides to hear witnesses for the future. There now appear the poet, who can feel it, the sculptor, who can see it, the musician, who can hear it, and the philosopher, who knows it. Their testimony thus conflicts, even though all testify to his coming. The Court dares not admit its indecision. Hence an endless succession of new complaints and witnesses. Torture and martyrdom ensue. The jury-benches are occupied by living creatures (*Lebenden*) who listen both to man-the-prosecutor

(*Mensch-Ankläger*) and the witnesses with equal mistrust. The jurors' seats are inherited by their sons. The dread finally seizes them that they might be driven from their benches. In the end, all the jurors flee, only the prosecutor and the witnesses remain behind. (GS, 11,1153–4)[37]

Benjamin places the above scenario, which he wrote under the impact of Kafka's *Trial*, in the tradition of the medieval mystery play. But whereas the latter dramatizes the fate of Everyman, whose soul wavers between God and the Devil, Benjamin's concern here is with the passion and possible redemption of nature at the hands of man, whose representative status has meanwhile become that much more ambiguous. Man no longer represents Everyman. He represents his client. It is now Gretchen, not Faust, who is the focus of attention.

In taking up nature's lament (*Klage*), Benjamin's script also harks back to the medieval 'literature of complaint' (*Klageliteratur*, GS, 1,316; OGTD, 137) and beyond that to the biblical song of lamentation (*Klagelied*). But its closest precedent is the German baroque *Trauerspiel*, the 'play of sorrow', which, according to Benjamin, finds its modern counterpart in Baudelaire's lyric poetry. In both these allegorical genres, transcendence is no longer what it once was. The heavens are clouded over by the 'low and heavy sky' of the *Spleen* poems, where an interminable cortège files slowly past 'without drums or music',[38] silently echoing the pomp and circumstance of baroque processions (GS, 1,298; OGTD, 298); and the 'majestic sorrow' of a 'passing woman' in 'deep mourning'[39] seems in turn to allegorize the god-forsaken sadness of what Benjamin, in his book on baroque *Trauerspiel*, calls 'Nature-History' (GS, 1,353; OGTD, 177). No glimmer of salvation relieves the gloom. Unlike a medieval mystery play or a classical tragedy, the baroque *Trauerspiel* knows no final end. Benjamin interprets the even number of its acts as indicative of endless mourning, repetitive lament, a trial forever deferred (GS, 1,316; OGTD, 137). Therein lies the deepest link between baroque *Trauerspiel* and the above scenario.[40] Endless delay is not merely the original cause but also the permanent condition of its legal proceedings, which thereby perpetuate the original scandal and serve only to reproduce themselves. The trial (*Prozess*) *is* the process, the endless procession of time itself, the wear and tear of due process which, in due course, includes 'torture and martyrdom' among its procedures. It turns out to be a trial in every sense.

So, too, does nature's complaint. The German word *Klage* has precisely the same double meaning as 'complaint' in English.[41] Benjamin's treatise on German *Trauerspiel*, completed two years before, refers not merely to nature's 'complaint', but also to the 'trial of the creature', whose 'complaint against death – or whomever else it may indict – is shelved at the end of the *Trauerspiel* after having been only half dealt with' (GS, 1,316; OGTD, 137). Nature's complaint has, in the process, become a legal one. But the double genitive implicit in the phrase 'trial of the creature' points to a telltale ambiguity. Is nature the subject or the object of her trial? If she is clearly the subject, she is still subjected to it. Throughout her trial she will be obliged to pay the costs. Unable to initiate proceedings in her own name for lack of a voice of her own, she is destined to remain an absent scapegoat even on her day in court. Whence her never-ending complaint. And yet her mute powerlessness has the power to undermine the very legitimacy of the law. No law can ever silence her plaintive plea, because it is the bad conscience of the law. In this sense, her deep sadness conspires with such contrary Brechtian virtues as 'trust, courage, humor, cunning, tenacity' to 'call into question every victory, past and present, of the rulers' (GS, 1,696; IU, 255).

Nature laments indefinitely, intransitively. But she does not pronounce judgment or complete a sentence. Nor does she exchange the position of an accusative object for that of an accusing subject. Her subjectless lament also remains practically without object. What she laments is something that has failed to materialize, namely the arrival of the Messiah, her promised bridegroom.[42] Pure mourning does not, Benjamin wrote in response to Scholem's essay *Über Klage und Klagelied*, necessarily end in complaint (*Klage*) (B, 182). Nature's mourning is a notable case in point. Her *Klage* is purely hypothetical: she *would* complain *if* she had the words. Her mourning is thus not a case of melancholia. For the complaints (*Klagen*) of the melancholiac turn out, according to Freud's essay *Mourning and Melancholia*, to be disguised accusations (*Anklagen*) turned back against the self.[43] Nature's lament, on the other hand, no more lends itself to accusation than her plaintive mourning leads to querulous complaint. The 'purity of her feelings' is devoid of all corrupting psychology, and points to the inherent limits of the law. Therein may lie something of that 'hope' that is certainly not 'for us' as psychological subjects or, concomitantly, as subjects before the law.[44]

In the above scenario, however, nature's immemorial plaint *does* assume the form of a legal complaint (*Anklage*) lodged on her behalf by a human prosecutor (*Mensch-Ankläger*) who lends her his voice. But the legalization of her lament serves merely to make matters worse. The trial will turn out to be a travesty of justice. Its ironical effect will be to place *itself* on trial. In the process, the very justice of divine Creation will be implicated.[45] For, in going to court over an unkept promise, the plaintiff is indirectly calling God's reliability into question. But – to return to the 'immense irony' that the court suspends over the 'questioner' – what right did she have in the first place to question the justice to which she must inevitably resort? If she is to be represented in court, nature has no other recourse except to the one animal that is possessed of the gift of speech. But does not man, by virtue of that monopoly, already belong to the other side? Does not (his) language harbour a built-in bias against the have-nots on behalf of the Logos? How can it presume to speak in their name? How is the justice it serves competent to decide on a pre-verbal complaint which mutely questions its authority? Do not its various officers, notwithstanding their adversarial roles, collectively form a clique? Should not, therefore, human justice exclude itself from the case? Is it not prejudged? If the monologic Word exercises a monopoly on justice, does it not by the same token have a monopoly on *in*justice? How can it therefore presume to represent the other without thereby compounding the original injustice? Does not that injustice already cry to high heaven? Who, on the other hand, can ever do the plaintiff justice if not the court in question? But the endless succession of new trials and tribulations to which the legalization of nature's complaint gives rise await a final judgment that will never come. The 'immense irony' that Benjamin had evoked in connection with the 'mythical origin of law' also hangs over the trial of nature. And here too it remains poised between gravity and farce, the *Trauerspiel* and the Jewish joke.

Nature lodges a complaint against the non-fulfillment of a promise: the Messiah has not come. Lamenting her interminable privation, she appeals to the law. But the court merely perpetuates, indeed ratifies, the delay. It is as if the absence of the Messiah cannot but prejudice the outcome of a trial devoted, precisely, to the issue of his non-appearance. 'The Court dares not admit its indecision.'[46] Its workings confirm the theological verdict on human justice that Benjamin had first pronounced in his *Critique of Violence*. Seeking refuge behind formalities and adjournments, confusing means with ends, such 'wavering subjectivity of judgment' (GS, 1,407; OGTD, 234) can assert its arbitrary authority only by an external show of force. Only 'by means of punishments' is it 'anchored in reality'. That 'torture and martyrdom' punctuate nature's trial should not, therefore, come as a surprise. They belong to the very logic of due process. Just as clock time in Baudelaire's poetry adds up, like falling snowflakes, to an avalanche, so an endless succession of legal delays here results in an accelerating fall. For, it is, according to Benjamin business as usual, the normal course of events that constitutes the 'catastrophe' (GS, 1,683). However 'deeply anchored in reality' it may be, human justice sinks ever deeper into a morass of signs. Reproducing the referential structure of the sign, referring its decisions from one session to the next, the court in turn betrays its promise. If nature is mute, human justice is both deaf and blind. But no Last Judgment, no bolt from the blue, will intervene to end the babble. It was, on the contrary, the non-arrival of the Messiah that occasioned the whole proceedings in the first place. Nor is it clear how even a Messianic intervention could remove the grounds for nature's complaint. For nature is the very ground of Creation. Unlike the proletariat, which can in theory be abolished, or the 'damned of the earth', who can in principle be saved, the earth itself would appear bereft of any future prospects. Its mourning would seem as inescapable as the laws of gravity. Even if Benjamin himself elsewhere salutes the resurrection of nature as the corollary of social revolution,[47] how do we know that this is not a further instance of human, all-too-human babble, the discourse of a 'philosopher' who claims to 'know' the Messianic future?

Benjamin wrote his *Idea for a Mystery Play* after reading Kafka's *Trial*. In both cases, the tortuous course of human justice is synonymous with an ever deeper regression into myth. For the court is nothing short of mythical. Its bureaucratic authority, far from ensuring impartiality, seems only to confirm the obscurity of its mandate. God no longer guarantees the 'objectivity' (GS, 11,151; O, 119) of translation. And it is in a very different, legal sense that man henceforth assumes the role of nature's 'spokesman'.[48] From being the 'lord of nature' called upon by God to 'give names to things' (GS, 11,144; O, 111), he falls to the rank of a professional advocate, a mere 'manager of things' (*Sachwalter*). He continues, certainly, to speak in nature's name. But, instead of doing her justice by reciting her name before the Lord, he inevitably betrays her cause. Like the phrase 'trial of nature', the compound noun *Mensch-Ankläger* (literally, 'man-prosecutor') contains two possible meanings, one of which ('prosecutor of man') may at any moment subvert the other ('human prosecutor'). Man-as-prosecutor indicts himself. It is in this inaudible irony that nature's complaint finds its most eloquent expression – an irony that enacts the judgment which human justice unwittingly pronounces upon itself. Instead of hiding its indecision behind bureaucratic procedures, language here *exhibits* its duplicity.

In God's 'heavenly Court', Benjamin had written two years before, 'self-confessed subjectivity triumphs over every deceptive objectivity of the law' (GS, 1, 407; OGTD, 234). One might conclude from this that artists make better spokesmen for nature than do her legal representatives. In the present instance, however, man turns out to be no more convincing as a witness than as a lawyer. It is true that the figure of the witness occupies a special place in Jewish tradition. Whether he sings God's praises (GS, 11,246) or gazes in mute horror at the catastrophe of history (GS, 1,697; IU, 259), Benjamin's *angelus novus* is a messenger of that tradition; and Baudelaire is termed a 'witness in the historical trial brought by the proletariat against the bourgeois class' (GS, V, 459). In nature's trial, on the other hand, not even the best-intentioned of human witnesses proves to be above suspicion.

The court decides to assemble expert testimony in the field of futurology. All the witnesses duly testify to the coming of the Messiah. What the artists merely *sense*, the philosopher already *knows* (*weiss*). Here too a classical hierarchy reasserts itself, one that has always granted philosophy pride of place as the final arbiter of truth. But the pretensions of philosophical systems to absolute knowledge, like historicism's 'lewd' (GS, 111,286) gestures towards 'universal history' (GS, 1,702; IU, 262), constitute an ideological abuse of legitimate Messianic aspirations. They amount to the premature 'anticipation', indeed the prostitution, of the true 'teaching' that is yet to come (GS, 1,207–8; OGTD, 28). System-builders, like the builders of Babel, usurp the Messiah's prerogatives, thereby erecting further monumental evidence of the fall into mere 'knowledge' (*Wissen*) (GS, 1,407; OGTD, 233). Just as fallen knowledge mistakes itself for unfallen truth, so philosophical systems amount to windy fragments masquerading as the whole. The upshot is not *less* but *more* fragmentation, a 'syncretism' (GS, 1,207; OGTD, 28) or 'esperanto' (GS, 1,1235) which merely parody the Messianic idea of a universal language and history. Concealing a chaos of conflicting idioms and disparate knowledge behind the tawdry appearance of an all-embracing synthesis, such phony Messianism merely documents the dispersal it claims to have transcended. As a theoretical system, Messianism is a contradiction in terms.[49] Such inflated claims paradoxically reduce it to another -ism, one which typically imagines it has resolved the babble of mere -isms.

Nor does the 'language of the poet', contrary to what is 'commonly supposed', enjoy any privileged ontological status *vis-à-vis* the redemption of nature (GS, 11,155; O, 121). Instead of 'purifying the words of the tribe' (Mallarmé), the poet here appears merely to have added to the chaos of signs; just as the musician and the sculptor seem in turn to have increased the confusion of artistic tongues.[50] No longer capable of translating the 'language of things into an infinitely higher language', they seem rather to have succumbed to the 'overdeterminateness' (*Überbestimmtheit*) that obtains in the tragic relationship between the languages of human speakers (GS, 11,156; O, 122). A gentle but inexorable irony thus deflates the pretentions of the whole cultural-humanist profession. Benjamin is said to have called philosophy the 'language of pimps'. Messianism, clearly, can also be a racket, for all its opposition to the status quo. The expert testimony of the 'theological professional' (B, 613) serves merely to reproduce a deteriorating situation. The artists may prefigure the coming of the Messiah, but their lasting contribution is, ironically, to help prolong the wait. His coming would perhaps, if anything, *upset* their calculations. 'May the Messiah come', it has been said, 'but I do not wish to see him.'

'Their testimony thus conflicts.' The common cause has disintegrated into yet another shibboleth. Is this because the differences between the muses, or the division of labour between the senses, originate with the fall from a previously undivided language? Or is it only during the subsequent history of the Fall that they have hardened into a conflict of faculties? As Benjamin here presents them, the various idioms of Jewish Messianism do not seem capable of being reconciled even among themselves, oriented though they are toward the Messianic 'reconciliation' (GS, IV, 15; IU, 75) of all languages. 'There is, in God's name', Adorno will later write to Benjamin, 'only the one truth' (B, 787); therefore all true, all truly radical, impulses must finally converge. Adorno would seem here to be urging Benjamin's own *Theologico-Political Fragment* upon its author. But in so doing he is slightly parodying it. *When* exactly are the differences to be resolved? For Messianic fulfilment is, according to that fragment, a matter of each passing moment. The knowing philosopher who claimed to reconcile the conflicting testimony of the other witnesses by referring them to some grand but indefinite future would thus emerge as another friend of the court.

The role played by the witnesses in Benjamin's scenario seems to point to a certain *embourgeoisement* of the Messianic impulse. The coming of the Messiah has become a largely academic question; and the professional utopians, as Georges Sorel might have called them, seem to prefer waiting for godot to losing their tenure. It is as if Bloch's 'principle of hope' had been consolidated into a (counter-) cultural institution, and thereby incorporated into the status quo. In the process, all possibility of a united opposition has been lost. Utopia is quietly jettisoned amidst the Babel that is officially dedicated to its realization. Its prophets can safely continue to decry the divisiveness that they themselves promote. The avalanche drags down everyone in its fall into the 'abyss of prattle' (GS, 11,154; O, 120), including the experts on the Fall, the certified eschatologists who have found accommodation in Lukács' 'Grand Hotel Abyss'. For all their conflicting unanimity about the Messiah's coming, they are here to stay. By the end of the trial, 'only the prosecutor and the witnesses are left'. There remains another, more endangered species that has been summoned to the trial: the members of the jury. Unnamed lay creatures of no fixed address who are simply referred to as 'the living', they bear a significantly indeterminate relation to the human race. Their sole qualification for jury duty is their bare, unaccommodated existence. But this is perhaps the one essential prerequisite for being able to give a sympathetic hearing to nature's complaint. Are not human(ist)s too entitled, too deformed by their professions, to be responsive to a cause so common as to extend beyond their shared humanity? Unlike the witnesses and the prosecutor, the jury betrays no human (conflict of) interest in the trial. Even so, the court's choice of jurors protects its own interests much better than the plaintiff's. Allowing her token representatives certain privileges, such as the creature comfort of a bench to sit on, it can at any time revoke them. Hence the jurors' increasing uneasiness about their alienable rights It is 'with equal mistrust' that nature's peers listen to the spokesmen for the absent plaintiff.

The fate that befalls them bears out their misgivings. During the initial phases of the trial, they manage to save their seats for the next generation; their place is inherited, like that of the painter Titorelli in Kafka's *Trial*. Such, then, is the only meaning that the Messianic categories of tradition and salvation still retain in the present context, whatever any of the witnesses may have to say on the subject. ('No-one', says Pascal, 'dies so poor that he does not leave something behind.' (cit. GS, 11,454; IU, 98)). Even as the jurors seek some modicum of permanence amidst disaster, they seem to suspect that no refuge is sacrosanct,[51] no sanctuary inviolable[52] and that they will not be allowed to camp indefinitely within the precincts of the court. Their visceral conflict of interest is that of knowing when to leave. Sooner or later the time will come for them to seek asylum from the law. The jurors will then become the outlaws of a system which ceaselessly perpetuates the expulsion from Paradise. Then, if not before, the systematic indecisiveness of the law will stand revealed for what it always was – a negative decision. 'In *The Trial*', Benjamin observes, 'postponement is the hope of the accused only as long as the proceedings do not gradually turn into the judgment' (GS, 11,427; IU, 129). Nature, for her part, never entertained such a hope. That she should have remained conspicuously absent throughout her ordeal, excluded from her own complaint, represented only by fast talkers and mute creatures, anonymously present only in the ensuing torture and martyrdom – all this amounts to a grimly ironical case of poetic justice. *De facto*, if not *de jure*, she is always in the process of losing her trial. If she *can* still win it, then only on the final appeal. But it was, precisely, the unavailability of the last instance, the non-appearance of the Messiah, which prompted her complaint in the first place. Meanwhile, the law continues to echo the serpent's empty promise to grant us knowledge of 'good and evil' (GS, 1,407; OGTD, 233).

Nothing is therefore less certain than the 'end' of history. The story Benjamin here sketches carries with it no sense of an ending. In the absence of the Last Judgment, the world ends not with a bang but an endless whimper. 'In the end, all the jurors flee, only the prosecutor and the witnesses remain behind.' The law buries the complaint, but the complaint undermines the law. Each thereby survives the other. Benjamin's inconclusive scenario anticipates the collapse of the law, and intimates the law of its collapse. If, as Hegel announced, world history is itself the Last Judgment ('Die

Weltgeschichte ist das Weltgericht'), that sentence amounts, on this showing, to the self-indictment of a world where 'progress in the consciousness of freedom' is synonymous with an endless fall. It progresses only as a funeral procession, a *Trauerspiel* filled with the lamentation of ghosts who return to haunt the scene of the crime.

> Ainsi que des esprits errants et sans patrie
> Qui se mettent à geindre opiniâtrement.[53]

'Foreign words are', according to Adorno, 'the Jews of language.' Nature – which speaks no audible language, not even a foreign one – might in turn be called the Jew(ess) of the Logos. She would thus be the Jew(ess) of Judaism itself,[54] the burnt offering or holocaust it bore within itself. Nature would in other words, *belong* to the Logos. Its muteness would not be alien to the Word but, on the contrary, its very own creation. For there is, outside the Logos, only nothingness. Or so the Logos says. Its logic dictates that there can be no other language beside it which might dispute the ascendancy of the Word; no outside language which does not bear the marks of the Fall; no alternative form of communication which might recover what got lost in the translation from lower to higher languages. To lodge a complaint is, on the contrary, to recognize the authority of the law. In lamenting language, nature does not, strictly speaking, contest it. For she is bereft not merely of speech but also of subjectivity. 'She' cannot, in other words, ever present herself; she can only be (mis)represented by others. To hear a *critique* of the Logos in her long-suffering lament would therefore be to put words in her mouth – the mouth she does not have. It would amount to projecting civilization's discontents on to nature, adding yet another 'pathetic fallacy' to the pile. For the 'confused words' (Baudelaire) that man thinks he hears her speak have, in effect, always been more or less dictated by her master's voice, even where they were voiced by a responsive witness, a poet for example, rather than a legal representative. Nature is thus forever condemned to submit to the vicarious whims of those who claim to speak on her behalf. So much so that the very metaphor of submission merely represents another, more sympathetic whim. Benjamin's whole scenario, aiming as it does to 'represent' history as a trial in which nature is the plaintiff, is itself another such fiction – one which is, however, calculated to expose our legal and cultural fictions for what they are.

It is, according to his early essay on language, 'for the sake of her redemption' that 'the life and language of *man* – not only, as is supposed, of the poet – are in nature.' The task is, accordingly, one of translation – from the 'lower' languages of creation into a 'higher' one (GS, 11,155,157; O, 121,123). Such translation is, however, inseparable from transcendence and transfiguration. It is therefore destined to idealize nature's complaint out of existence. Suppressing what it does not sublimate, it finally dissolves her indistinct lament into the 'ultimate clarity' of 'God's word'. But, after all has been said and done, it will be an unredeemed nature – not the prosecutor or the witnesses – that will be left behind, in all her abject materiality, to haunt a Logos that inevitably failed to be as good as its word. Such is 'that irredeemability of things, that recalcitrance, that heaviness of things, indeed of beings, which in the end allows merely a little ash to survive from the efforts of heroes and saints' (cit. GS, 1,334; OGTD, 157). If evil resides in the very resistance of matter, then it must be endemic to Creation. Prior to all objection, the abjection of the object constitutes its law of gravity. Nature's complaint would thus somehow resist her own inertia.

For nature, far from shunning redemption, plaintively aspires to it. As her trial wears on, however, her prayers seem increasingly destined to go unanswered. With the 'sickening of tradition,' Benjamin observes in connection with Kafka, 'the consistency of truth has been lost' (B, 763; IU, 143). But what if a certain inconsistency were internal to the truth? 'The language of nature', Benjamin's early essay on language triumphantly concludes, 'is comparable to a secret password that each sentry passes to the next in his own language . . . until in ultimate clarity the word of God unfolds, which is the unity of this movement [*Sprachbewegung*]' (GS, 11,157; O, 123).[55] The complaint of nature, on the other hand, is comparable to a secret password hidden *within* the official one. It bears witness to a chronic condition. Logocentrism secretes its own 'unhappy consciousness'. Hegel's 'labour of the concept' coincides with Freud's 'work of mourning'. If the Word can only work through nature's mourning, such mourning cannot ever be 'worked through'. The sentries may relieve one another, but they cannot relieve nature's pain. Powerless to end the suffering it engenders, the divine Logos can only recycle it. The Hegelian 'patience of the concept' cannot outlast that of nature – a patience which, in Benjamin's mystery play, assumes the proportions of a Passion. Nature's lament would thus call for a new *Aufhebung*, a second coming of the Word. But how would the second differ from the first? How could the Logos 'brush' itself 'against the grain' (GS, 1,697; IU, 257) – that is, from below – when, by definition, it descends from on high? Does not the reconciliation of spirit with matter fail to the very extent that the former unilaterally identifies the latter? Is there not always a remainder which escapes all theological summation? Nature is the 'other', the other of the Word, indeed 'its' other. But it is not a negative Hegelian moment that is cancelled out as the Word comes full circle. Her lament is the stumbling-block which trips up all such speculative flights.

But if redemption is to be, it can come about only in and through the Word. Nature's plea is, in this sense, as 'idealist' as it is 'materialist'. Too Jewish not to aspire to speech,[56] she is not *in*spired by it. It is only upon man that God has bestowed 'the *gift* of language' (GS, 11,148; O, 114). In so doing, God refrained from naming him: 'He did not wish to subject him to language, but in man God set language, which had served *Him* as the medium of creation, free from himself [*entliess frei aus sich*]' (GS, 11,149; O, 115). Nature, on the other hand, *is* subjected to language. In naming her, man does not confer on her the gift of language. It is not within his power to give her voice. To try to do so, to 'breathe the breath' (GS, 11,147; O, 114) into her would be to parody God. It would be a ventriloquist's trick. Incapable of *bestowing* (*verleihen*) speech on nature, man would merely *lend* (*leihen*) her his anthropomorphic voice.

Were it somehow possible for man to bestow language on nature, this would have to amount to more than a mere loan. 'To "endow with language" is more than to "have her speak".' It involves nothing less than granting the beneficiary the benefit of the gift – namely, freedom, without strings attached, without puppetry or ventriloquism. But how is it possible to have, or let, her speak (*faire parler les silences*) without, in the process, *making* her speak ('*machen, dass sie sprechen kann*'), and thereby reducing her once again to silence (*macht sie verstummen*)? What is the precise difference between the gift and the loan of speech? Or, alternatively, between a good loan and a bad one? Was not even the original gift of language, from God to man, already fraught with ambiguities? Even if such distinctions can be maintained, what actual difference do they make? 'It is a metaphysical truth', the essay on language announced, 'that all nature would begin to lament if it were endowed with language.' However apodictic its tone, this oracular thesis clearly rests on an univerifiable hypothesis.[57] Hence, indeed, the 'metaphysical' quality of its 'truth'. What, then, is the status of Benjamin's 'idea' for a mystery play? Is not the very idea of 'representing' the complaint of nature doomed to misrepresent it? To burden her with yet another spokesman? To pose, along with the artists and the philosopher, as a further Messianic witness to her plight? The author of such an aesthetico-philosophical scenario cannot, in short, avoid being implicated in it. This is perhaps why he left it as an 'idea', one that both invites and defies representation; and why he kept his own version to a strict minimum. Even if he were, as Benjamin claims the storyteller to be, the authentic 'spokesman' (*Fürsprech*) for created things' – the 'just man' (GS, 11,459; IU, 104,109) as opposed to the legal professionals – he would still remain the master of his literary creation. Try though he might to place his mastery in nature's service, he would never be able to eliminate the ontological inequality between them. It is already a daunting task for the bourgeois socialist to betray his origins in favour of the class for which he speaks.[58] How much more implausible for man to act as nature's mouthpiece. If 'there is no document of civilization which is not at the same time a document of barbarism' (GS, 1,696; IU, 256), can any statement ever be made on nature's behalf that does not bear the ineradicable traces of a certain imperialist humanism?

Is it, then, sheer utopianism – as well as the most insidious form of perjury – to claim to take 'the side of things' (Ponge)? Is the 'complaint' of a personified nature anything more than a case of projection motivated by pity and guilt?[59] If this were indeed the case, would it not still be better to lend nature a voice than to strip her of her last remaining attributes, thereby reducing her to a speechless, nameless 'thing in itself'?[60] It is all too easy to read civilization's own discontents into nature's eternal silence, and thus to add to the burden she – 'she'? – already has to bear. But there is no way out of anthropomorphic metaphors. And the fear of lapsing into them tends to promote a worse injustice than the one it seeks to avoid. Nature's lament is easily dismissed as a 'pathetic fallacy', an arbitrary poetic fancy or metaphysical self-indulgence wholly lacking in rigour or objectivity. Enlightened reason claims to have outgrown such archaic projections. But was it not the Fall, 'the triumph of subjectivity and the onset of an arbitrary rule over things' (GS, 1,407; OGTD, 233), that, according to Benjamin, reduced nature to the abject status of an object-for-a-subject, the *Sache* of a

Sachwalter, and inflicted on her another, sadder silence? 'Subjectivity' and 'objectivity' would constitute mirror opposites, two abysmal consequences of an original catastrophe; and the so-called demythologization of the world would be the 'storm . . . we call progress'. The appeal to such reified objectivity would thus be another way of gagging nature's lament. 'The removal of any echo of "lament" from history', Benjamin remarks in a related context, 'marks its final capitulation to the modern concept of science' (GS, 1,1231). Anyone who still discerns that lament is accordingly diagnosed as hearing voices. Deaf to all complaint, 'science' would deny its existence. In dismissing it as a pre-scientific projection of human responses on to nature and history, positivism would, however, merely betray its own projective arbitrariness. Like the court, it conceals its subjectivity behind objective appearances. Had the court summoned 'scientific' as well as 'humanist' testimony, the result would have been much the same.

If Benjamin's scenario implicates itself in the story it tells, this by no means invalidates the idea of representing nature's complaint. Doing so is, admittedly, to act as another of her representatives; not to do so is, however, to refuse to hear her complaint, to dismiss it out of court.

Nature's spokesmen unwittingly testify against themselves, the witnesses no less than the prosecution. Their Messianic babble accommodates itself all too smoothly to the functioning of the legal system. Even before they begin to contradict one another, their testimony is already compromised. If 'cultural treasures' are the 'spoils' of the 'victor' (GS, 1,696; IU, 256), then even the most militant aesthetic, the most radical utopianism, is in danger of speaking for the powers that be – for those who have the say. By the end of nature's trial, only those who speak remain. Seen from below, human justice is class justice, the legalization of millennial exploitation. It is the lowest of the low, the substructure, base matter and archaic mother of all materialism that pays the price of progress. While culture dreams of its reconciliation with her, nature continues to carry her spokesmen on her back. On *their* backs they may, in turn, sometimes feel the weight of her 'familiar glances' (Baudelaire). They may have the last word, but her silence will surely engulf their prattle.

Nature's 'theological' lament is, in this sense, more 'objective' than the 'scientific' arguments against its existence. Such objectivity is not the one imposed on her by the Fall; it is one that passively resists it. If her silent plea, which is not without Jewish overtones,[61] echoes human concerns, it is also a voice from beyond. Beyond projective tautology, beyond all vicious, hermeneutic circles, beyond human representation and control, nature laments. She laments what they all do to her. But anthropomorphism is open only to an immanent critique. Only from within human language can resistance to it still be articulated. Such is the circular structure of the Word, which admits nothing beyond itself. Such is, at all events, its own self-authorizing version of the story, the story it tells itself, the view from above. The theological complexity of nature's plight thus foreshadows Benjamin's much later account of the relation between the victors and the defeated. According to the *Theses on the Philosophy of History*, the strengths of the oppressed 'will forever call in question every victory that has ever fallen to the ruler'. But such retroactive effects cut both ways: 'Even the dead will not be safe from the enemy if he wins. And this enemy has not ceased to be victorious' (GS, 1,694–5; IU, 255).

This is not to imply that the Logos is itself the Antichrist. Salvation only exists in and through theology. But would it not also consist in being saved *from* theology? For nature to be able to speak, the god-given order of things would have to be revolutionized. But that is unthinkable. In 1935 Benjamin will, on the other hand, refer to the 'complete upheaval' that his earlier theological thinking has had to undergo 'in order to sustain, with all its strength' his 'present state of mind' (B, 659). Theology is to be converted into materialism; and the resulting tensions between them are to energize the common cause. Nowhere in Benjamin's writings are theology and materialism, melancholy and revolution, ultimately at odds with one another. The early theological melancholy which dwells on the passion of matter persists in the riveted gaze of the 'angel of history' on 'the triumphal procession which leads today's rulers over those who today lie prostrate' (GS, 1,696; IU, 258). However 'idealist' its aspirations and unalterable its predicament, the lament of nature foreshadows the 'claim' that history has on the 'materialist historian (GS, 1,694; IU, 254). The emphasis falls, on the eve of both World Wars, on the suffering inflicted by the progress of the world on those that carry the burden. Each time, the 'Messianic cessation of happening' (GS, 1,703; IU, 265) hardly lasts much longer than the time which will be allotted, at war's end, to observe a brief silence at the tomb of the unknown soldier. Deaf to the mourning it leaves in its wake, the triumphal procession remains a funeral procession. History remains 'Nature-History', 'prehistory' (Marx), a prehistoric allegory of itself. It is, for all its 'progress', a case of arrested development, at once over- and under-developed, both too stunted and too advanced to be capable of Messianic fulfilment. Our modern condition is already foretold by the predicament of nature – a parallel which is sadly indicative of the all too natural state of history. The Logos could function without let or hindrance (but such hindrance seems to be the very condition of its functioning) only if it could spirit away the passive resistance of matter. Conversely, matter could be subversively materialist only if, as in Marx's version of the proletariat, it were able to abolish itself as object and become the subject of its fate. What both of these equally impossible hypotheses have in common is that nature would have to be transformed beyond all recognition.

If the complaint of nature is the underlying ontological motivation for a certain 'creaturely' materialism, historical praxis would seem powerless to redress it – as powerless as the *angelus novus* who is carried off by the progress of the Fall. Yet 'only for the sake of the hopeless is hope given to us' (GS, 1,201).[62] Conversely, Benjamin's essay on Kafka includes intimations that the only hope lies *with* the hopeless, namely with hapless creatures – a hope that is 'not for us'.[63] In his final jottings, on the other hand, Benjamin resurrects the Messianic hope for a world in which 'the confusion deriving from the Tower of Babel is allayed', and the original, prelapsarian language has been restored – one which is 'understood by all men like the language of birds by Sunday's children'. The Messianic world 'is this language itself', a universal language which is also universal history (GS, 1,1239). Just as, according to the *Theses*, a 'redeemed humanity' will, in the fullness of time, receive the 'fullness of its past' (GS, 1,694; IU, 254), so a redeemed nature will partake of an all-inclusive language which will finally give nature and history their due. Malebranche called attentiveness 'the natural prayer of the soul'. In such attentiveness, Benjamin writes, Kafka 'included all living creatures, as saints include them in their prayers' (GS, 11,432; IU, 134). In a world where such prayers were granted, nature would no longer have any cause for complaint.[64] But would Paradise regained afford her a 'bliss' that was not, this time around, 'only of an inferior degree'? Or would the whole process begin all over again?

Does Benjamin's Kafka-inspired 'mystery' belie his earlier theological thinking? Or is it a kind of negative theology? Can Kafka's Judaism be said in this context to subvert that of Marx? Was the revolutionary work of the 'old mole' already undermined by a work of mourning even before Benjamin became a 'Marxist'? Do they not rather work together? If Kafka remains as crucial to him as Brecht, writes Benjamin to Scholem, 'then not the least of the reasons is that he espouses *none* of the positions which communism rightly attacks' (B, 605). According to one of those positions, which Marx attacked in his *Critique of the Gotha Program*, nature is thought to 'exist gratis' (GS, 1,699; IU, 261). Instead of uniting to put an end to the exploitation of man by man, the proletariat would merely have to make common cause with the bourgeoisie in order to share in the proceeds of their joint exploitation of nature. Shifting the burden of the class struggle on to nature's back, social-democratic ideology would, under the guise of a classless humanism, amount to an identification with 'the victors' (GS, 1,696; IU, 258). Benjamin, for his part, continues to side with the defeated. Placing himself at the crossroads between two materialisms whose respective concerns are the living creature and dead capital, he visualizes their collaboration, that of the hunchback with the machine (GS, 1,693; IU, 255), as a 'kind of labour which, far from exploiting nature, is capable of delivering it of the potential creations slumbering in its womb' (GS, 1,699; IU, 261).[65] Instead of violating Creation, modern productive forces would enable it to come into its own. The idea of such technological midwifery no doubt seems a far cry from a theological understanding of nature's complaint. Absolute respect for her inviolability can, however, hardly serve as an alibi for not interfering in her aggravated violation. Whatever misgivings old and new, ontological and ecological, versions of nature's plea may have about one another, they too surely belong together.

But could the spirit of Judaism, happily procreating with nature, effectively preside over their joint emancipation? Patriarchal, monotheistic, logocentric and monological though it is, might the spirit nevertheless be capable of healing its own wounds? It is, after all, a Jewish sensibility which here tells of the redress sought by nature from Judaism, and which seems to recognize in her exclusion something like a forewarning of the history of the Jews.[66]

Benjamin also defines Judaism, in entirely traditional terms, as having made a decisive break with myth. To what extent, however, are its ensuing taboos, necessary though they may have been to such demythologization, mythical in turn? Refusing to tolerate alien, pagan gods, a jealous God reduces nature to silence. But the past

> carries with it a temporal index by which it is referred to redemption . . . there exists a secret agreement between past generations and our own. On earth we were awaited. Like every generation before us, we have been given a *weak* Messianic power, to which the past has a claim. (GS, 1,693–4; IU, 256)

The most archaic and Messianic of claims is arguably that of nature. One of the tasks awaiting Benjamin's generation was perhaps to complete the deliverance of Judaism from the dictatorship it had been forced to impose on the mythical order. Such would have been, beyond their respective divergences, the project shared by Benjamin, Scholem and Adorno.[67] 'Myth will persist', wrote Benjamin, 'as long as a single beggar remains' (GS, V, 505). The hunchback dwarf of German nursery lore who prays inclusion in the child's prayer is such a mythic beggar. But very little, it seems, is needed in order for myth to save itself. In the opening parable of the *Theses on the Philosophy of History*, the little hunchback has turned into the grand-master, the past master, of theology. Like nature, he carries the burden of history on his back; and his plea echoes her wordless lament. But, by some saving grace, the figure that once appealed for redemption has now become its secret agent. Could it then be that nature's lament contains the 'secret password' of redemption after all?

NOTES

1 Reference to Benjamin, *Gesammelte Werke* (henceforth GS), edited by R. Tiedemann and H. Schweppenhauser (Frankfurt 1974); *Briefe* (henceforth B), edited by G. Scholem and T. W. Adorno, 2 vols. (Frankfurt 1966). Wherever possible, references to Benjamin's work in English have been given to standard published translations: *Illuminations* (henceforth IU), trans. by H. Zohn (London 1979); *The Origin of German Tragic Drama* (henceforth OGTD), trans. by J. Osborn (London 1977); *One-Way Street and Other Writings* (henceforth O), trans. by E. Jephcott and K. Shorter (London 1979); References to Benjamin: Schweppenhäuser, *Reflections* (henceforth R) trans. by E. Jephcott (New York 1986). In many instances these translations have been modified.

2 Since the tree of knowledge has always been translated as *Baum der Erkenntnis*, but *Erkenntnis*, as opposed to *Wissen*, is, in Benjamin's terminology, a *positive* term, Benjamin on one occasion adds inverted commas to it: *Baum der 'Erkenntnis'* (GS, 1,407). The tree promises *Erkenntnis*, but delivers only *Wissen*.

3 In naming Creation, man is, however, merely following God's lead:

the rhythm by which the creation of nature (in Genesis 1) is accomplished is: Let there be – He made (created) – He named. . . . [The act of creation] originates with the creative omnipotence of language, and in the end language incorporates the created, as it were, and names it. Language is thus both the creative and the crowning principle, it is word and name. In God the name is creative because it is word, and God's word is cognizant because it is name. 'And he saw that it was good', that is: he had known it through the name. The absolute relation of name to knowledge exists only in God, only there is the name the pure medium of knowledge, because it is at bottom identical with the creative word. This means: God made things knowable in their names. Man, however, names them according to knowledge (GS, 11,148; O, 115)

Thus even man's names, which are the 'divine inheritance (*Erbteil*) of human language' are a 'mere reflex' of the divine Word: 'The name comes no closer to the word than knowledge to creation' (GS, 11, 144, 149; O, 111, 116).

4 Baudelaire's *Oeuvres Complètes* (hereafter OC), Pléiade edition, ed. by Y.-G. le Dantec, Paris 1968, 11. Language is not merely 'communication of the communicable, but at the same time symbol of the incommunicable. This symbolic side of language is connected to its relation to the sign, but also extends in certain respects to the name and to judgement' (GS, 11, 156; O, 123). A 'doctrine of the sign' which *extends* to names is presumably to be distinguished from the arbitrary sign which is the *degradation* of the name. It is, at all events, the *name* which is to be correlated with the *symbol*, whereas the arbitrary *sign* is, in turn, associated with *allegory*. Both allegory and the arbitrary sign are connected to the categories of evil, nothingness, and abstraction, and are accordingly at home in the Fall' (GS, 1, 407; OGTD, 234). Benjamin's verdict on the Romantic devaluation of allegory on behalf of the symbol does not, however, in any way contradict his equally categorical condemnation of a 'bourgeois' semiology predicated on the arbitrary nature of the sign (GS, 11, 150; O, 116). Appearances to the contrary, these two objects of his attack are two sides of the same coin, like Romantic sentimentality and bourgeois positivism. The one side behaves as if the language of Paradise were still available; the other treats the present, all too ordinary state of language as the norm. Thus, each in its own way conceals the effects of the Fall. To the 'vulgar' mystifications of Romantic symbolism Benjamin opposes the 'idea' of allegory and, correlatively, an authentic, namely theological, notion of symbol (GS, 1,337 ff; OGTD, 159 ff). Thus, allegory and symbol, properly understood, are complementary. Whereas the former thematizes the fall of language, the latter intimates its divine origin. The symbol (literally, 'partaking of a whole': the 'fragment of a vessel', (GS, IV, 18; IU, 78) points to a unity of language beyond its communicative dimension (*Mitteilung*, literally 'division with', 'participation'). Such a unity, which is perhaps prior to the division into name(s) and divine judgment (*Urteil*, literally 'original division'), would be synonymous with the name of the indivisible Jewish God. No semiology could, presumably, get close to the absolute self-presence of this monologic Word.

5 Cf., on 'monologism', Mikhail Bahtin, *The Dialogic Imagination*, University of Texas Press, 1981. Cf. also the following passage from Gérard de Nerval's *Voyage en Orient*, quoted by Sarah Kofman in *L'Enigme de la femme*, Paris 1980, 271–2 (*The Enigma of Woman*, Cornell University Press, 1985, 225):

Go back to the initial struggles of the monotheist religions which proclaimed the degeneracy of woman out of hatred for Syrian polytheism, in which the feminine principle predominated under the name of Astarte, Derceto or Mylitta. The earliest source of evil and sin was traced back even earlier than Eve herself; those who refused to conceive of an eternally solitary creative God were told of a crime, committed by the ancient divine spouse, so great that after a punishment that had caused the whole universe to tremble, all angels or earthly creatures had been forbidden from ever speaking her name (. . .) this wrath of the Eternal one destroyed even the memory of the world's mother!

(Not even) in the beginning was the Word (that suppressed the woman's name.)

6 Cf. Jacques Derrida's translation of the Hegelian term *Aufhebung* by *releve*, which means, among other things 'relay'; and Alan Bass's translator's notes in Jacques Derrida, *Margins of Philosophy*, University of Chicago Press, 1982, 19–20, 43. Derrida's most extended discussion of *Aufhebung* is in 'The Pit and the Pyramid: Introduction to Hegel's Semiology', ibid., especially 88 ff.

7 Benjamin's critique of nominalism is contained in the 'Epistemo-Critical Prologue' to his book on German *Trauerspiel* (GS, 1,220 ff; OGTD, 39 ff.), with a 'neo-Platonic' theory of Ideas. The *Erkenntniskritische Vorrede* is an implicit critique of the alleged knowledge to be derived from the so-called tree of knowledge (*Baum der 'Erkenntnis'*).

8 Differentiation does already exist in the limited plurality of names, but it accelerates after the Fall: 'The paradisiac language of man must have been one of perfect knowledge; whereas later all knowledge once again infinitely differentiates itself in the multiplicity of language, was indeed forced to differentiate itself on a lower level as creation in the name' (GS, 1,152; O, 119).

9 Cf., on the nomadic nature of the sign and the ancestral 'palace' of the 'oldest logoi', B, 329; and, on *différance*, Derrida's essay of that title, op. cit., 1–28.

10 If language, in falling from grace, becomes, 'in part at least, a *mere* sign' (GS, 11,153; O, 120), the remaining part ensures that 'language never gives *mere* signs' (GS, 11,150; O, 117).

11 Benjamin interprets this notion of (Friedrich) Schlegel's as follows: 'the historian turns his back on his own age, and his seer's gaze is set ablaze by the peaks of earlier generations as they recede ever further into the past' (GS, 1,1237). The angel of history is such a prophet.

12 'Le monde va finir', in OC, 1262–5. As an allegory of 'progress', the tower of Babel may also be compared to Baudelaire's description of a 'progressive' newspaper, *Le Siècle*, as a 'vast monument of stupidity, leaning towards the future like the tower of Pisa' (OC, 1070). In the above-mentioned prose piece Baudelaire equates 'universal progress' with 'universal ruin' (OC, 1263).

13 A formula of Fichte's cited around the same time by Georg Lukács in *The Theory of the Novel* (trans. Anna Bostock, MIT Press, 1971, 153), where the petrified world of 'second nature' is described, in almost identical terms, as a 'charnel-house of long-dead interiorities' (64).

14 It is at this point that our reading parts company with that of Gershom Scholem, who sees *only* the crypto-theological dimension of Benjamin's historical materialism.

15 Cf. Benjamin's 'Theologico-Political Fragment' GS, 11,203–4; O, 155–6. It is in this perspective that Benjamin sees the *Communist Manifesto* as a surrealist one which calls on reality – not to 'sublate' (*sich aufheben*) or 'overcome' (*sich überwinden*) but – to 'outdo' itself (*sich übertreffen*) (GS, 11,310; O, 239).

16 Baudelaire, OC, 950.

17 CF. GS, 1,398; OGTD, 224–5.

18 The 'old wisdom' that 'all nature would begin to lament (*klagen*) if language were conferred upon her' is also invoked in Benjamin's short essay 'The Meaning of Language in Tragedy and Trauerspiel' (GS, 11,137–40). Written in the same

year as the essay on language, it nevertheless puts a somewhat different construction on nature's lament. Tragedy, Benjamin there argues, is 'the drama of the dialogic word, which is the 'bearer of meaning'. *Trauerspiel*, on the other hand, articulates feelings which neither originate nor culminate in language but are destined to pass through it on their way elsewhere. Language is not only the bearer of meaning. It also has a 'pure life of feeling, in which it purifies itself from the sound of nature into the pure sound of feelings. (...) It is nature which rises into the purgatory of language for the sake of the purity of its feelings' (GS, 11,138). Its ensuing lament is a transitional phase on the way to music, which marks the 'rebirth of feelings in a super-sensuous nature' (139). *Trauerspiel*, however, blocks this circular movement. It is 'not the spherical passage of feeling through the pure world of words, culminating in music, back to the liberated mourning of blissful feeling; but on the way nature finds itself betrayed by language, and this immense inhibition of feeling becomes mourning (*Trauer*)' (138). Thus, rather than seeking to express itself in language, nature's mourning now seems to be occasioned, or at least deepened, by its contact with language – the medium which seemed at first to hold out the promise of purifying its feelings. 'It is,' Benjamin writes, 'the circle of feeling which is closed in music, and it is the duality of the word and its meaning which destroys the calm of deep longing and spreads sadness over nature' (139). In the essay on language, on the other hand, the emphasis falls on the circular movement of the Logos, which translates lower languages into higher ones, be they Adamic words or the various arts. Thus, birdsong is translated into human song (GS, 11,156; O, 122). Here, however, the sounds of nature are dammed up on their way to musical consummation. 'Thus, with the ambiguity of the Word, with its *meaning* (*Bedeutung*), nature began to stumble, and while Creation wanted to pour itself out and in pure feeling, man bore its crown. This is the meaning of the king in *Trauerspiel*, and of its political intrigues (*Haupt-und Staatsaktionen*). They represent the inhibition of nature, a kind of immense blockage of feeling, which suddenly discovers in the word a new world, the world of meaning and unfeeling historical time; and here too the King is both man, an end (*Ende*) of nature, and king, the bearer and symbol of meaning. History is synonymous with meaning in human language; this language freezes into meaning; tragedy threatens; and man, the crown of Creation, is preserved for feeling only by becoming king, a symbol as bearer of this crown. And the nature of *Trauerspiel* remains a torso in this sublime symbol; mourning fills the sensuous world in which nature and language encounter one another' (138–9). According to Benjamin's version of the Fall, history, meaning and nature's mourning all stem from the fall of language. But this version of nature's lament tells a significantly different story. It is almost as if it were being told this time from the perspective of nature rather than that of the Logos. For it is not so much the fall of language into meaning as language itself, *qua* meaning, which causes her mourning; there is no suggestion here that language can be anything other than meaning; the 'intimation of mourning' that nature felt at being named is correspondingly amplified by her subjection to meaning. Adam is likewise replaced by the king, the man who wears the crown of nature. Instead of translating its mute language into Adamic names, human language now betrays its pure feeling, blocks its passage, and thereby provokes its mourning. Language thus seems to be inherently divided between meaning and its undertones, the 'endless resonance' (140), the 'sound' that it suppresses; and the man-king who represents both nature and history emblematizes this conflict. The protagonist of the *Trauerspiel* would thus be language itself, allegorically embodied by the king. 'Mourning conjures itself up in *Trauerspiel*', writes Benjamin, 'but also redeems itself' (139). But the conflict between history and nature, meaning and sound,

cannot find release within language itself. 'The rest in *Trauerspiel*', observes
Benjamin in another essay 'Trauerspiel and Tragedy', 'is music' (GS, 11,137). If
tragedy, according to Nietzsche, is born of music, it is in music, according to
Benjamin, that *Trauerspiel* finds redemption. It is, he writes, 'the place of the
actual reception of word and speech in art; the powers of language and of hearing
still carry equal weight; indeed, everything finally depends on the ear of the
lament, for only the word that is deeply heard becomes music' (GS, 11,140).
Thus, the lament of nature, which figures in Benjamin's logocentric theology as no
more and no less than an arresting parenthesis, emerges here as the core of
Trauerspiel. Nature does not, on this reading, aspire to language but to the
condition of music. For Kafka, too, according to Benjamin, 'music and singing'
hold out what hope there is (GS, 11,416; IU, 118). On the other hand, the trial of
nature, as Benjamin will visualize it, holds out no prospects of redemption. After
the legal babble has finally died down, the rest is silence.

19 OC, 82.
20 Cf. Baudelaire's warning to his reader in his *Epigraphe pour un livre condamné*:

Mais si, sans se laisser charmer,
Ton oeil sait plonger dans les gouffres,
Lis-moi . . . (OC, 163)

The pitfalls of such fascination are described in *L'Irrémédiable*:

Une Idée, une Forme, un Etre
Parti de l'azur et tombé
Dans un Styx bourbeaux et plombé
Où nul oeil du Ciel ne pénétre;

Un Ange, imprudent voyageur
Qu'a tenté l'amour du difforme
Au fond d'un cauchemar énorme
Se débattant comme un nageur,
. . .
Tête-à-tête sombre et limpide
Qu'un coeur devenu son miroir!
. . . (OC, 75–6)

Such a *tête-à-tête* trapped in endless self-reflection – 'La conscience dans le Mal!' –
is the precise opposite of the liberating self-encounter envisaged by Benjamin. The
declared 'Platonism' of his method seems calculated to protect his 'Idea' of
Trauerspiel from a like fate.
21 Cf. OC, 11. Conversely, *Correspondances* may be read as enacting the return of the
repressed. Nature's unnerving look suggests, in this context, that she is not merely
the inert matter of man's oblivious domination but also his immemorial *mater*.
22 Samuel Weber was the first to juxtapose Benjamin with Derrida in 'Lecture de
Benjamin', *Critique*, August-September 1969, 699–712.
23 Baudelaire, *La Vie Antérieure*, OC, 17.
24 'The allegorical signifier is prevented by guilt from finding its fulfilled meaning
(*Sinnerfüllung*) within itself' (GS, 1,398; OGTD, 224).
25 *The Theory of the Novel*, 29.
26 For Hegel, too, *immediate* can be synonymous with *abstract*, but only in a negative
sense, within a quite different series of oppositions. In Benjamin's early essay on
language, 'immediacy' (*Unmittelbarkeit*) is opposed to 'mediateness' (*Mittelbarkeit*,

literally 'mediation through means'), and not, as in Hegel, to dialectical 'mediation' (*Vermittlung*). Only with the Fall does language cease to be a 'medium' (*Medium*) and become a 'means' (*Mittel*). *Vermittlung* is cognate with *Mitte* ('middle'), not *Mittel*. The Hegelian 'middle' is the 'labor of the concept' which unfolds the 'World Spirit'. Its negativity nevertheless distinguishes it markedly from the positivity of the Word. Both, however, share the same self-relaying circularity.

27 The verb *richten*, which means not merely 'to judge' but also 'to condemn', 'to direct' and 'to destroy', nicely sums up the performative force of divine judgment.

28 'Efface the traces' is the motto of the 'destructive character' (GS, IV, 396–8; O, 155–6), who tests the world for its 'worthiness to be destroyed'. He would doubtless subject theology to the same test – if it were worth his while to do so. But is not his judgment on the world also a crypto-theological one, which recalls nothing so much as the divine judgment on human prattle?

29 The same scheme is at work in the early Lukács. The novel cannot regain the lost Paradise of epic concreteness except by pursuing abstraction 'to the very end' (*The Theory of the Novel*, 71). The 'immanent magic' invoked by Benjamin is *not* Lukács' 'immanence of meaning': meaning, in Benjamin's narrative, coincides with the Fall. Both narratives nevertheless share much the same teleology.

30 Benjamin's underlying theological anarchism in legal matters is most extensively expounded in his early essay *Critique of Violence*, which does not shrink from a global condemnation of the state, the law and the largely unacknowledged violence which preserves their existence. Such mediated violence is not criticized from the standpoint of pacifist non-violence, but in the name of another, immediate form of violence – one which, however, has non-violence as its ultimate goal. Two antithetical forms of immediate violence are distinguished: mythical and divine. The mythical violence of the gods is not a means to an end but a 'manifestation of their existence'. But, 'far from inaugurating a purer sphere, the mythical manifestation of immediate violence proves to be fundamentally identical with all legal violence' (GS, 11,199; O, 150). To this complicity between legal and mythical, modern and archaic, violence Benjamin opposes the purer immediacy of divine violence. 'If mythical violence institutes law, divine violence annihilates it . . .; if the former threatens, the latter strikes . . .' (ibid.). Thus, 'God's judgement on the company of Korah (. . .) strikes them unannounced, without threat (. . .), and does not stop short at annihilation' (ibid.). The 'highest manifestation' of such 'pure violence' that is available to man is said to be 'revolutionary violence', which breaks with myth, suspends the law, abolishes the state and founds a 'new historical epoch' (GS, 11,202; O, 153). 'Once again all the eternal forms which myth bastardized with law are open to pure, divine violence. It may manifest itself in a true war as well as in the divine judgement of the multitude on the criminal' (GS, 11,203; O, 154). If there can be no doubt that revolutionary violence is possible, Benjamin argues, 'it is not equally possible or equally urgent for men to decide when pure violence realized itself in a particular case' (ibid.). But how, then, are they going to be able, in a particular case, to distinguish, between the 'divine judgment of the crowd on the criminal' and the mythical vengeance of lynch justice, between pure and impure forms of immediate violence? Benjamin's essay, which rests its case on the self-evidence of that distinction, concludes by forcefully restating it one last time. The mythical violence which institutes laws is, it announces, to be called *die schaltende* – the present participle of a verb that connotes arbitrary rule; the violence that preserves laws is termed *die verwaltete* – 'administered', 'administrative, and thereby mismanaged, *ver-waltet*; and divine violence is named *die waltende* – from a verb that connotes higher governance. What is striking here is that Benjamin, in

order to call arbitrary and non-arbitrary violence by their proper names, should have resorted to a bold and untranslatable play on words. The distinction it reinforces is, of course, implicitly presented as anything but arbitrary. Does it not name the difference between mythical arbitrariness, its perpetuation in modern legal bureaucracies, and divine justice? And is not the creative (*prägende*) violence of the name emphatically distinguished, in the 'Epistemo-Critical Prologue' to the book on *Trauerspiel*, from the arbitrary introduction of 'new terminologies' (GS, 1,216–17; OGTD, 36–7)? Benjamin's closing word-play is thus clearly intended to be as far removed from 'play and arbitrariness' (GS, 1,217; OGTD, 37) as was Adamic naming. What he has done is to uncouple the idiomatic expression *schalten und walten* (which means 'to do as one pleases') and to transform a tautological echo effect into a rhyming opposition. He has also drawn on the theological connotations of the verb *walten* (as in the expression *Gnade walten lassen*, 'to let mercy prevail') in order to intimate the non-violent telos of divine violence. But in distributing the two synonymous halves of *schalten und walten* between the opposite poles of mythical and divine violence, Benjamin almost seems to be daring us – like God in Paradise – to question his judgment. 'Yes', his word play seems to say, 'they echo one another: I tell you so myself. But this does not mean any blurring of the distinction. The poles remain poles apart. The rest is arbitrary play. I condemn it in advance.' Benjamin's all-important distinction between arbitrary and non-arbitrary violence rests, in short, on the authority of his own say-so, on the formidable strength of his word, on the word of the Word.

31 Benjamin's philosophy of language is of a piece with his critique of violence. The enemy is, in both instances, 'bourgeois': the bourgeois conception of language and of violence. Just as 'the most elementary relation underlying all legal order is that of ends and means' (GS, 11,179; O, 133), so the prevailing conventionalist theory of language reduces it to a 'means of communication' (GS, 11,144; O, 111). Means are associated in both these cases with the arbitrary violence of the social contract. Divine violence, on the other hand, is the 'insignium and seal, never the means of sacred execution' (GS, 11,203; O, 154). True violence, like true language, is pure immediacy. Instrumental means are as foreign to the former as fallen signs are alien to the latter. But not all means are instrumental, nor all signs fallen. The last page of the essay on language refers, without further elaboration, to the connections between the 'language of art' and the 'doctrine of the sign', and to the relation between the sign and the 'symbolic side of language' (GS, 11,156; O, 123), while the essay on violence speaks of 'the actual sphere of "agreement", namely language', as the 'realm of pure means' (GS, 11,192; O, 143).

32 Cf. the following late jotting: 'The apocryphal phrase of one of the Gospels – "Where I meet you, I shall judge (*richten*) you" – casts a peculiar light on the Last Judgment. It recalls Kafka's jotting: the Last Judgment is martial law (*ein Standrecht*). But it also adds something to it: the Day of Judgment would not, in this case, differ from all othe others. . . . Every moment is one of judgment over particular preceding moments' (GS, 1,1245). Thus, every judgment is to be made in the immediate present, instead of being indefinitely delayed; and every present constitutes a moment of judgment over certain definite moments of the past.

33 Cf. Jacques Derrida, 'Différance', op. cit., 1–27.

34 How are we to interpret the 'immense irony' that the tree of knowledge represents – a 'sign [*Wahrzeichen*] of judgment over the questioner' which is at the same time a 'sign [*Kennzeichen*] of the mythical origin of law'? Did it all start *with* or *before* the Fall? Did man initiate all subsequent legal proceedings by wanting knowledge of good and evil, and thereby questioning God's judgment? Or did God do so by placing the tree in the garden as a kind of suspended sentence? But how is such suspension to be reconciled with the alleged immediacy of divine judgment? It is,

according to the *Critique of Violence*, only mythical violence that is 'threatening'; divine violence strikes 'unannounced'. Does this distinction hold good for God's original act of judgment?

35 Part of this passage is a quotation from *Critique of Violence* (GS, 11,198–9; O, 150), where Benjamin adds that the modern principle that ignorance is no protection against the law points to the continuity between the unwritten laws of ancient fate and the mythical workings of modern legislation. This is confirmed by K's experience with the law. 'One is sentenced', he observes, 'not only in innocence but also in ignorance' (cit. GS, 11,412; IU, 114). It is true that Adam, for his part, knew that he was sinning. But does it not take a considerable amount of casuistry to posit an absolute distinction between *his* punishment and the mythical one visited on ancient heroes such as Niobe and Prometheus for 'provoking fate' (GS, 11,197; O, 148)? Divine justice, as Benjamin portrays it, seems alternately utopian and totalitarian. But 'ambiguity' is, according to his *Critique of Violence* (GS, 11,198–9), characteristic of the *mythical* order. The Logos is supposed to speak with one voice, and one voice only.

36 It would follow from Kafka's equation of original sin with the complaint about it that he should, for his part, remain studiously neutral on the subject – except when, as in the letter to the father, he occupies the position of the son.

37 Also cited in Gershom Scholem, *Walter Benjamin – Die Geschichte einer Freundschaft* (Frankfurt 1975, 180–1).

38 OC, 70–1.

39 OC, 88.

40 There likewise exists, according to Benjamin, an affinity between the structure of the Athenian trial and that of Greek tragedy. The latter is, however, 'both a portrayal and a revision' (GS, 1,295; OGTD, 116) of the legal proceedings, and thereby points beyond its mythical material. But whereas such a 'struggle against the daemonic character of the law is bound up with the word' (GS, 1,298; OGTD, 118) of the tragic hero, nature's struggle against the law will also be one against the word. In *The Meaning of Language in Trauerspiel and Tragedy* (GS, 11,137–40), Benjamin had explored these two antithetical relations to language, which give rise to two different types of trial. Whereas tragedy represents a 'definitive (*einmaliq*) resumption of the tragic trial before a higher court' (GS, 1,298; OGTD, 119), *Trauerspiel* opens up the possibility of an *indefinite* resumption of the proceedings. 'If tragedy ends with a decision – however uncertain it may be – there resides in the essence of *Trauerspiel*, especially in the death-scene, an appeal of the kind that martyrs utter' (GS, 1,315; OGTD, 137).

41 Grimms' dictionary, which contains a long entry under *Klage*, suggests the original connection between these two meanings: 'Complaint before court, here too, the outcry with which one blames the one who has done one wrong, and calls upon the judge's help; hence also the Old French *claime* . . . (cf. Fr. *réclamer*)'.

42 Cf., on nature as a 'bridal bed', GS, IV, 147; O, 104; and also the Talmudic legend of the exiled princess waiting for her Messianic bridegroom in a village whose language she does not understand (GS, 11,424; IU, 126). Pierced 'through and through' by the name of the Father, a hostage to the fallen language of Adam and his sons, a Gretchen-like nature awaits Messianic redemption from a 'secret password' that will no longer pass her over.

43 Sigmund Freud, *Gesammelte Werke*, Frankfurt 1946, vol. 10, 434. Freud specifically refers to the 'old sense' of these words.

44 Cf., in this context, Benjamin's remarks on Kafka's story *The New Attorney*. What is new about Bucephalus, a horse turned legal scholar, is that he 'no longer practises law' (GS, 11,437; IU, 139). It is as a scholar, not as an attorney, that he 'remains

true to his origins'. 'The law which is studied and no longer practised is the gate to justice' (ibid.).

45 'I would recommend', wrote Scholem to Benjamin in 1931, 'that any study of Kafka begin with the Book of Job or at least with a discussion of the possibility of divine judgment, which I take to be the sole subject of Kafka's work' (Scholem, op. cit. 212–13).

46 Indecision, admitted or concealed, is, according to Benjamin, endemic to the law. In *Critique of Violence*, he refers in passing to the 'ultimate undecidability of all legal problems' (GS, 11,196; O, 147). The Kafkaesque trial of nature would thus exemplify the normal workings of the legal system.

47 Cf. Benjamin's unhesitating defence, in the eleventh Thesis, of Fourier's apparently extravagant ideas about nature's untapped potentialities (GS, 1,699; IU, 259).

48 Only the 'storyteller', who resembles not so much a lawyer as a saint, could truly be called the 'spokesman (*Fürsprech*) for created things' (GS, 11,459; IU, 104). Therein he embodies the 'just man', and presides over a fairytale theodicy in which 'all souls' may be thought to enter Paradise (GS, 11,458; IU, 103). In *such* a world, nature would seem to have no cause for complaint. The storyteller plumbs 'the hierarchy of the creaturely world' (GS, 11,460; IU, 104). But was it not the hierarchical structure of Creation that prompted nature's complaint?

49 Cf. B, 430 on Ernst Bloch's 'system (!) of materialism'; and Scholem, op. cit., on Benjamin's response to Bloch's 'system of theoretical messianism'.

50 The language of art ranks lower, in Benjamin's theology, than human language in general: 'art, not excluding poetry, does not rest on the ultimate essence of linguistic spirit [*Sprachgeist*] but on the linguistic spirit of things' (GS, 11,147; O, 114). This follows logically enough from the hierarchical structure of the Logos. But nature's lament constitutes a mute challenge to that hierarchy, one which might theoretically have reversed the respective positions of artistic language and human language in general. Who, after all, can better listen to nature than those who translate the 'linguistic spirit of things'? Why then do the artists *not*, in Benjamin's scenario, make the best witnesses, the most credible experts on the future? Is this because 'the Jews were prohibited from foretelling the future' (GS, 1,704; IU, 264) as well as from making graven images? Or is it that the artists' claims to speak on nature's behalf echo those of the lawyers, display the same *déformation professionnelle*, and play a similar role in nature's trial?

51 With the loss of an inviolable site, justice regresses behind the mythical stage. It had advanced beyond it, according to Benjamin, when the altar became the sanctuary of the sacrificial victim. The silence of the tragic hero is similarly inviolable. The 'testimony of a mute suffering' indicts the gods who, by a now familiar irony, are transformed from the accusers into the accused (GS, 1,286,288; OGTD, 107,109).

52 There exists a photograph of Norbert Elias receiving the Adorno prize with his suitcase beside him. Such are the conditioned reflexes of the refugee.

53 Baudelaire, OC, 71.

54 Cf., on the problematic of the Same and the Other in the relationship between Jewish thought and the Greek Logos, Emmanuel Levinas, *Totality and Infinity*, trans. Alphonso Lingis (Pittsburgh 1969), and Jacques Derrida's essay 'Violence and Metaphysics', in *Writing and Difference* trans. Alan Bass (Chicago 1978), 79–153.

55 The idea of a 'secret password' (which the Kabbalah sometimes identifies with the name of God) corresponds to a notion of tradition as the transmission of a hidden truth from one generation to the next: 'Kabbalah' means 'tradition'. Hence the

'secret agreement between past generations and the present one' (GS, 1,693; IU, 254). The transmission of the Logos and that of tradition undergo the same crisis.

56 'We discussed, from very disparate viewpoints, whether the particular relationship which binds Jews to language can be explained by their age-old preoccupation with holy scripture, by Revelation as a fundamental linguistic fact, and its impact upon all spheres of language' (Scholem, op. cit., 136).

57 Certain concepts come into their own, writes Benjamin, 'if they are not from the outset exclusively referred to man' (GS, IV, 10; IU, 70). It is no accident that the example chosen should be the Jewish injunction never to forget, or that such a requirement should be said to find adequate fulfilment only in 'God's remembrance'. Like the 'metaphysical truth' about nature, which also demands to be engraved on our memories, so categorical an imperative cannot be effaced by any empirical contingency. The gulf that here opens up between the ethical and the real is also what separates the Jew from his God.

58 Cf. *The Author as Producer*, GS, 11,700–1; *Understanding Brecht*, trans. by Anna Bostock (London 1973) 102–3.

59 This is clearly not Benjamin's position. 'And even where there is only the rustling of plants, a lament is to be heard.' Nature's lament is not, in this ontological scheme of things, a projection. It could be shown how, when faced with as 'noumenal' a 'phenomenon' as aura, Benjamin does not feel constrained to choose between nominalism and realism.

60 In the *Program for a Coming Philosophy*, Kantian criteria nevertheless figure as the bar before which all philosophical experience will for ever have to validate itself (GS, 11,100). Benjamin immediately adds that such experience can no longer be limited by the horizons of the Enlightenment. Yet how could an experience as 'noumenal' as that of nature's mourning be effectively submitted to Kantian criteria? Would she fare any better before the tribunal of Kantian reason than she does with the court?

61 In a letter to Scholem inspired by the latter's unpublished essay on the Hebrew song of lamentation (*Klagelied*), Benjamin writes in 1918 that in his own essay on 'Trauerspiel and Tragedy' of two years before he, too, had, on the basis of his Jewishness, come to recognize lament and mourning as a valid 'order' in its own right. In German, he goes on, lament finds significant expression only in the *Trauerspiel*, which is considered 'practically inferior' to tragedy. 'I was', he adds, 'unable to reconcile myself to this, and did not see that this hierarchy was as legitimate in German as the reverse probably was in Hebrew' (B, 181–2). His later work on the German baroque *Trauerspiel*, a genre that had been systematically devalued by German literary historians, would thus be dedicated to the rehabilitation of a 'Jewish' undertone in German literature – one which was increasingly making itself heard in modern literature. With the modern 'death of tragedy', the 'hierarchy' between the two genres could no longer be maintained.

62 Cf. the final redemption of the baroque allegorist, a dialectic of extremes which reverses his fall (GS, 1,406–9; OGTD, 233–5). This Kierkegaardian leap of faith may be compared to the neo-Pascalian wager on Marxism which Lucien Goldmann proposed in *The Hidden God* as a way of resolving the antinomies of bourgeois consciousness.

63 Cf. GS, 11,414; IU, 116, and B, 617–18, 763–4. Benjamin observes that there is hope in Kafka's world only for those who 'have not yet been completely released from the womb of nature,' for 'the unfinished and the bunglers' (GS, 11,414–15; IU, 117).

64 Historical materialism should doubtless not *rely* on the prayers of the saints, but it may not, to Benjamin's way of thinking, be able to *do without* them. It is easy to understand why Brecht should have mistrusted Benjamin's 'judaisms' to the point

of criticizing his Kafka essay for promoting 'Jewish fascism' (*Understanding Brecht*, 110). Kafka's version of the categorical imperative– 'Act in such a way as to give the angels work to do' (cit. B, 748) – is, however, entirely compatible with Brechtian pragmatism. Instead of passively waiting for the Messiah to come, we are, according to the *Theologico-Political Fragment*, to go to the opposite extreme of all Messianic spirituality by pursuing our profane impulses with undeviating intensity (GS, 11,203–4; O, 155–6).

65   In such a Fourierist paradise, 'wild beasts would enter man's service' (GS, 1,699; IU, 259). Man would thus be *master* of Creation once again. Amidst their seeming reconciliation (Marx's 'naturalization of man' and 'humanization of nature'), would not the old inequality persist even into utopia? But how could we honestly wish it any other way?

66   This would not be the first time in the Messianic tradition that an analogy had arisen between the historical experience of exile and the innermost structure of Creation. Cf., on the relationship between the expulsion from Spain and the Lurianic Kabbala, Gershom Scholem, *Major Trends in Jewish Mysticism*, New York 1961, chapter 7. But the Lurianic system locates exile at the heart of Creation only in order to renew Messianism from within. In Benjamin's thinking – on the other hand? – the tremors of history seem to correspond to structural faults within theology itself. Nature's exile is ineradicably inscribed in the logic of the Word. It is, as it were, internal exile, an internal Jewish matter. Is nature, then, not merely the Jew(ess) as scapegoat but the scapegoat of the Jews? How to square such structural exclusion with the all-inclusiveness to which any self-respecting Messianism has often laid claim?

67   We are here tentatively applying to Judaism the larger scheme developed by Theodor Adorno and Max Horkheimer in *Dialectic of Enlightenment* (New York 1978), according to which myth is already enlightened, and enlightenment still mythical. Cf., in this context, Scholem's project of rescuing 'mythic' dimensions of Jewish mysticism from the oblivion perpetrated by the assimilated rationalism of the modern 'science' (*Wissenschaft*) of Judaism (op. cit., 22–4, *passim*).

INDEX